THE INTERPRETATION OF HISTORY

THE INTERPRETATION OF HISTORY

BY

L. CECIL JANE

Author of "The Nations at War," etc.

GYAN

Published by

GYAN

Gyan Publishing House
5, Ansari Road
Daryaganj, New Delhi-110002
Phone: 011-47034999, 9811692060
E-mail: books@gyanbooks.com

Distribution Network
gyanbooks.com
India, USA, Canada, UK, Australia, France

ISBN : 978-81-212-6342-9 (PB)
First Published, 1915

2nd Impression 2022

Printed at: Gyan Press, Delhi.

THE INTERPRETATION OF HISTORY
Author: L. CECIL JANE

THE INTERPRETATION OF HISTORY

BY

L. CECIL JANE

Author of "The Nations at War," etc.

To

SIBYL

PREFACE

As its title may indicate, this book is an attempt to discover some underlying factor, in accordance with which History may be interpreted and the occurrence of all events explained. Of the ambitious nature of this attempt I am fully conscious, but it appears to be well worth making, and any apology for having made it would savour of insincerity.

Chapters I to V contain a statement of the theory that the factor is to be found in the existence of a mental conflict as to the means by which happiness is to be attained, between the idea that content is to be found in complete submission, "Universalism," or in complete self-assertion, "Individualism." It is argued that this conflict determines the conduct both of individuals and of those associations of individuals which form nations.

Chapters VI to XI endeavour to show how far this theory is justified by the past history of Europe and of England, and in Chapter XII an attempt is made to interpret the tendencies of the present day.

A detailed narrative of events hardly enters into the scope of the book, and I have in general confined myself to discussing the broad current of events, only entering into detail when to do so seemed to be necessary. For a certain inevitable allusiveness, I must therefore apologise.

Since the completion of this book in the spring of 1914, events of paramount importance have occurred. I have not altered the body of the book, but have added an appendix, "The Conflict in the Future," in which an attempt is made to indicate what may be expected to be the ultimate influence of the present European War upon the future of mankind.

I am unwilling to omit this opportunity of expressing my thanks to my friend, Mr. Maurice C. Blake, for his valuable criticisms and suggestions, and to my late secretary, Mrs. H. W. Rhodes, for patient and unwearying help.

L. CECIL JANE.

71 High Street, Oxford,
February 1915.

CONTENTS

THE INTERPRETATION OF HISTORY

I

THE MEANING OF HISTORY

THE necessary preface to the study of History must be a correct idea of the nature of the subject to be studied. History may be described broadly as a record of the past actions of mankind and of the working of human institutions. It deals with all the activities of man; it is concerned not only with the material but also with the intellectual and moral development of the world.

History, however, if it has any value, is something more than a mere record of that which has occurred. It is of little profit to know that Napoleon was defeated at Waterloo, or that in 1832 the Reform Bill became law. A chronicler who narrates the bare events of a series of years does little to advance human knowledge; he contributes still less to the profit of the human race. But a chronicler is not an historian. The latter must give something more than a record of events. He must discover the connection between one event and another, and not only between two events more or less closely united in point of time, but also between events separated, it may be, by centuries. It is a truism to say that every event which occurs has a direct bearing upon the whole future of the human race; that there must be some definite connection between the battles of Salamis and Trafalgar, between the careers of Julius Cæsar and Gladstone. We often speak of events which have changed the world's history. But it is certain that had any given event not occurred, the whole subsequent history of mankind would have been different. Nothing is more certain than that if Aristides had not been ostracised, the history of France in the eighteenth century would not have been that which it was. How it would have been modified, whether more or less, no man can say, since Aristides was ostracised. It may even appear that to connect two such events is fanciful and that their relation is non-existent. Certainly the bearing of the one upon the other is not easily traced.

Yet a little thought will often reveal a clear connection between two apparently unconnected events. To take but one example. The victory gained by Don John at Lepanto was directly responsible for the defeat of the Spanish Armada, and less obviously but quite as certainly for the victories of Nelson. Lepanto was the last great triumph of the oared galley. It so impressed the Spanish naval constructors with the excellence of that type of vessel that they ignored the fact that it was unsuited for oceanic war. Thus while England produced a new species of ship, the frigate, Spain still constructed galleys, and in 1588 she paid the penalty. The fleet of Philip II was unsuited for warfare beyond the Straits; for the attack on England he had to employ converted merchantmen, and they were easily out-manœuvred and crushed by the superior English ships. And the start which England had secured in the art of naval construction profited her in all the wars which followed; from the fighting point of view, she had become and remained the foremost shipbuilding nation in the world. If it had not been for the victory of Lepanto, Spain might have built ships suited for the new warfare. As it was, England first began to build the right type of vessel; when other nations imitated her, she had the advantage which years of practice were bound to give her.

In such a case as this, the connection between the two events is clear. But even when it is not clear, even when it cannot be discovered, it must none the less exist. To assert that it does exist is only to assert that the continuity of History is a real thing, that the history of modern England cannot be fully understood without a knowledge of the history of those empires which passed out of existence while England was yet in a state of profound barbarism.

This continuity of History is to-day an admitted fact. No one contends that the history of eighteenth-century England can be understood without a knowledge of the Anglo-Saxon period. It is just as clear that the Anglo-Saxon period cannot be understood without an appreciation of the peculiar character of the English conquest of Britain, without some knowledge of the history of the Roman Empire. And the Roman Empire itself was influenced by contact with Greek civilisation; Greek civilisation was in its turn modified by contact with Persia and the East. Hence from the study of English history in the eighteenth century we are led back by insensible degrees to the study of the remotest ages of antiquity; History becomes one continuous whole.

6 It is almost useless to study the history of one nation to the exclusion of that of other nations. It is still more useless to study the history of one century without reference to the centuries which precede and follow it. As the ultimate causes of any event may be traced back through the centuries, so the ultimate effects of any event may be traced onwards. The results of the sixteenth-century Reformation are felt to-day; they

will be felt in A.D. 3000, as long as the world endures. History has no end. We who are now alive are watching the working out of events which occurred a thousand years ago. We are, as it were, actors in a drama, imperfectly acquainted with the scenes which have been already acted, knowing less of the purpose of the scenes which are in progress, and almost wholly ignorant of the final development of the plot.

And if History possesses any value, it lies in this, that it may supply some clue as to what the future will bring forth. It is commonly said that from History statesmen may derive guidance, be warned of those things which they should avoid, saved from error and pointed to the right path. It is the function of the historian to make known the lessons of the past, and in doing so to reveal so much as he can of the future.

The imperfection of human nature, the real paucity of human knowledge, makes it impossible that the future should be wholly known. But the signs and warnings are there, waiting to be read. By careful consideration of the past many errors may be avoided.

If, however, the historian is to fulfil his function, if he is to wrest from the future some of its secrets, he must be more than a mere chronicler. It is not enough that he should bring to his task diligence and accuracy, that he should record truly the events of the past. That he should, as far as possible, do all this is no doubt necessary, but he must do more. He must be competent to analyse causes and results, to estimate characters and motives. And as History is a drama, he must also be gifted with something of the dramatic instinct. That instinct will aid him to discover the connection between events divided by centuries of time, to take a wide view of the past, to grasp that which is really essential, to discard that which is really trivial.

But though possessed of all these qualities, the historian will yet fail, if he has no principle of interpretation, if he discovers no explanatory factor enabling him to reveal the plot of the drama. He must find the true cause which has determined human conduct in the past, which will determine human conduct in the future, which has led and which will lead nations to pursue a particular course. If this explanatory factor can be discovered, the historian may hope to gain some clear idea of that fate which the future has in store for us. Without such an explanatory factor, his quest will of necessity be vain.

II

THEORIES OF HISTORY

THE need for some such explanatory factor has been generally recognised. Optimists have sought for it in a theory of consistent progress; pessimists in a theory of consistent retrogression. To one theorist every age is better than that which preceded it; mankind advances out of darkness into light; there is hope that perfect happiness will be ultimately attained. To another, the condition of the world grows constantly more evil as the race falls ever further away from an original golden age; the increase of wickedness promises that the wholesale destruction, foretold by some, will be richly deserved.

The optimist draws attention to the wider diffusion of political power, the increase in the material well-being of mankind, the spread of civilisation. But if it may be readily admitted that self-government is in general preferable to despotism, it must also be admitted that self-government is liable to degenerate into bureaucracy, and that the tyranny of a corrupt and selfish clique is at least as deadening and oppressive as the tyranny of a single man. Again, material prosperity has been bought at a price. Men tend more and more to herd together in great towns, there to live in an atmosphere so unnatural and so unhealthy that the physique of the nation deteriorates and only by means of improved sanitation and increased medical skill are appalling plagues prevented. The exodus from the country has aroused the gravest fears in the minds of statesmen. Improved means of communication have largely destroyed the original simplicity and quiet of rural life. The growth of civilisation has produced new economic wants; it has produced also new forms of disease more insidious, if less deadly, than the older plagues with which medical science has successfully contended. One of the characteristics of the present day is the prevalence of nervous diseases; that prevalence is justly attributed to the strain of modern life. If progress has been made, it has not been without its accompanying evils. He would be a bold man who should assert that the world is really happier to-day than it was a century ago.

And any consideration of History makes it clear that there has been nothing in the nature of consistent progress. It is assuredly untrue to say that one century has been even generally superior to that which preceded it. The golden age of Greece was certainly a period of greater intellectual and material well-being, of greater happiness, than the vicious period of the successors of Alexander. The age of the Antonines was a happier time than that of Diocletian and Constantine; in the Dark Ages men looked back with legitimate regret even to the period of the declining Roman Empire. If it be asserted that since the world emerged from the Dark Ages, progress has been consistent, it is easy to quote instances to the contrary. In England, there was certainly a marked deterioration in the Lancastrian period from the period of the Plantagenets. It may be contended that in most things which go to make for the good of the nation, the Stuart period was inferior to the Tudor. In France, the progress of the country was retarded by the Wars of Religion; the age of Louis XV shows a marked decline from that of Louis XIV. Two centuries hardly sufficed to enable Germany to recover from the miseries inflicted by the Thirty Years' War. In Italy, the degradation of the seventeenth and eighteenth centuries compares unfavourably with the age of Lorenzo de Medici. Russia had half emerged from barbarism when she was hurled back into misery by the Time of the Troubles. In no country has there been any semblance of consistent progress. The rule has rather been that progress up to a certain point has been followed by deterioration, even if that deterioration has culminated in renewed progress. And only a shallow observer would argue that because progress has been more or less consistent for a century or so, therefore the days of deterioration have passed, that there is to be no further interruption in the peaceful development of mankind.

The obvious flaws in the theory of consistent progress perhaps served to produce the theory of consistent deterioration. But this theory is even more obviously false. It is absurd to deny that advance has been made and is being made in all the arts of civilisation, that material progress has occurred and is occurring. And if more regard is to be paid to moral than to material considerations, it is certain that human sympathy has deepened, that the present age is at worst less openly cruel than that which preceded it. The tortures of the Middle Ages, the cruelties of the Spanish Inquisition, are an impossibility at the present day. Even the pessimists themselves admit that some progress has been made. They are inclined to fix the period at which the supposed deterioration set in at some fifty, one hundred or two hundred years ago. They refer generally to their childhood or to the days of their fathers as the golden age, and each successive generation advances the date at which the "good old times" ended.

And if the theory of progress is not justified by History, still less is the theory of deterioration. A trivial instance will serve to show that the "good old times" existed largely in the imagination. At the present day nothing is more common than the assertion that domestic servants have become familiar, lazy and improvident, whereas some fifty years ago they were models of all that could be desired. But writing in the early eighteenth century, Defoe complains of exactly those evils which are lamented by the modern mistress. He also found that domestic servants were too elaborately dressed, were impertinent, and were ready rather to lose their situations than to submit to any correction. He too longed for servants such as he had known in his childhood. And no doubt Defoe's father and grandfather made precisely the same complaints.

It would be absurd to deny that the world has lost something of its original simplicity and honesty. Advancing civilisation does tend to destroy certain virtues which are found among the savage races. But those virtues, exaggerated in themselves, were counterbalanced by vices now equally extinct; and at the same time there has been a distinct increase in the comforts and amenities of life. Indeed, the "good old times" are not improbably all the better because they exist only in memory. The most convinced pessimist would perhaps regret his fate if he found himself suddenly compelled to live in those conditions, the disappearance of which he so much deplores.

Nor is there any ground for supposing that the limit of advance has been reached or is about to be reached. Whatever evils may be discovered in the existing political system of any country, there is no doubt that open tyranny is becoming yearly less possible. In almost every state the government is forced to submit its policy to the criticism of its subjects, and though it is true that those subjects may be deceived, the dictum of Abraham Lincoln is also true, " You can fool all the people some of the time, and some of the people all of the time, but you cannot fool all the people all of the time." Justice is also more widely diffused; it is on the whole less possible for the guilty to escape or for the innocent to be condemned. Probably at no period of the world's history have the weak been so efficiently protected against the aggression of the strong. Every day some new advance in material prosperity has to be recorded; some new invention serves to increase man's power over the forces of nature. It may be admitted that the present is no golden age, that it has in it evils unknown in the past. But it must also be admitted that it certainly approximates quite as nearly to the golden age as has any other period; that there are many evils which were rampant a hundred years ago which have to-day ceased to exist.

To both the optimistic and the pessimistic theory, bowever, the most serious objection is that they are a like untrue to human nature. Any view of History which disregards human nature must be unjust. A state cannot be considered apart from its members. the very existence depends upon their consent, its laws and institutions are expressions of their will, and if the policy of the state varies, that variation must be the result of a variation in the ideas of the citizens. It is time that the opinions of the citizens do not always, or oven normally, find immediate expression; but it is also true that no government, no law, no institution can andure, no line of policy be long pursued, save with the consent of the members of the state. No theory of History which ignores the individual can supply the true explanatory factor.

And the life of the individual is no record of persistent progress or persistent deterioration. We escape from the ignorance of childhood by sacrificing its innocence; moral loss is the price paid for intellectual gain; "he that increaseth knowledge, increaseth sorrow." Absolute progress and absolute deterioration are alike unknown. In any given course of action there is alike good and evil; we have to balance the good and evil, making our choice with such skill as we may. Our life thus becomes a conflict; we are perpetually weighing pros and cons, striving to choose the lesser of two evils, often failing. This conflict is the determining factor in the life of man. And since nations are but aggregations of individuals, united in a certain special manner, the determining factor in the life of nations also is this same conflict. If the nature of that conflict can be accurately determined, the factor explanatory of History will be discovered.

There is nothing new in the conception of the life of man, and of History, as a conflict. Those who have recognised the falsity of the optimistic and pessimistic theories have sometimes suggested that History is a record of a struggle between the forces of progress and those of reaction. But a question at once arises as to the meaning of "progress" and "reaction," and this question is often too arbitrarily answered. It is, for example, frequently taken for granted that progress has been made when political power is more widely diffused, the argument being that greater liberty is thus secured to the individual, and with greater liberty, greater justice and greater happiness.

But the rule of the many may be as tyrannical as that of a single man or as that of a section of the community. Legislation which penalises the rich is not uncommon where political power has been secured by a majority, and such legislation is as unfair and as pernicious as any legislation penalising the poor. In a debased democracy, corruption and jobbery are at least as rife as in an oligarchy or a tyranny. It may be doubted whether a system under which legislation depends upon bribery, open or concealed, is an advance upon a system under which legislation depends upon the caprice of a despot or the interest of a governing class. Yet in every case where the legislative power is in the hands of men dependent on the will of an electoral majority, bribery is almost inevitable. In England to-day no sane man believes the professions of disinterestedness put forward by political candidates. No sane man believes that the would-be M.P. kisses babies from love of those babies, or subscribes his guinea to the funds of a local cricket club from genuine interest in that club's welfare. The kisses and the guinea, and the golden promises in the election address, are all a form of bribery. The candidate is concerned to persuade the electorate that they will profit individually if they elect him. They know that he wants something from them, and they hope to be paid in some manner for giving him that something. And as for the measures which he so vigorously supports and condemns, it would be the height of absurdity to imagine that the candidates, put forward by any political party, sincerely believe their own assertions, or that they hold all measures advocated by their side to be good, all those advocated by their opponents to be bad.

In the days prior to the Reform Bill, votes were bought openly, constituencies sold themselves to the highest bidder. To-day the electorate is larger; open bribery is forbidden by law, and is in any case too expensive to be practised. Candidates are forced to resort to indirect bribery. They pay the debts of chapels in the constituency which they hope to represent; they promise to patronise local tradesmen; they entertain largely, not as candidates, but as holders of some municipal office. There is here a system of indirect bribery, coupled with a large measure of hypocrisy; and it is not easy to see that the new method is any great advance upon the older and more direct. Nor does the House of Commons at the present day contain a better type of member than it did in the early years of the nineteenth century. It is at least arguable that it does not represent the true opinion of the country any more thoroughly than it did prior to the Reform Act.

And a wider diffusion of political power may result, and often has resulted, in anarchy. In such a case, it is difficult to contend that progress has been made from earlier conditions when, if power was in the hands of a few, a settled government at least guaranteed security of life and property. It is equally difficult to contend that there has been any retrogression when the anarchy is ended by the concentration of power in the hands of one man or of a small minority. In England during the Lancastrian period there is no doubt that parliament had a far greater share in the government than it had possessed under Edward I or Edward III. But if progress had therefore been made, it had been made at the cost of good order; it had certainly not increased either the happiness or the prosperity of the people. Under the Tudors, the executive was strengthened; the powers which parliament had secured under Henry IV were taken from it. Yet few will be found to assert that the age of Henry VIII and Elizabeth shows a deterioration from that of the Lancastrians.

In short, though a greater diffusion of political power may be and often is a sign of progress, it is not so invariably. On occasion the most real progress may consist in a limitation of the share of the people in their own government. The progress of one age may be the reaction of the next; that which one man regards as reaction may to another appear to be progress. It is, perhaps, not too much to say that this must be so, that progress and reaction are merely relative terms.

To describe History, therefore, as a record of a conflict between the forces of progress and those of reaction is in effect to say nothing. In every age there is both advance and decline; there is also a constant conflict. But the nature of that conflict has yet to be determined, and it can be determined only by consideration of the individual man. It is in the conflict which makes up the life of the individual, which determines his conduct, that the explanatory factor in History must be found. For the life of the nation is in reality a replica of the life of the individual, and that conflict which is found in the life of each man will be found also in the life of each state.

III

THE CONFLICT IN THE LIFE OF THE INDIVIDUAL

THOSE who have regarded the life of man as a conflict would seem to have been led into error as to the nature of that conflict. There is an apparent contrast between the animal and spiritual sides of human nature, between what are described as the higher and lower instincts. And it has therefore been concluded that the conflict is between these two sides of man's nature, between instincts which are practically those of the brute beasts and instincts which belong to a somewhat higher plane. Theologians especially have insisted upon this conflict. They have argued that in so far as man gives rein to his physical passions, he sinks to the level of the brute; that in so far as he restrains and masters those passions, he raises himself towards the divine level. The restraining motive is divine. If man does curb his natural passions, his success is attributable to the grace of God working in him. From this it follows that what may be described as animal instincts are evil, what may be described as truly human instincts are good. And the conflict in each man is between the good and evil instincts which alternately sway him.

Up to a certain point, all this is admittedly true. Man assuredly should exercise some measure of restraint over himself. If he does not do so, he certainly sinks below the human level. But it is not in a struggle between these two instincts that the true conflict which makes up man's life is to be found.

In the first place, the so-called animal instincts are not wholly evil. A man who had so curbed them that they had become extinct would be only an imperfect man; as Gibbon says, "The virtues of the clergy are sometimes more dangerous than their vices." The end to be desired is not extinction but reasonable restraint. Nor are the animal and spiritual sides of man necessarily in conflict with each other. It is frequently the case that a man's intellect, all his alleged higher qualities, are utilised to gratify his animal passions. And there are many men in whom the animal instincts are so weak that no real conflict can be said to exist.

But the most fundamental objection to this view of the life of man is that it ignores the fact that man's distinguishing characteristic is his possession of reason. An individual may cease to use his reason, but at the moment when this occurs, he practically ceases to be a man; he becomes a mere brute. And it is only on very rare occasions that a man does allow his reasoning faculties to become dormant. It is, therefore, in a mental conflict that the struggle which makes up man's life is really to be found. The conflict between reason and passion is not a mental conflict. It is a contest between the mind, that is, between the humanity of a man, and instincts which are only quasi-human. Such contests do not make up a man's life; they occur only when he has almost ceased for a while to be a man. The real conflict is to be found in the mind, in those forms of mental activity by which man is most profoundly moved.

And of all the activities of the mind, religion and love are certainly those by which a man is most profoundly influenced. It has always been for religion and for love that men have been most ready to die, to make the most supreme sacrifices. If, therefore, it is possible to discover the motives which determine a man's attitude towards religion, which induce him to give his love, it is possible also to discover the true nature of that conflict which makes up his life.

It has been said that if God did not exist, it would be necessary to create Him; in other words, mankind has always experienced the need for guidance by some higher power. Men shrink from the responsibility of facing the problems of life unaided; they would almost rather submit to a despotism than assume the burden of absolute private judgment. And there are many who, feeling the littleness of man in comparison with the immensity of the Universe, the brevity of human life in face of eternity, are driven to seek consolation in the belief that some deity orders their life and shapes them for some greater destiny than existence for a few short years on one small planet, whirling, they know not whither, in the boundless realms of space.

Dogmatic religion owes its existence and its vitality to man's realisation of his true insignificance. "What is man that Thou art mindful of him, or the son of man that Thou so regardest him?" This is the keynote of all religion. It cannot be that the Universe, that all the wonders of nature, exist by some chance; that man, whose intellect even if developed to its highest capacity still cannot comprehend a billion years, is the most highly developed being. Rather it seems inevitable that above and beyond all else there is a supreme Being, a God, to Whom men must yield complete and unquestioning obedience. And the peculiar gift of man is that he can realise his limitations, realise that there is One far above him, in Whom he "lives and moves and has his being." Man does not lose, but gains by admitting his inferiority to God, by recognising the obligation of obedience. He finds the perfection of his own nature in the realisation of its limitations; he is most truly man when he accepts the guidance of that Being to Whom he owes his very existence. God the Creator is worshipped before God the Saviour; the Deity Who guides us in this life is more real and vital than the Deity Who is to give us an existence when this world has passed away.

The reality of this desire for guidance, for control, is seen especially in the vitality of the Roman Church. The creed of that Church denies explicitly the right of the individual to judge for himself, and in that very denial lies its strength. Men feel that they cannot face the problems of everyday life unaided, that they are still less able to face the problems of eternity. And to such the Catholic Church brings a message of great comfort. "Only believe" has been that Church's motto; "all things are possible to him that believeth." Here is the solution of every difficulty which might trouble the mind of man; all can cast themselves on the Church, and the Church will guard and guide them. The desire to be controlled, to submit, is gratified to the fullest extent.

And only in so far as a Church gratifies this desire can it have vitality. In the sixteenth century, the right of private judgment was asserted; men were bidden to cast away the shackles of authority, to choose for themselves. New Churches arose, and in them the law of liberty was to prevail. Yet it was not long before the very opponents of authority themselves asserted the right to guide. Calvin was hardly less dictatorial than the Pope whom he attacked; Protestants have coerced the heretical as readily as have Catholics. Such was the necessity of the case. Those who became Lutherans or Calvinists were not less desirous of guidance than those who held to Rome. If denied that guidance, they would have drifted back to the Church from which they had parted. Dogmatic religion must gratify the desire to be ruled.

At the same time, there have always been some who have prized the right of private judgment above all things, who have resented even divine interference with their absolute liberty of thought and action. The mythology of all nations bears witness to the permanence of this desire for freedom. It led Eve to eat of the Tree of Knowledge; it led Prometheus to snatch fire from the sun. And when we pass from the age of myth to that of History, the basic force in all resistance to an organised Church, the origin of all heresy, has been the reluctance of the individual to surrender his freedom of thought. He desires to be equal to his spiritual guides, to be equal even to the Deity; he seeks to be master of his own fate. It is for this reason that the doctrine of transubstantiation has always been selected for attack by the enemies of the Catholic Church. That doctrine places the priest in a position far superior to that of any of his flock; they may be powerful in this world, but he alone can perform the daily miracle of the Mass. Those who would assert their freedom, who would refuse obedience, are forced to deny first of all the exceptional position of the priesthood. Only so can they justify their demand to be allowed to judge for themselves; only so can they satisfy their desire to rule.

Irreligion is no more than the expression of that desire. Those men are irreligious who do not feel the need for guidance from without. They prefer rather to rely upon themselves and to fall into error, than to surrender their intellectual liberty and be led along the right path. To them it seems better to die in a state of mental freedom than to live in a state of mental servitude. They aspire to be as God; they find a certain inspiration in the thought that if they fall they fall in battle against an almighty power; that if they die, they at least die free.

When, therefore, man approaches the consideration of religion, he is faced with two logical alternatives. He may render that complete submission which Catholicism demands, or he may assert that complete independence which Agnosticism claims. Anything short of complete submission or complete independence is a compromise, and as such lacks both combative force and vitality. Protestantism has succeeded just in so far as it has partaken of Catholicism. The negations of Luther would not have secured the permanence of his protest; it was the dogmatism of Calvin which in reality prevented the complete triumph of the Counter-Reformation.

And it is indeed clear that no Church can accept the logical outcome of the right of private judgment. If it did so, it would fall forthwith into a state of anarchy and its extinction would be inevitable. Lutherans, Zwinglians, Calvinists were alike forced to become illogical. Denying on the one hand the authority of the Catholic Church, they on the other hand asserted the authority of the Bible, of the Bible as interpreted at Wittenberg, Zurich or Geneva. And only by gratifying in this way the desire to be ruled, did Protestantism maintain its existence; only, that is, by ceasing to admit that right of private judgment which had been the watchword of the original resistance to Catholicism.

The fact is that Catholicism is one logical position; the only logical alternative to it is Agnosticism. The one position gratifies the desire to be ruled to the fullest extent; the other gratifies the desire to rule. There never has been, and, unless human nature changes entirely, there never can be a time when the whole race either accepts or rejects dogmatic religion. There must always be revolt against mental servitude; the right of private judgment must always find its champions. And yet it is, perhaps, those who assert this right most emphatically who are also most prone to seek relief from the responsibility which they have assumed. In other words, men waver between their desire for external guidance and their desire for freedom from all control, and because they so waver Catholicism and Agnosticism must always exist, gratifying as they do two deep and enduring desires.

It is probable also that between these two there will always lie a body of uncertain opinion. Those who are passing from one extreme to the other rest for a time in an illogical *via media;* the success of the Anglican Church is evidence of the large number of men who are passing through the transitional stage. Yet the tendency in members of such Churches will be to move in either one direction or the other; some will approximate more and more to Catholicism, others to Agnosticism. And it may be noted that Anglican ecclesiastics themselves readily admit that a very large percentage of the professed adherents of their Church are in fact "indifferent," that is, are in reality Agnostics. This is exactly what might be expected. A middle course satisfies neither the desire to be ruled nor the desire to rule; it is, therefore, less able to command devoted support than Catholicism or Agnosticism. It is hardly too much to say that in reality the world is divided between the two logical opinions; that many are unconscious Catholics or unconscious Agnostics, while professing allegiance to some middle Church.

A consideration of religion, therefore, brings to light a definite mental conflict in the mind of mankind. That conflict is between the desire to rule and the desire to be ruled, and the attitude which any individual adopts is determined by the degree to which he seeks or rejects external guidance. And whenever one desire has been fully gratified, almost before it has been so gratified, a natural reaction sets in. It is well known that the convinced Agnostic is not unreadily converted to Catholicism; the most sturdy rebel is liable to become the most devoted subject. Recent converts have always tended to become the most violent of persecutors. And it is equally true that the convinced Catholic tends to revert to Agnosticism. Those revolts against Catholicism, which have attained the largest measure of success, have in general been led by men once devoted adherents of the Church which they afterwards laboured to destroy. The reaction when it occurs is violent. Men turn from one extreme to the other, the human intellect failing to grasp and hold fast the golden mean of moderation.

As religion is one of the great mental activities of man, so love is certainly another. By that emotion, whether existing between the sexes or between members of the same sex, the mind is profoundly moved. And if the determining factor in human life is to be discovered, the means by which man is influenced to give or to withhold love must be discovered first.

Yet this quest may well appear to be hopeless. The sentiment of love seems to be too elusive, too unreasoning, to be brought under any rules. It arises without adequate cause, endures when every argument opposes its endurance, ceases as inexplicably as it begins. It resembles a disease; it defies all attempts at analysis. And in a measure it is physical rather than mental; the product not of the brain but of that vague something which, for want of a better word, men call "heart." Only those who have never loved, it may seem, would attempt anything so impossible as to explain what love is, how it comes into being, by what means it is either maintained or destroyed.

But it will also be admitted that there is a certain kinship between love and religion. In early times, love was constantly deified; Christianity itself asserts that "God is love." A man's devotion to his mistress may be unreasoning, unquestioning, blind. Yet it is little more unreasonable than the pietist's devotion to his Deity. Indeed, the popularity of the worship of goddesses, the introduction of sex into the religion of most, if not all, races, almost suggests that men and women have often found in their religion the satisfaction of their natural craving for love. And the existence of this community between the two emotions makes it possible, if not probable, that the motives which govern a man's attitude towards religion govern also his attitude towards love. In other words, there may be in love the same conflict between the desire to be ruled and the desire to rule.

On the one hand, a man desires to submit his will to some external guidance. He may find that guidance in some conception of a Deity. But there are some who need more obvious, more palpable guidance than that afforded by an unseen being. Their faith is weak; they long to touch and handle the being to whom they will submit. In such cases, a man inclines to deliver himself over to the control of another human being, whether of his own or of the opposite sex. He finds that peace and happiness, which is the goal of his desires, in obeying the lightest wish of some other mortal. For him love takes the place of religion, and his devotion to his deity is possibly the more real because he feels that his god is a being of like passions with himself.

Or again, the assertion of the right of private judgment towards the Deity is not enough to gratify man's desire to rule. Even if the very existence of God be denied the longing is still unsatisfied, since men wish to have authority over some being that they can see. They long to feel that their assertion of independence is against some one who would control them; they long to compel obedience from some other mortal. And in love they find the desired subject; they find scope for the exercise of their power, whether positively, that is, by compelling obedience, or negatively, that is, by refusing to obey.

It is well known that love between husband and wife has greater strength than love between brother and sister. This may be attributed to the fact that in the former instance the sense of possession is more fully gratified. There is a feeling of certainty which cannot exist so long as it is realised that at any time possession may cease. In other words, the more fully an object is possessed, the more fully will the desire to be ruled and to rule be gratified. And even in the case of physical love, the determining factor is the sentiment of possession, except perhaps in the case of merely transient passion which cannot justly be regarded as love at all. A man desires to possess, to control some beautiful object; or he desires to be enslaved by that object. There is still the same root motive, the desire to be ruled or to rule. And the only difference between the more physical and the more mental forms of love is that the exciting cause of the emotion is in one case the body and in the other the mind. It matters little whether it is the contemplation of a beautiful form or of a beautiful nature which serves to arouse the desire to be controlled, or the desire to control.

The origin of love, then, is to be found in the contact of two natures, which happen for the time being to satisfy the dominant desire in each other. One seeks to be ruled, the other seeks to rule: the would-be ruler finds a suitable subject, the would-be subject a suitable ruler; and love results. The emotion is also naturally fickle. The gratification of any desire leads to satiety. Men weary of being ruled or of ruling; they turn from the person who has fully gratified the one desire to find a person who will fully gratify the contrary desire. It has been generally recognised that complete identity of tastes and of opinions is as unsatisfactory a basis for love as is complete dissimilarity. Constant friction will certainly destroy affection; a complete absence of friction will destroy it almost as readily. Love, indeed, is only enduring in those rare instances where two natures are so attuned to each other that satiety occurs simultaneously in each case, when the one who has been ruling wearies of rule at precisely the moment when the one who has been ruled wearies of subjection.

Alike in religion and in love, then, there is a perpetual conflict between the desire to be ruled and the desire to rule. This conflict makes up the life of man; his conduct is determined by the predominance of one or other of these two desires. Men are met by the necessity of making a choice. They may seek that peace which is born of submission to external guidance, or they may seek the satisfaction to be derived from consciousness of mental independence. But the peace secured by submission tends to become irksome; the stress involved in the constant exercise of private judgment grows wearisome. Upon the gratification of either desire, a natural reaction ensues. Those who have given implicit obedience turn hastily to the other extreme and refuse to give any obedience at all. Those who have ordered their lives without external aid are eventually oppressed by the weight of responsibility which they have assumed, and seek relief in complete subjection.

The reaction from one course to the other is often startlingly rapid. A man who has surrendered his will to the guidance of a Church or of an individual suddenly finds that the degree of submissiveness demanded is more than he can give. At once, he begins to question the perfection of his guide; no sooner is that question asked than faith in the guide is weakened, and the revolt which thus begins will be the more violent in proportion as the submission was the more complete. Or again, a man who has prided himself on his independence, who has scorned even divine guidance, is often moved by some great calamity to abandon entirely the right which he once so zealously asserted. Faced by some insoluble problem, a man naturally seeks advice; brought into conflict with the untamed forces of nature, he finds his only hope of safety in an appeal to the Deity, Whose very existence he has perhaps denied. And if it be, as it so often is, that he secures real or apparent relief from his appeal for help, he is led to surrender entirely that independence in which he formerly found satisfaction if not content.

But the reaction may also be gradual. Many a man has fallen little by little under the control of some external power, hardly realising that he has surrendered anything of his original independence, until he has already fallen into a position of servitude. The process of conversion to belief in a particular creed is constantly extremely slow; the habit of reliance upon the judgment of others develops insensibly. And the converse is equally true. Those who have been devoted members of the Church come gradually to neglect that Church's commands, until at last they find that what was once all-important has sunk into a mere form. Children slowly learn to free themselves from the control of their parents. Those, who are no longer children, insensibly emancipate themselves from the guidance of some once trusted friend.

Whether, however, the reaction be rapid or gradual, it is not the less inevitable. Men seek happiness perpetually; they never attain it. To the generality of mankind, perfect happiness appears to lie in the mean between the two extremes, in a judicious combination of submission and liberty. The submission should not become servitude; the liberty should not become anarchy. To accept direction is in some cases manifestly wise; to assert independence of thought and action is in some cases also wise. But human nature is imperfect, nor do men succeed in maintaining so exact a balance between the gratification of the two desires. A man who has suffered from submission tends to refuse all submission. A man who has unwisely rejected direction tends to distrust his own judgment in all things. We hasten from one extreme to the other; our life remains a never-ending conflict.

And that conflict is intensified by the fact that there are never wanting some who advocate extreme courses. Believing that while human nature remains what it is, its imperfection renders the search for happiness vain, they seek to modify human nature. They look for such modification through the medium of the complete gratification of one or other of the two desires. Some trust that the most complete assertion of independence will produce the wished-for result; they attribute all unhappiness to men's lack of confidence in their own judgment. Others believe that happiness is to be found in complete resignation of their own will to that of the Deity, that the extreme of self-abnegation will root out the seeds of misery, misery being no more than the result of man's failure to accept the all-wise guidance of his Father in Heaven. And thus every man, who has experienced sorrow as the result of submission or of assertion of independence, finds at least some among his fellow-men ready to encourage him to pursue that extreme reaction to which his very nature inclines him.

But whether or no an eventual change in human nature may be effected, while it remains as it is, neither desire can ever secure a complete victory. The extreme of submission and the extreme of independence alike weary men. A passionate courtship rarely, if ever, culminates in a happy marriage. A convinced Agnostic is never unlikely to be converted to Catholicism. There is nothing stable in the life of man; the search for happiness never ceases because it is never successful; death overtakes each one of us still vainly struggling to find perfect content.

Special stress has been laid upon the existence of this conflict in religion and in love, since they are the two great mental activities of man, since by them man is most profoundly moved. But the same conflict of desire appears in every relation of life. Men offer a more or less instinctive opposition to whatever hampers their freedom of action; even the most sober-minded feel occasionally that "stolen waters are sweet, and bread eaten in secret is pleasant." To forbid trespass is often to induce it; the defrauding of a public body is almost universally regarded as venial. There is probably no one who has never felt a desire to free himself from the cramping fetters in which society holds him, who has not, that is, desired complete independence.

Nor is the longing to live in a state of anarchy restrained solely by acquired habits of submission or by a fear of pains and penalties. Obedience is often the outcome not of compulsion, but of inclination. There is no reason for supposing that immunity from punishment would in all cases produce crime. It is rather true that men at times delight in the surrender of their self-will.

And since the conflict of desire is perpetual, since man is, as it were, in a constant state of reaction from one extreme to the other, his attitude is frequently inconsistent. A man who loyally obeys a Church is not necessarily also controlled by his wife; one whose public life is marked by independence of attitude may well be most subservient in his private life. But though this is the case, it is also true that at any given moment a man is tending either towards a more complete surrender of his will to the guidance of others, or towards a more complete assertion of his independence. He is constantly moving towards one extreme or the other, and the inconsistency which appears is due mainly to divergence between his public and his private life. His attitude towards each tends to become the same. If he is an advocate of complete submission to a Church, he will probably tend also to be guided more readily by his friends. But though the tendency is towards assimilation, it is also true that at any given moment the divergence may be great.

To each desire, indeed, there is a dual aspect. Many, who are content to submit to external authority in all their relations with others, insist upon their independence of thought. Others, believing that content of mind can be attained only by submitting their very thoughts to direction, are reluctant to exercise their private judgment in any relation of life. And the dual character of the two emotions is seen even more clearly in the desire to rule. Men wish to determine their opinions without regard for others. But action is the expression of opinion; without action, opinion seems hardly to exist. And since the life of an individual can never be entirely isolated from the lives of other individuals, no sooner does action begin to correspond with opinion than men are brought into contact or into conflict with their fellows. A man's desire to rule himself develops into a desire to rule others; to the internal aspect of the desire, an external aspect is added.

Finally, the conflict of desire is largely sub-conscious. It is not to be supposed that men are always, or even generally, aware of the real motives for their conduct. That conduct seems to be irrational, determined by trivial causes, as often as not traceable to no particular cause. But the true motive is always the conflict of desire. Men are able to detect this fact in others; they are often inclined to ignore or to deny its existence in their own case. A Catholic will easily attribute the attitude of the Agnostic to his wish to be even as God; he will with more difficulty appreciate the fact that his own conduct is determined by his longing for guidance. The Agnostic will be equally alive to the fact that the Catholic is prone to submission; it will not be so clear to him that he himself glories in his sense of revolt. But it is only in accord with human nature that men should be more able to detect the motives and the faults of others than to analyse correctly their own conduct. They are not the less swayed by the conflict of these two desires because they are unconscious of the fact.

IV

THE CONFLICT IN THE NATION

WHATEVER view may be taken of the origin of society, whatever character may be assigned to the state, it is certainly true that all states are aggregations of individuals. And since this is so, the conduct of states is ultimately regulated by that factor which regulates the conduct of individuals. History, the record of a nation's life, is, then, also the record of a conflict between the desire to be ruled and the desire to rule. Every state, like every individual, enters upon the search for happiness, and in that search is driven to make its choice between the alternatives of submission and independence.

That choice has to be made both in the settlement of the internal organisations of the state and that of its external relations. At home, the alternatives are self-government and despotism; abroad, splendid isolation and inclusion in a commonwealth of nations. There is certainly the mean between the two extremes, but that mean is the ideal, and as the individual fails to secure the ideal, so the aggregation of individuals fails. All states search vainly for the perfection of happiness; no state has achieved that perfection. They are foredoomed to failure by reason of the very fact that they are aggregations of human beings, because human nature is in its essence imperfect.

For this reason, the internal history of any state is

characterised by a constant rearrangement of the balance of political power. That rearrangement may be almost insensible, as it has been in England; it may be rapid, the outcome of violent revolution, as it has been in France. But whether it be gradual or sudden, it is none the less always occurring. If at any given time a state is a despotism, there is present in it a tendency towards a wider diffusion of political power. The executive will be gradually weakened, until at last it has become so weak that it can no longer perform its original function of maintaining order, and anarchy supervenes. From this state of anarchy, there will be a necessary reversion towards despotism, and so the life of nations proceeds in a never-ending cycle. Like individuals, states pass from extreme to extreme. Convinced of the evils of despotism, they seek refuge in anarchy; weary of anarchy, they look for relief in despotism. The conviction that one system of government is bad produces a more or less violent reaction towards its antithesis. And though perhaps aware that happiness lies in the mean, nations are as unable as individuals to secure that mean.

History abounds with obvious illustrations of the working of this law Under the *ancien régime*, France experienced all the calamities attendant upon the possession of unfettered power by a single individual. The Revolution occurred, and jealousy of the executive served to produce anarchy. From that anarchy, from the evils attendant on the lack of all settled government, the country was rescued by Napoleon. But he established an absolutism probably more real and more complete than that which had been destroyed by the men of 1789. In the period which elapsed between the meeting of the States-General and the establishment of the Empire, France passed rapidly from one extreme to the other and back again to the starting-point. There are possibly few examples of equally rapid changes, but in reality France merely crowded into a few years the inevitable experience of many.

In the external relations of states, the same process is observed. Choice has to be made between the acceptance or refusal of inclusion in a corporation of nations. On the one hand, a state may recognise its obligations to consider not merely its own interest, but also that of the world at large. On the other hand, it may deny this obligation. When the disadvantages of international entanglements are experienced, an isolated attitude is adopted; when the peril of isolation is realised, safety is sought in some alliance, and the advantages of inclusion in a corporation of states are once more appreciated. Here, as in internal policy, the problem is to choose between two ideals, between that submission which will give peace and that independence which will prevent the action of the state from being hampered by considerations alien to it.

It is this persistent conflict which makes up History. Nations seek happiness and in doing so fly to extremes; experiencing the evil of one extreme, they turn to the other. The apparent triumph of one desire is rather anticipated than followed by a reaction in favour of the gratification of the contrary desire. History is a record of oscillation, of a vain and unending search for political happiness. The explanatory factor in History, the factor which reveals the true motive for the conduct of nations, is to be found in the recognition of this conflict between the desire to be ruled and the desire to rule.

If a term be sought to describe this desire to be ruled, it may at first sight appear to be found either in "Cosmopolitanism" or "Socialism." But there are objections to the employment of either of these two terms, objections which become apparent when the implications of the two terms are considered and compared with the implications of the phrase "the desire to be ruled."

Cosmopolitanism is the term applied to a certain attitude adopted by the members of one state towards the members of other states. It suggests a breaking down of the barriers between nations. The interest of any given state is subordinated to that of the world at large. Questions even of national honour are to be submitted to some arbiter, since the sacrifice of the individual community is preferable to the infliction of distress upon many peoples.

All this will be the outcome also of the gratification of the desire to be ruled, since the corporate nature of human society is regarded as axiomatic. But the term "Cosmopolitanism" suggests no special relationship between the government of a particular state and the citizens of that state. It is concerned only with external relations. On the other hand, the gratification of the desire to be ruled does involve a very definite relationship between ruler and subject; it implies the complete subordination of the individual.

To the use of the term "Socialism" there are even more serious objections. Above all, Socialism has become a word used in current political controversy, and suffering the fate of all such words has acquired a sinister meaning to some, a specialised meaning to others. As used generally to-day, it contains the idea not only of the subordination of the individual to the community, but also that of resistance to the arbitrary government of a single man. It suggests a particular economic policy; it upholds the superior political right of one section of the productive community.

But the desire to be ruled, though it may be gratified under an oligarchy or under a democracy, may be and has been equally gratified under a despotism. And though the desire to be ruled does not preclude the organisation of society upon a collectivist basis, neither does it preclude the organisation of society upon a capitalistic basis.

There is no doubt that a state, in which the desire to be ruled holds sway, will tend to be cosmopolitan in its attitude towards external affairs, and socialistic in its attitude towards internal affairs. But much is implied by "Socialism" which does not necessarily result from the desire to be ruled; much results from the desire to be ruled which is not implied by "Cosmopolitanism." No term in general use, indeed, exactly connotes the desire to be ruled, and for this reason a term, "Universalism," may be used in an arbitrary sense to cover all that is implied by the desire to be ruled.

Universalism has an external and in internal aspect. Externally, it implies the subordination of the interest of any particular state to that of the world at large. All nations are regarded as members of one corporation; they recognise some common superior. That superior may be definite or indefinite. In the Middle Ages, it was found in the Holy Roman Emperor or in the Pope; more recently, it has been found in international law or in the Hague Tribunal. The degree of intimacy in the relationship of state with state will vary directly with the authority of the recognised superior. But to that superior some ultimate obedience must be paid, even if it be at the cost of some limitation of national independence. And since nations are at least united in a species of loose confederation, the arbitrament of war will tend to be replaced by the arbitrament of some individual or of some tribunal, war being nothing more than the result of the pursuit by a state of its own interests without regard to the interests of humanity in general.

Internally, Universalism implies the subordination of the individual to the community. The province of government will be extended. Education and the conditions of labour will be the care of the state. Pushed to its logical extreme, Universalism will entrust the ruler with the direction of the most private activities of his subjects. Government will tend towards despotism; liberty will be valued less highly than the complete organisation of civic life.

The despotism, however, will not necessarily be that of a single man. Universalism really implies the possession of absolute power by the state, which may find its embodiment in one man, or in the few, or in the many. The truly necessary implication in the theory is the wide extension of the province of government; there is no necessary implication as to the form of that government. The universalist has no preconceived ideas as to the organisation of the executive or legislative power; he demands only that the individual should be controlled by the community, and that the interest of all should be considered as in every case of paramount importance.

As a term has been created to cover all that is implied by the desire to be ruled, so a term must be created to cover all that is implied by the desire to rule. Those who would gratify this desire insist upon the importance of the individual state as against the whole human race, of the individual citizen as against the whole community. And the desire to rule may therefore be described as "Individualism." But it must be observed that the term is used in an arbitrary sense to connote ideas which it does not normally connote. It covers not only the relations of citizens with the community, but also the relations of communities with one another. Like Universalism, Individualism has an external and an internal aspect.

Viewed in its external aspect, Individualism implies the adoption by a state of an entirely independent attitude towards other states. Nations are " in a state of nature." They deny, or at least disregard, the corporate character of human society; they assert their own sovereign power; they recognise no common superior. They will make peace and war as seems best in their own eyes. International law will be observed only in so far as it seems to accord with the private interests of a particular state. If alliances are made at all, they will be as between equals, involving no sacrifice of ultimate liberty of action. Even the idea of such an alliance is perhaps antipathetic to the truly individualist state, since any alliance imposes some external obligation upon the contracting parties.

Internally, Individualism implies the restriction of the province of government within the narrowest possible limits. The citizens will be left free to order their own lives. Logically, education and the conditions of labour should not be regulated by the state. If a man desires to live in complete ignorance, if he wishes to sell himself into slavery, the state should not interpose its veto. Only if the liberty of the individual threatens the dissolution of the commonwealth, will the interference of government be justifiable.

There are, indeed, some individualists who hold that in no circumstances should the citizen be coerced. They preach a creed of anarchy. But inasmuch as anarchy clearly destroys all state-organisation, it may be disregarded. The vast majority of mankind, differing widely as to the true limits of the province of government, are yet agreed in believing that some government is necessary, and therefore that there must be some coercion of the individual. The real dispute is as to whether that coercion should be applied only when it is absolutely unavoidable, or should be the rule rather than the exception. The individualist practically holds that coercion by the state is a necessary evil, justifiable only in the last resort.

V

GENERAL CHARACTER OF THE CONFLICT

HISTORY would be a far simpler subject, far more readily understood, if nations adopted at any given time a consistently universalist or consistently individualist attitude. But in actual fact, nations are as inconsistent as individuals; their conduct is as wavering. Such, indeed, must be the case, since they are aggregations of human beings. And so it is frequently, almost always, the case that a state which is universalist in one aspect is individualist in the other. An extension of governmental authority at home is normally coupled with the adoption of an independent foreign policy; the admission of obligations towards foreign states is normally accompanied by an assertion of the rights of the individual citizen as against the community.

The most perfect example of internal Universalism is possibly afforded by a complete despotism, but it is abundantly proved that such a despotism is very far from generally admitting any external control of its policy. During the Middle Ages, when the theory of the universal sovereignty of the Emperor or of the Pope was most widely admitted, the internal organisation of states was generally individualist in character. The central government was too weak to meddle with the course of life in the districts under its nominal control, and the citizen was left very largely to provide for his own safety. And when resistance to the claims of Emperor or Pope began, it came first from those states which at home had become universalist. As the power of the central government in any country was increased, as the sphere of that government was extended, so obedience was more and more reluctantly accorded to the external power, the corporate character of human society was more and more disregarded. The last traces of the old mediæval conception of the unity of Christendom were destroyed in England by Henry VIII and Elizabeth, by the very sovereigns who most widely extended the limits of state interference at home. The Act of Supremacy was followed by the Poor Law and the Act of Apprentices.

It is also often the case that the party in a state which most zealously champions the rights of the individual is also most eager to submit all external disputes to some arbiter. The members of the Peace Society in the Victorian age were recruited mainly from sturdy individualists who objected even to such apparently necessary interference as was seen in the Factory Acts. And in the past, the churchmen who preached the doctrine of the universal supremacy of the Pope asserted with equal vigour their own individual rights; Becket stood quite as much for his own liberty of action as for the abstract principle of the freedom of the Church from all secular control.

At the same time, there is always in every state a body of opinion favouring the acceptance of Universalism or of Individualism to the fullest extent. The gratification of the desire to be ruled in one aspect produces a general spirit of submissiveness; the gratification of the desire to rule produces a general spirit of independence. Peoples who have cast off a foreign yoke tend to organise their government upon a popular basis. Switzerland, the Dutch Republic, and the United States are instances of the internal result of a war of liberation. When an internal despotism has been destroyed, there is an immediate tendency towards self-assertion as against foreign states; a struggle for mere independence is not infrequently followed by a war of aggression abroad. The history of France after 1789 supplies the most remarkable instance of this fact; other examples may be discovered in the case of Sweden under the Vasas or in that of the Dutch Republic after the final deliverance from Spain.

It seems to be equally true that a despotism is on the whole ultimately less able to resist foreign aggression. The despotism exists only by reason of the prevalence of the desire to be ruled. Where that desire has attained ascendancy, though the government may pursue an independent policy, the people tend to be indifferent, careless whether or no they fall under the foreign yoke. The cities of Greece which had successfully resisted the Persian invaders accepted the Peace of Antalcidas after their spirit had been crushed by Lacedæmonian harmosts. The Italian republics which had defeated Frederic Barbarossa at Legnano offered little opposition to the Valois and the Habsburgs after they had fallen under princely government. The opposition to French aggression, whether under the Bourbons or after the Revolution, came generally from those states which had rejected internal Universalism.

Every state, therefore, tends to become wholly universalist or wholly individualist. But it never actually reaches the logical conclusion. The extreme of Universalism is despotism at home and subjection abroad; the extreme of individualism is anarchy at home and unceasing war abroad. The evils of these extremes are obvious; they are in general soon realised, so that no sooner does the state approach the complete gratification of one desire than a reaction begins in favour of the gratification of the contrary desire. The nearer a nation has approached to complete Universalism the more violent will be the reaction towards complete Individualism; the nearer a state has approached to anarchy the more thorough will be that despotism by which the anarchy will eventually be subdued.

The history of France strikingly exemplifies this truth. Louis XIV could declare with considerable justification, "*L'état, c'est moi*"; he aspired to acquire an ascendancy over Europe, and France seemed to be wedded to the idea of internal Universalism. The reaction, which set in during the reign of Louis XV, culminated in the Revolution. The absolute monarchy was replaced by an executive so weak as to be unable to curb the most exaggerated licence. The policy of armed aggression was for a moment abandoned; instead, an altruistic crusade was undertaken to deliver all nations striving to be free. The violence of the French Revolution was, in short, proportionate to the completeness of the despotism which it shattered. And an interesting contrast is afforded by the English Revolution of 1688. Then it was not necessary to overthrow an established system; it was merely necessary to prevent the modification of that system into an absolutism. Consequently the Revolution of 1688 was orderly and calm, unattended by any of those excesses which a century later heralded the birth of the new France.

In all countries and at all times two tendencies are at work; the gratification of one desire inevitably produces a reaction towards the gratification of the contrary desire. At any given moment one desire is more powerful than the other. But as one attains the mastery, that mastery is undermined by the appearance of the other. In the interplay of these two desires the conflict which constitutes History is found, the secular conflict betweer Universalism and Individualism.

As individuals seem to oppose instinctively whatever hampers their entire freedom of action, so states are moved to seek complete liberty. They chafe at the limitation of that liberty by treaties, regarding any advantages which may be derived from the acceptance of some obligation as being more than counterbalanced by the evil of a certain measure of external control. They are restless under the curb of international law. They are reluctant to subordinate their own interest to that of the generality of mankind. They desire to rule. And those sacrifices which are commonly described as having been made in the cause of national prestige or of national self-sufficiency have in reality been made at the call of Individualism.

The conduct of nations, however, is often actuated by the desire to be ruled. One of the most remarkable phenomena in the internal history of all countries is the fact that no strong government has yet had to face a revolution. The Stuart and Bourbon monarchies had become weak before they were seriously attacked; Metternich was successful until he lost his grip of affairs; the strength of the Empress Dowager long postponed a probably inevitable outbreak in China; Abdul Hamid was secure on his throne till premature old age crept upon him. Even tyranny secures voluntary and disinterested support, if that tyranny is not merely the capricious assertion of authority by a power conscious of its real weakness. An absolutism begins to tremble on that day on which it learns to pardon; the worst crime in a despot is a readiness to make amends. Amiability has frequently been the salient characteristic of rulers who have met their death at the hands of a revolutionary mob, or who have experienced the destruction of their absolute power. Louis XVI was essentially virtuous and essentially weak; he paid the penalty of weakness. At the present day, Nicholas II is certainly inspired by a sincere zeal for reform; during his reign the autocracy of the Tsar has been impaired and the very existence of Tsardom has been imperilled. Nor can the ready obedience given to strong government be explained by Rousseau's dictum that "a slave loses everything in his bonds, even the wish to escape from them"; it is too widespread, too permanent.

This inclination to obey is not confined to the sphere of internal politics. In the Middle Ages, nations submitted to many inconveniences rather than sacrifice their ideal of a united Christendom. Even in the midst of the Becket controversy, Henry II shrank from joining Frederic Barbarossa in the recognition of an anti-pope. The ending of the Great Schism was welcomed throughout Europe, even though it was clear enough that a pope with an undisputed title would be better able to check the growing liberty of national Churches than a pope with a rival at Avignon. After 1815, even England only broke with reluctance from the Quadruple Alliance, and Alexander I was ready to risk his throne and life rather than disturb the concert of Europe by independent action in the Eastern Question. More recently, the strength of the wish for that concert of Europe has been illustrated in the policy adopted by the great powers towards the Balkan problem. It is, indeed, a fact that the desire to be ruled is a sentiment ingrained in mankind, and therefore ever-present in nations, no less than the desire to rule.

Whether the relations of state with state, or of the state with its members, be considered, it will be found that Universalism and Individualism always have their advocates. There will always be some eager to limit, some eager to extend the province of government. While some will always be ready to sacrifice everything in the cause of national independence, some will always find that independence too dearly purchased at the cost of even the most moderate defensive precautions. Liberty and subjection each gratify one side of human nature. If men glory in freedom, they glory also in self-abnegation. The conflict of desire is secular.

And the intensity of that conflict is increased because the gratification of either desire can be readily justified. Some subordination of private interest to the public good is essential; only an extreme anarchist will contend that murder and theft should go unpunished. If the state is to exist at all, it must exist to perform certain functions, and even if those functions are restricted to the mere safeguarding of life, limb and property, their performance will yet destroy the absolute liberty of the individual. But if it be once admitted that some state interference is not only legitimate but actually necessary, it can be claimed that the limits of such interference are indefinable. The universalist can accuse his critics of attempting to draw an arbitrary distinction between liberty and licence.

And the same accusation can be brought against the universalist himself. There is probably no one who believes that the state is able to deal with every conceivable circumstance, who denies that something must be left to private effort. If citizenship is not to degenerate into servitude, a certain liberty must be allowed to the individual; even Hobbes left him the right of self-preservation. But the term "self-preservation" is susceptible of widely different interpretations. To some it may connote the bare right to exist; to others, the right to an existence in which the highest faculties can be developed. The universalist, therefore, may be charged with drawing an arbitrary distinction when he attempts to define the degree to which the state is bound to respect the passions and prejudices of its members.

The gratification of either desire can thus be defended on the ground of necessity. It can be defended also on the ground of intrinsic excellence. Universalism regards all nations as members of one corporation; they must unite to promote the general well-being of mankind. Altruism becomes the guiding principle in international politics. And from the citizens of each state a like altruism is demanded. The individual must so order his life as to cause no injury to his fellows; he must even do more, and seek their welfare rather than his own. The interest of the community is preferred to that of any of its members; the function of government is to make the good of all the care of each.

Such a conception could hardly fail to win support. The imagination is almost necessarily fired by the thought of a world united in pursuit of one lofty ideal, of nations forgetting their mutual jealousies at the call of a high mission, of the citizens of every state abandoning the pursuit of their petty interests to adopt an enlightened patriotism. To many, the conception makes an especially strong appeal. Those who recoil from the horrors or who deplore the economic waste of war see a vision of mankind delivered from so great and so unnecessary a scourge. Those who lament the prevalence of misery and want, or who are disgusted by the spectacle of advance retarded by selfish opposition or misdirected effort, find hope of rapid progress through the agency of state control. A dream of universal altruism will delight the enthusiast. Self-sacrifice is admittedly meritorious in private life; it seems unreasonable to suppose that in public life it is altogether evil. Universalism, the apotheosis of political unselfishness, should rather be regarded with respect and admiration, as benefiting the world at large and ennobling the individual.

But the gratification of the desire to rule appears to be equally ennobling; Individualism also makes a strong appeal to the imagination. There is something magnificent in the thought of a single state, standing alone, defying all the world. And while the corporate conception must tend to destroy patriotism, in the accepted sense of that word, Individualism fosters patriotism, since it regards nothing as more important than the prestige and prosperity of a particular state. Internally, a spirit of self-reliance is encouraged in the people; they are saved from the danger of becoming "a spoon-fed generation."

Nor are there wanting those who feel that a victory gained by external aid is almost as harmful as a defeat, who believe that the best interests of a nation are served by complete release from all foreign entanglements. And at home, the obvious evils of grandmotherly legislation supply an argument against all state interference. It is suggested that the evils which it has sought to remedy are the result of human nature, and that human nature cannot be changed by Act of Parliament. It is contended that true progress has always been the outcome of private initiative, that every limitation on the right of the individual to stand alone reduces his power of doing so. Initiative may well be cramped or even destroyed by state interference. And the loss thus sustained will tend to be absolute rather than relative, since the action of government is often blind and only too frequently vitiated by care for the interest of a particular section of the community or by attention to the immediate needs of some political party.

Universalism and Individualism are thus equally capable of defence, equally open to attack. Since only a minority of mankind believes either in a complete despotism or in a state of complete anarchy, the logical application of either theory produces an impossible situation; no state could ever exist permanently upon a wholly universalist or wholly individualist basis. So it is that the conflict between the two desires, in any case inevitable and eternal, is rendered more vigorous and more intense.

The permanent factors in the conflict between Universalism and Individualism are found in human nature. But in the conflict there are also occasional or historical factors, predisposing circumstances which at any given time incline men towards the gratification of one or other of their two primary desires. While these circumstances are produced by the prevailing tendency in the human mind, there is still a certain interaction. Men are inclined to give rein to a particular desire; they establish institutions which favour the accomplishment of their wishes. Those institutions fulfil their purpose and by so doing increase the desire, since up to a certain point appetite is whetted by gratification. But presently that point is reached at which gratification produces satiety, and then reaction follows. The order of life is conflict; cessation of conflict would be death. Whenever, therefore, the complete triumph of one desire appears to be imminent, a reaction in favour of its antithesis begins. The conflict is renewed with increased vigour, that renewal being, as it were, compelled by the very instinct of self-preservation.

Thus there are factors which normally assist the growth of Universalism; there are factors which normally assist the growth of Individualism. But there are not, and there cannot be, factors which invariably assist the growth of either the one or the other. The very institutions which men create to gratify a particular desire tend at the last to quell that desire; they accomplish their purpose too effectually, they gratify the desire too completely. The desire to be ruled produces a despotism and by that despotism is fostered, until the exaggeration of despotism leads to a reaction towards anarchy, and the desire to rule gains ground at the expense of the desire to be ruled.

Among those factors which normally assist Universalism, the first place must be assigned to simplicity of mind, which naturally favours the desire to be ruled. Those who possess this simplicity seek guidance and are eager to obey. Averse from debate, they tend to support despotism, the absolute rule of one man being the least complex form of government, since under it no question as to the rights of subjects or the ultimate seat of authority can arise. It is not without reason that political education has been discouraged in despotic monarchies. Nothing can be more valuable to a despot than that his subjects should be unable to discover any ground for resisting his unfettered rule.

Simplicity of mind favoured the establishment of despotism in the earliest times and the eventual domination of the world by the Roman Empire. That Empire itself was the second great historical factor making for Universalism. The whole civilised world was, or appeared to be, under one government; that government repeatedly defeated attempts to destroy it. It therefore made a deep impression on the human mind, such an impression that even when the work of destruction had been accomplished, men were very slow to realise what had occurred. The barbarians could not imagine an order of things in which universal dominion had no place; they conquered provinces and established kingdoms, but they were overwhelmed by their very success. It was incredible to them that an institution, for centuries victorious over all its enemies, the very mirror of ordered stability, should have passed away like a dream of the night. The Roman Empire, in fact, survived its own death.

But the opinion that the Roman Empire was eternal did not owe its prevalence solely to the depth of the impression which that Empire had made on the minds of the barbarians. The same opinion was also zealously propagated by the Christian Church. From the moment when St. Paul declared that the creed which he preached knew no distinction between Jew and Gentile, Christianity had become essentially cosmopolitan in character; it could not be identified with any one tribe or nation. And while dogmatic religion necessarily inculcated habits of obedience, since it owed its very existence to willingness to obey, the doctrine of the Church demanded that converts should recognise their unity as children of one Father in Heaven. The Teutonic races were turned from the worship of gods, peculiar to particular tribes, to the worship of one God, common to all mankind. And in the process of conversion, they learnt also to disregard the barriers between states, to believe that all Christians were ultimately subject to the rule of the Roman Emperor, the vicegerent of the Almighty. Presently, it is true, the West found it hard to recognise in the ruler of Constantinople the lord of the world. But the Church devised a way of escape from this difficulty; the creation of the Holy Roman Empire and later the gradual elaboration of the doctrine of papal supremacy served to maintain the ascendancy of Universalism.

Without, however, an entire modification of human nature, it was impossible that continued gratification of the desire to be ruled should not produce a reaction. As time passed, doubts arose as to the actual excellence of a system which had once seemed to be ideal. And these doubts were increased by every error which the Emperors or their representatives committed. Among the causes which contributed to weaken the hold of Universalism on the human mind, a prominent place must be assigned to the faulty system of taxation under the later Empire. The curials, tax-collectors, were reduced to starvation; they inclined to hope that the imperial government was not eternal, to question whether a government which inflicted such misery on them was indeed necessary to the world. And though they failed to put their new ideas into practice, though they still bowed to authority, they were not the less ready to give rein to their desire to rule, to discover hitherto unsuspected virtues in a condition of anarchy.

Even the barbarians themselves showed traces of this spirit of resistance. If the majority humbly accepted the political theory of the Church, some regretted that freedom of action which they had enjoyed as pagans amid the forests of Germany. They were moved to regret the loss of gods whose care it had been to promote the welfare of a particular tribe. They were reluctant to believe that all those ancestors, whose deeds they had been taught to admire and emulate, were burning for ever in Hell. Some at least felt that they would rather suffer torments with the heroes of old times than share in the joys of a Heaven which seemed to be suited only to weaklings and women. They were disinclined to subordinate their interests to those of the Emperor; martial spirit led them to despise a monarch who cowered behind impregnable fortifications, whose mercenary armies they could invariably defeat. Individualist ideas were not wholly destroyed even by the combined influence of imperial prestige and ecclesiastical authority. Among the barbarians, the Vandals never accepted Universalism;

all tended occasionally to render mere lip-service to it; the spirit of nationality survived; the conflict did not cease.

And when, after the establishment of the Holy Roman Empire, Individualism seemed to be well-nigh extinct, it was revived by the force of necessity. Threatened by the raids of the Northmen, districts were compelled to provide for their own defence. There was no hope that an appeal to the Emperor would bring effectual help; there was no time to seek imperial sanction for such measures as had to be taken. Left to their own resources, the provinces tended more and more to forget everything except their own immediate interests, and this growth of local sentiment was encouraged by the increasing difficulty of communication between the different parts of the Empire.

Nor did the Church entirely oppose the resultant decentralisation. When the Papacy had been degraded by the vices of the Popes and by the undue influence of notorious women, those bishops who sincerely desired the advancement of religion could hardly turn to Rome for encouragement or guidance. The princes of the Church began to pursue an independent policy. But by doing so, they necessarily assisted the progress of Individualism, of that "political heresy" which officially they condemned.

Nothing indeed is clearer than the fact that the operation of those agencies, which tend normally to favour the gratification of one desire, is frequently confused. Simplicity of mind generally fosters Universalism, increased intellectual activity generally fosters Individualism. But it would be entirely incorrect to assert that the individualist is necessarily either more intelligent or better educated than the universalist. Rather is it true that, when once a certain point has been reached, the same result is produced by education and lack of education. A man simple in mind readily submits to guidance; a people simple in mind is peculiarly susceptible to external influence and so inclined to obedience. But it is equally true that a man whose mind is highly developed is painfully conscious of his own limitations and therefore also ready to seek direction; that a nation which has attained a high degree of civilisation will often sacrifice something of its independence in order to avoid war, which it feels to be a crude and extravagant method for attaining a given end. Though increasing civilisation, any intellectual development, tends at first to favour Individualism, it tends ultimately to produce a reaction towards Universalism, which had made a potent appeal in the original period of ignorance and barbarism.

Again, the conception of the Roman Empire, on the whole, promoted the desire to be ruled and was opposed to the spirit of nationality. But the Universalism which prevailed under the Empire was external rather than internal; local independence was rather strengthened than crushed. On the other hand, when the spirit of nationality developed, royal power developed simultaneously; that is, the growth of external Individualism was accompanied by an equal growth of internal Universalism.

Even the influence of the Church was not wholly on the side of the desire to be ruled. Among the causes which led to the definition of Individualism, a foremost place must be assigned to the quarrel between the Empire and the Papacy. There are not wanting instances of the clergy resisting external Universalism; in every dispute with the Popes, kings found some ecclesiastics enlisted on their side. And the Popes themselves, by supporting suffragans against their metropolitans, did something to sap the strength of internal Universalism. That very development of free thought, which was so opposed to the political theory of the Church, in one aspect assisted the desire to be ruled. Only with the help of a strong monarchy could local clergy hope to assert their independence against the might of the Papacy, and accordingly those who most vigorously opposed Universalism abroad were often driven to preach that theory at home.

The complexity of the conflict is extreme; the action of the different factors is frequently most obscure. One illustration of this may be given. Commerce normally favours the growth of Universalism, externally because it tends to break down the barriers between nations, internally because its prosperity so largely depends upon strong and efficient government. But war is an expression of Individualism, and the most frequent cause of war has been commercial rivalry; the assertion of national independence has often been principally due to the economic evils resulting from alien rule. And since nothing affects commerce more disastrously than that irregularity of taxation, which is constantly the outcome of arbitrary government, the commercial class has frequently been the first to advocate resistance to that strong central authority which at an earlier date it had most assisted to create.

This complexity is natural. Human nature is admittedly complex, and the conflict between the desire to be ruled and the desire to rule is the outcome and expression of human nature. Men are swayed by feelings over which they have little control, the meaning of which they hardly understand. Those aggregations of men, which we call states, are swayed by similar feelings and understand them no better. History, the life-story of nations, can never be simpler than the life-story of each individual man.

As might be anticipated from its very complexity, the conflict between Universalism and Individualism follows no immutable course. It would be idle to assert that the gratification of the desire to be ruled abroad is invariably accompanied by the gratification of the desire to rule at home; it would be equally idle to assert that the converse is invariably true. It is altogether impossible to define absolutely the lines along which the reaction against the dominant theory will proceed; all that can be said is that the reaction will infallibly occur.

But at the same time, if every allowance be made for numerous exceptions, it is perhaps possible to indicate what may be described as the normal course of the conflict. That course the conflict generally follows, though by no means invariably. For as there is infinite variety in the nature of the individual man, so there is infinite variety in the history of that conflict which makes up man's life. And there is the same variety in the history of aggregations of men; the conflict no more pursues an invariable course in the case of states than it does in the case of an individual.

Certain probabilities may, however, be suggested. A state which is as nearly as possible entirely universalist will generally adopt external before internal Individualism. For the assumption of an independent attitude towards foreign powers, a strong government at home is almost essential, so that the existence of such a government often encourages the inauguration of an isolated foreign policy. The premature gratification of the desire to rule at home, before independence has been asserted abroad, will not infrequently either perpetuate or produce a state of subjection to some external power.

On the other hand, in a state which is as nearly as possible entirely individualist, the reaction also tends to begin externally. The ultimate evil produced by the exaggeration of Individualism is anarchy, and the ultimate consequence of anarchy is normally foreign conquest. But foreign conquest supplies a complete gratification of the desire to be ruled, so that external Universalism follows upon that inability, whether material or mental, to resist foreign aggression, which is produced by too extreme gratification of the desire to rule. The history of Poland supplies a striking illustration of this fact.

Such may be described as the normal course of the conflict. But there are certainly numerous instances of the conflict pursuing a different course. Internal Individualism has often fostered a love of independence so intense as to render a nation proof against all attack; internal Universalism has sometimes so deadened the spirit and cramped the energies of a people as to render that people an easy prey to foreign aggression. The slightest comparison of the history of the Swiss Confederation with that of the ecclesiastical states on the Rhine will suffice to supply evidence of this truth. A state which has become entirely individualist has often begun the reaction by ending a condition of anarchy productive of every evil short of foreign conquest; such was the work of Gustavus III in Sweden. A country which has become wholly universalist has often first destroyed the despotism which hindered all free development. After the Congress of Vienna, the overthrow of the Metternich system was accomplished rather by the revolt of peoples than by any reversal of the foreign policy of governments.

The utmost, therefore, that can be said is that there appears to be a normal course which the conflict in nations follows, though deviation from that course is frequent. And it must always be remembered that the process of reaction from one extreme to the other may proceed so evenly in external and internal relations as to make it morally impossible to decide where the reaction first began or where it first attained completion.

VI

THE CONFLICT IN EUROPE: I. TO THE CORONATION OF CHARLES THE GREAT

THE struggle between Universalism and Individualism dates from the moment at which man became man, and will continue until human nature is changed out of all recognition. But in its earlier stages the conflict was hardly apparent; it existed but was not defined. Desire is always felt long before it is expressed, such expression demanding a relatively high level of intelligence. Particularly is this true of anything in the nature of political desire, and it would have been indeed surprising if primitive man had possessed the intellectual capacity necessary for the enunciation of a theory.

And when political ideas began to find verbal expression, at first Universalism alone was clearly defined. It is a theory easily stated and positive in character, whereas Individualism is essentially negative and rendered more difficult of exposition by its very insistence upon the right of private judgment. The theory of subjection had thus an initial advantage as against the theory of independence.

That advantage was increased by the character of primitive man. His mind was receptive rather than active. He was prone to superstitious reverence, reluctant to assume the burden of personal responsibility; he was inclined by nature to obey those upon whom ability or good fortune had conferred a real or apparent superiority. Absolute monarchy was therefore the earliest form of settled government; in the first ages of mankind, the desire to be ruled was far stronger than the desire to rule. And this fact is almost sufficient in itself to account for the apparent absence of conflict in the remotest period of History.

Even Universalism itself long remained undefined. The subjects of the ancient monarchies of the East were as devoid of all initiative as are their modern representatives, the inhabitants of Asia Minor, Syria and Egypt. Their half-developed minds could evolve nothing in the nature of a political theory. Oriental despotism was the only form of government which they could understand; they obeyed their rulers because they could hardly realise the possibility of disobedience. If some objected to the practical slavery in which they lived, their objections took the form of somewhat purposeless revolt; a victory for the malcontents merely resulted in the substitution of one despot for another. Political debate remained unknown to the peoples of the East, until long after they had fallen under the influence of western civilisation; such traces of political institutions and theories as are found among them to-day have been recently imported from Europe.

The Greeks were cast in a different mould. Their virile genius early prompted them to discuss the science of politics, and they formulated the universalist theory as the true solution of the problem of the relationship between the state and the individual. They carried that theory, indeed, to an unusual extreme. Nowhere is the province of government so widely extended as in the ideal polities of the Greek philosophers. Plato and Aristotle, differing in many respects, agree in committing to the care of the state the regulation of the whole life of the citizen; the government is to them the agency by which men are to be guided to that higher life, for the attainment of which political society exists.

On the other hand, there are comparatively few traces of a conception of external Universalism; the policy of the Greek republics was individualist in spirit. Certainly the Hellenes did regard themselves as one people; non-Greeks were rigorously excluded from participation in the Olympic or Isthmian games. They even professedly recognised a species of common superior in the Amphictyonic Council. But the authority of that body was only nominal, and though signs of a corporate spirit may be detected in the centuries which elapsed between the semi-mythical days of the siege of Troy and the period of the expedition of Alexander, yet Individualism was certainly in the ascendant so far as external relations were concerned. A widely extended empire was generally identified with barbarism. Almost compelled by the physical geography of their country to live in small and isolated communities, the Greeks found in the city-state the only possible existence for civilised man. Internal Universalism alone really attained definition in ancient Greece.

A new situation was created by the victories of Rome. For all practical purposes, the whole civilised world was brought under a common government. Roman citizenship was gradually extended until Caracalla granted it to all his subjects. And since the advantages of law could be enjoyed only within the Empire, it was not unreasonably held that beyond the imperial frontiers men were little better than brutes. If the large measure of local self-government granted to the provinces and cities somewhat impaired the ascendancy of internal Universalism, that of external Universalism was established. The deification of the Emperor was no more than the emphatic expression of man's reverence for the embodied majesty of world-wide dominion.

But the continuance of that reverence, was speedily imperilled. The deified Emperor was, after all, only one among a crowd of gods and goddesses, and a form of worship which the virtues of the Antonines rendered popular and almost legitimate became absurd in the age of their successors. The imperial office suffered in reputation when it became the prize of successful intrigue, when it was disputed or shared by rival claimants. The vices of some Emperors, and the incapacity of others, seemed to destroy their claim to be the embodiment of the imperial idea. And an almost fatal blow was struck at the whole system when Elagabalus attempted to make personal an apotheosis which had in reality been the apotheosis of an office. Diocletian laboured to restore the prestige, which had been lost, by shrouding the person of the Emperor in mystery. But the elaborate ceremonial of his court caused as much offence as it did admiration; his colleague Maximinian failed to work cordially with him, and the failure was completed by the civil wars which followed his abdication.

At this critical moment, however, Christianity intervened to complete the work which the armies of the Roman Republic had begun. The Church laid down the proposition that God rules the world through a human vicegerent, and found that vicegerent in the Emperor. His authority was held to have received the explicit sanction of Christ and of the apostles. The former had issued the command, "Render unto Cæsar the things which be Cæsar's." St. Peter had coupled obedience to earthly rule with the service of God. St. Paul had condemned resistance to constituted authority, and had not hesitated to appeal to the judgment of Nero. The

Empire, too, was almost co-extensive with civilisation and with Christendom. If some converts dwelt beyond its frontiers, their numbers and importance were slight, nor would they have seriously disputed the assertion that all Christians were subjects of Rome; rather they regarded themselves as exiles in a barbarous land.

From the very first, the Church taught the duty of obedience even to a persecuting Emperor, so long as that obedience did not involve the denial of Christ. And when the conversion of Constantine had removed this obvious danger, Christian theologians hastened to develop their political theory on essentially imperialist and therefore universalist lines. The Emperor was degraded that he might be exalted. He was deprived of an unconvincing divinity to be endowed with a new supremacy as the chosen representative of the Almighty, and the imperial office gained all, or more than all, that its immediate holder lost. Those who might have been revolted by the idea of an imperfect god accepted their subjection to a veiled theocracy, the sanctity of which could not be impaired by any deficiencies in a human lieutenant. And into a veiled theocracy Christianity converted the Roman Empire. It was regarded as a divine institution, co-eternal with the world. The end of imperial rule would be the end of all human government, the prelude to the Second Advent and the personal reign of Christ.

During the period of the Greek republics and of the Roman Empire, Universalism thus appeared to have secured not only definition, but also an unquestioned supremacy. That supremacy, however, was in reality incomplete; the inevitable conflict existed, and its existence was only concealed because Individualism was undefined. It would be manifestly absurd to suppose that at any time all men preferred subjection to independence, and, as might be expected, examples of individualist tendencies are not lacking in this period.

It has been already suggested that the Universalism of ancient Greece was almost entirely confined to the relations of the community with its members; the external policy of the Greek republics was conceived in the contrary spirit. Even during the crisis of the Persian wars, Thebes and other states were found to be ready to support the invader. This willingness to submit can hardly be regarded as an example of universalist ideas, since there was no community of sentiment, nor corporate feeling, between the civilised Greeks and their barbarous neighbours. It was rather an assertion of Individualism. The Medising cities rejected the idea of subordination to the leadership of Lacedæmon and Athens, and hoped for greater freedom of action when those aspiring states had been crushed by Darius or Xerxes. The same individualist spirit found expression in the constant resistance offered to any state which attempted to control or to unify the Hellenic race. Athens, Lacedæmon and Thebes alike failed to establish a permanent supremacy in face of the persistent opposition of the majority of the other cities. And other illustrations of the prevalence of external Individualism in Greece are supplied by the almost perpetual isolation of Argos, by the refusal of the Lacedæmonians to share in the expedition of Alexander, and by their later resistance to Philopœmen and the Achæan League.

Nor was internal Individualism wholly unknown. With the doubtful exception of Lacedæmon, there is no trace of a "constitutional" opposition in Greece, and the extant political writers unanimously preach Universalism. But the frequency of seditions in the majority of the Greek cities shows that the spirit of resistance to government was by no means dead; it may well be that the stability of the Lacedæmonian constitution was in some measure due to the fact that in Lacedæmon alone was the necessary safety-valve supplied. The individualist theory, too, appears to have found support even from political thinkers. The contempt poured by Plato upon extreme democracy, "where horses and asses have learned a wonderfully free and magnificent way of walking," suggests the existence of a school of individualists so extreme as to be practically anarchists. And Aristotle's eagerness to prove that the state is natural, the defence which he offers for slavery and ostracism, indicate that internal Universalism had been assailed and that the contrary theory had obtained at least verbal expression.

Individualism, however, made little progress in the period following the age of Plato and Aristotle. At first the authority of those philosophers justified sufficiently the control of the citizen by the state; presently, a certain mental weariness seemed to overcome the world. Patriotic zeal was lessened by the very magnitude of the Roman Empire; the character of the imperial government hindered or prevented political discussion. The edict of Caracalla vulgarised, and hence reduced the value of, Roman citizenship; the chief privilege of the citizen became the obligation to pay taxes.

At the same time, men ceased to find the expression of their highest development in political association. The Stoics and the Epicureans agreed in recommending men not to turn aside from the pursuit of their private interest. To one school, society was hardly worthy of a philosopher's attention; to the other, the cares of citizenship were little more than a hindrance in the pursuit of happiness. Aristotle had found the highest form of existence in membership of a state, the truest joy in the activities of political life. Marcus Aurelius admits that those who are called upon to share in the task of government must labour to do their duty; he seems to regret that any one should be so called, to envy those who are freed from the cares of public life. And this political melancholy is characteristic of the age in which he lived. A tendency to distinguish between the citizen and the individual appeared, and if deliberate criticism of the universalist theory was still practically unknown, the ground was yet being subtly prepared for the assertion of Individualism.

Nor was this work of preparation altogether hindered by the Church. While the Empire was pagan, full citizenship was almost impossible for the sincere Christian; he could not perform those sacrifices on the altar of the Emperor which were the recognised test of allegiance. Even after the conversion of Constantine the difficulty did not entirely disappear. Idolatry was no longer demanded, but the favour shown to Arianism by the imperial government served to alienate the orthodox from their rulers. Indeed, during the reigns of Constantius II and Valens, the hostility of a large part of the clergy towards the government produced a situation not far removed from civil war; the persecution of Athanasius severely taxed the loyalty of the Church. Ecclesiastics, too, not unreasonably dreaded a conflict between religion and patriotism. They laboured to fix the thoughts of their disciples upon the world to come, and by so doing they tended unwittingly to undermine an institution to which they both professed and felt loyalty. Under their guidance, men learnt to care more for the salvation of their own souls than for the preservation of the Empire. Monasticism and asceticism became popular; they were alike inimical to true citizenship, since those who turned aside from the pleasures of an active life could hardly be expected to perform its duties. Despite the arguments put forward by Augustine in the *De Civitate Dei*, there is no reasonable doubt that the triumph of Christianity did accelerate the collapse of imperial power in the West. Had as many Roman citizens embraced the military as embraced the monastic profession, a far more serious opposition might have been offered to the barbarian invasions. Had the soldiers of the Empire displayed that degree of self-sacrifice and enthusiastic devotion which was exhibited by the hermits of Egypt or the pillar saints of Asia Minor, it is more than probable that the invaders would have been hurled back into the forests from which they emerged.

Yet even the cataclysm of the fifth century did not destroy the ascendancy of external Universalism. The barbarian invaders had come into contact with Rome before they passed the Rhine and Danube. They had been profoundly impressed by the law and order of the Empire, by its recuperative power and by its apparent perpetuity. Accustomed to the social and political vicissitudes of a migratory life, they were astonished at the spectacle of organised government and enduring institutions; their desire for plunder and their contempt for the imperial army were sensibly modified by a feeling of respectful wonder. Service under the Emperor became almost more honourable than victories gained over him; titles granted by the Emperor were prized as highly as trophies won on the field of battle.

This inclination towards respect and obedience was intensified by the conversion of the barbarians to Christianity. Though the missionaries who laboured among them were for the most part Arians, they none the less instilled into the minds of those whom they converted to doctrinal heresy the orthodox political theory of the Church. The influence of superstition increased the existing reverence for the Empire. The barbarians felt their inability to destroy an institution, in which they found the perfection of human wisdom and in which their spiritual masters taught them to recognise the working of the mighty hand of God. There is an oft-quoted saying of Athaulf, king of the Visigoths, to the effect that he aspired to be the foremost defender of that Empire which he had once hoped to destroy. Athaulf did no more than express the sincere longing of the majority of his fellow Teutons. The invaders eagerly adopted external Universalism; with the inevitable zeal of recent conversion, they became its most passionate supporters.

Thus, while the provinces actually became the seat of new monarchies, they remained theoretically part of the Empire. With the exception of Gaiseric the Vandal, each king secured imperial recognition and based his claim to the obedience of the provincials upon some commission granted by the Emperor. It was held that the deposition of Romulus Augustus by Odovacar meant nothing more important than the recognition in the West of the sole rule of the Emperor Zeno. Even Theodoric the Ostrogoth accepted the position of an imperial lieutenant in Italy, as Wallia the Visigoth had done in Aquitaine and as Gunthar the Burgundian did in the Rhone valley. If Chlodovech ruled the Franks as a national king, he would himself have been the first to admit that he ruled the Gallo-Romans by virtue of the vague gift of "the ornaments of the consulship," which he had received from the Emperor Anastasius. Accomplished facts were indeed ignored; it was held that nothing had changed. By some strange political alchemy, barbarian tribes were converted into Roman armies, barbarian kings into Roman proconsuls. It was universally believed that the extent of the Empire was undiminished, the power and authority of the Emperor unimpaired.

And however harassed that Emperor might be, he never even mentally abdicated his lordship of the world. No sooner did an opportunity arise for the practical reassertion of dormant rights, than every effort was made to bring facts into accordance with theory. During the last agony of the Empire in the West, Marjorian, in place of consolidating his position in Italy, preferred to attempt the restoration of his authority in Gaul and Spain, and the recovery of Africa. Anthemius allied with Leo I in order to overthrow the Vandals. And after the abdication of Romulus Augustus, the resources of the Empire in the East, which even the careful government of Anastasius had hardly rendered adequate for the defence of such lands as remained to the ruler of Constantinople, were expended lavishly in an attempt to regain the provinces of the West. Justinian, rather compelled by a sense of duty than actuated by mere lust of glory, despatched Belisarius to Africa and Italy. His efforts were crowned with partial success; the kingdoms of the Vandals and Ostrogoths were overthrown, that of the Visigoths was shaken. Imperial prestige was revived; external Universalism acquired additional strength.

And since the supremacy of the Emperor seemed to be hardly inconvenient and unlikely to be more definitely asserted, there was little inducement to formulate a theory in which that supremacy should have no place. So accustomed had mankind become to the universalist idea that, though the conflict continued, the assertion of external Individualism was fitful and inconclusive. Of those barbarian kingdoms which inclined to deny imperial claims, the Vandal and Ostrogothic were destroyed, the Visigothic weakened and a prey to constant civil war. The Franks remained. But though they at first both attacked the imperialists in Italy and set an example of independence by coining money not bearing the Emperor's head, their kingdom in a manner owed its eventual permanence to a denial of its own existence.

While, however, external Universalism thus maintained the ascendancy which it had acquired, internal Individualism made rapid progress. The Roman Empire had never been a highly centralised state; its decline and fall served to increase that local independence which the imperial government had rather fostered than attempted to crush. Districts were driven to provide for their own defence. The Venetian and "Armorican" republics, the curious autonomous state which seems to have existed in Auvergne, and the short-lived "kingdom" of Syagrius are examples of the new organisation of states upon individualist principles, since in every one of these instances membership of the Roman Empire was not only admitted but also prized.

The barbarian states, too, had this characteristic in common, that they allowed a large measure of self-government to their subjects. The Roman provincials were accorded their own law and, when once the conquerors had settled in their midst, suffered little interference beyond the obligation of paying taxes. Over their Teutonic subjects the kings had but a limited authority. A ruler of marked personality was perhaps sometimes absolute, but a ruler of less capacity was hardly more than president of a council of turbulent warriors. Even the ablest monarchs were often driven to conciliate rather than to command; the story of the vase of Soissons is typical of the relationship between the barbarian kings and their subjects. In some other cases, royal authority was far more restricted than it was among the Franks. At least after the conversion of Reccared, the government of the Visigoths rested practically with the synods of the Church; the great ecclesiastics in Spain were all-powerful. The period was, in short, a period of external Universalism and internal Individualism.

This ascendancy of external Universalism was assisted by the rise of a new power. It was only natural that the Popes, as bishops of the imperial city, should enjoy a pre-eminent position in the Christian hierarchy, and from an early date they claimed spiritual supremacy over the provinces of the West. It was asserted that St. Peter had been specially entrusted with the care of his Master's disciples, that the Popes had inherited the plenitude of the Apostle's power, and that they were therefore Vicars of Christ, the ecclesiastical counterpart of the Emperor. These claims had been already admitted to a great extent when circumstances almost compelled the entrance of the Pope into the domain of secular politics. The recovery of Italy by Justinian was soon followed by a new invasion; the greater part of the peninsula was occupied by the Lombards, and their control of the passes of the Apennines practically cut off Rome from such other districts as still acknowledged the authority of Constantinople. Neither the Emperor nor his immediate representative, the Exarch of Ravenna, was able to afford much assistance to the ancient capital of the Empire. The city was forced to provide for its own defence, and the Popes to supply the place of an imperial governor, adding the character of diplomatist, and even of general, to that of bishop. Rome, threatened by the Lombards, was probably saved from capture by the peace which Gregory the Great concluded with Agilulf. The service thus rendered was gratefully acknowledged by the Italians, who thenceforward looked rather to the Papacy than to the Exarchate for help and guidance. Had the Popes so inclined, they might almost have destroyed the last traces of imperial authority in their city. But they possibly feared to attack the accepted political theory of the Church, and they were in any case wedded to external Universalism by the very nature of their office. Christianity is a cosmopolitan religion; the head of western Christendom could have no part in national life, and any open assertion of independence towards the Emperor would at that date have involved the creation of a national, externally individualist state in Italy.

Hence, even when the Lombards abandoned Arianism and accepted orthodoxy, thus removing one possible objection to union between themselves and the Papacy, the Popes still continued to maintain a hostile attitude towards them. They continued to profess their allegiance to Constantinople, despite the fact that they were alienated from the Emperor by the Iconoclastic Controversy. Even when they called upon Pippin to deliver them from the increasing power of the Lombards under Aistulf, the request for help was so ambiguously worded as to leave room for the opinion that the Frankish king was only invited to act as an imperial lieutenant. The Popes, in fact, remained consistent champions of external Universalism.

That theory soon came to need powerful advocacy. Irene blinded her son, Constantine VI, and usurped the throne of Constantinople, assuming the title of Empress and by implication claiming to be as much the vicegerent of the Almighty as any of her predecessors had been. The idea of feminine rule was unfamiliar; such women as Pulcheria and Martina, who had practically governed the Empire, had cloaked their authority under the name of some male relative. Consequently, even the East was disturbed by the conduct of Irene, and though she was for a while recognised, that recognition was hardly given with enthusiasm. The political conscience of the West was still more profoundly shocked. The imperial throne was considered to be vacant, and the duty of supplying that vacancy was held to devolve upon those subjects of the Empire who were not so dead to shame as to accept a woman's rule.

This opinion, however, would probably have failed to secure definite expression, and still more probably have failed to effect definite results, if it had not been adopted by the Pope. As it was, that ingenuity which had recently produced an autograph letter from St. Peter to Pippin was now employed to profit from the usurpation of Irene. Already attracted towards the Carolingians by benefits received and the hope of further advantage, the Pope proceeded to deny the capacity of a woman to rule. The crimes and sex of Irene were declared to have created a vacancy in the Empire; by a convenient fiction, the right to fill that vacancy was conferred upon the mongrel population of the papal city, who were announced to be the senate and people of Rome. The one candidate upon whom the choice could reasonably fall was opportunely present; he appeared before a mob excited by the progress of a great religious festival. On a memorable Christmas Day, Charles, king of the Franks, already Patrician of the Romans, was hailed as Emperor by the intoxicated congregation at St. Peter's, and the Pope at once recognised the voice of the people as the voice of God. Leo III placed the imperial crown upon the head of his friend and benefactor; the Holy Roman Empire came into being.

The coronation of Charles might well have destroyed the supremacy of external Universalism. In the West, many who had yielded obedience to an Emperor whose wishes could be ignored with impunity, were moved to resist an Emperor whose commands were reinforced by overwhelming military strength. Already the power of Charles had excited revolt in Aquitaine and in Bavaria; now Venice and Beneventum alike attempted to assert their independence. In the East, the deposition of Irene and the accession of Nicephorus weakened the constitutional ground upon which the theory of a vacancy had been based. Two rival claimants to the lordship of the world appeared, each declaring himself to be the legitimate successor of Augustus and Constantine VI, each stigmatising the other as an usurper. Mankind received an embarrassing invitation to make its choice between them, and the rejection of both would not have been surprising. But the desire to be ruled was still stronger than the desire to rule. The arguments and influence of the Church prevailed; external Universalism rather gained than lost by the accession of Charles, since the theory was once more brought into closer accordance with fact.

VII

THE CONFLICT IN EUROPE: 2. FROM THE CORONATION OF CHARLES TO THE FALL OF THE HOHENSTAUFEN

NOT only did external Universalism survive the coronation of Charles, but for a time after that event even internal Universalism made some progress. Already the displacement of the Merovingians by Pippin had been accompanied by an increase of royal power in the Frankish kingdom. Charles the Great directed his energies towards a further strengthening of the central government. Though the very extent of his dominions compelled the delegation of authority over the provinces to dukes and counts, he attempted to secure the subordination of these lieutenants. Hunold in Aquitaine, Tassilo in Bavaria, were reduced to obedience. The *missi dominici* were instituted, officials of the court sent at intervals through the Empire to supervise the local administration and to check any tendency towards independence in the provincial governors. But the system was short-lived. During the reign of Lewis the Pious, the *missi* received or usurped the position of counts; life officers were made hereditary, occasional appointments became permanent posts, and in the more distant districts of the Empire practically independent principalities were gradually established. This decentralising process was hastened by the civil wars between Lewis and his sons, and by the incapacity of successive Emperors. The day of internal Universalism had not yet dawned.

On the other hand, external Individualism did not at

once develop even as a result of that political maëlstrom into which the western world was plunged by the weakness of the Carolingian dynasty and the attacks of Saracens and Northmen. The Treaty of Verdun has often been regarded as one of the epoch-making events of History. In reality, the recognition of the titular supremacy of Lothar is more remarkable than the acquisition of actual independence by Lewis the German and Charles the Bald. The document marks not so much the birth of Germany and France as the postponement of the death of the imperial conception in those two countries. The position of Emperor remained the highest reward of successful ambition, the vain prize for the sake of which every king was ready to neglect his immediate duties and his true interest. The reunion of all the Frankish states under Charles the Fat shows how slight was the belief in national monarchies, nor is it too much to say that if the Emperors of the ninth century had possessed the ability of an Otto the Great, the Treaty of Verdun would have remained entirely unexecuted. External Universalism gratified the world despite the destruction of imperial prestige; external Individualism struggled very slowly towards recognition.

For this continued ascendancy of the desire to be ruled, the Church was in great measure responsible. Kings, unable to protect their own immediate dominions from Northmen and Saracens, secured and degraded the imperial office; their utter weakness emphasised the unreality of the Empire, and the provinces, driven by that weakness to provide for their own defence, might well have forgotten the conception of the unity of Christendom. But at the moment when society appeared to be fast tottering to dissolution, the Popes effected new spiritual conquests. Britain was reunited with Europe; the rudest barbarians were softened by the gentle influence of the Christian faith; the untamed fierceness of the Northmen was subdued by the devoted zeal of unarmed priests. The Church produced a unity more real than that which had been forced upon reluctant tribes by the military prowess of Charles the Great; in the West, the Popes reigned without a rival. But they were inevitably cosmopolitan, forbidden to sympathise with national aspirations by the very nature of their office. Denying the right of private judgment in religion, they were prohibited from favouring it in politics. They were compelled to champion external Universalism, of the merits of which they had become the only exponents.

Nevertheless, the Popes were ultimately instrumental in securing the definition of external Individualism. As their prestige increased, they remembered that Leo had placed the imperial crown on the head of Charles, and they claimed the right to dispose of that prize for which earthly monarchs so eagerly contended. In the garden of Gethsemane, St. Peter had produced two swords; these swords were now declared to symbolise the temporal and spiritual powers, to indicate the dual headship of the Christian world. If the Emperor were supreme in secular affairs, the Pope was supreme in ecclesiastical; there was at least equality between the two vicegerents of God.

This hypothesis at first presented no difficulty. The Emperors were too weak to interfere with the interests of the Papacy; the city of Rome was in reality independent. On the other hand, despite such cases as the intervention of Nicholas I in the matter of Waldrada and the consequent excommunication of Lothar II, the Popes in general could not yet aspire to dictate even to a feeble monarch. They lacked material force; their strength depended upon moral prestige. And at this period the Papacy became not less degraded than the Empire. The tiara was a gift with which disreputable women gratified their lovers, and in such circumstances there was no likelihood of a conflict arising between the two heads of Christendom. Each was too weak to attempt any effective assertion of authority over the other. It seemed infinitely more probable that both Emperor and Pope would disappear; that mankind would revolt against a theory which exalted into the position of vicegerents of the Almighty an Italian princeling and an immoral bishop.

External Individualism, in fact, began to develop from the moment when Charles the Fat proved his utter unworthiness to be the successor of his great namesake. His deposition was followed by the foundation of several independent monarchies, and in the vacancy of the imperial throne only a dubious homage was rendered to Arnulf of Germany, as the possible heir to the dormant title. But the desire to be ruled, the sense that the Christian world should have some determinate head, produced a remarkable reaction in favour of external Universalism. For a while, the Emperors were obscure nonentities, and the abler rulers found their energies sufficiently employed in combating the attacks of the Northmen. Yet when Henry the Fowler had restored a measure of order to Germany, when Otto had crushed his rebellious nobles and given at least transient stability to his kingdom, the first use made of the new power thus acquired was to attempt the revival of the Holy Roman Empire. In place of completing the consolidation of a national state, Otto followed the example of Justinian. He entered Italy and received the imperial crown at Rome. His action is evidence of the continued influence of the universalist theory; his personal capacity and the military strength of Germany made the

Emperor once more a real factor in the affairs of all the states of western Europe.

And the first use which was made of the revived imperial power by Otto and his successors was to effect the reform of the Papacy. A series of Popes, nominated or practically nominated by the Emperor, restored that reputation which the vices of the lovers and son of Marozia had well-nigh destroyed. But the reformed Papacy forgot its obligations to the Empire. Realising their strength and the potentialities of their position, the Popes resented the idea that they had any earthly superior; they became unwilling to admit even that they had an equal in the person of the Emperor. They insisted on the superiority of spiritual over temporal power. They argued that since the imperial crown could be received only at Rome and from their hands, they created Emperors and that the created must be controlled by the creator. Such claims naturally roused opposition; a contest which fills the history of the Middle Ages began between the secular and ecclesiastical heads of Christendom. And this contest was nothing more than the inevitable reaction against the long-continued ascendancy of external Universalism. For though the two principals were alike universalists, their allies and helpers were in a measure conscious or unconscious exponents of Individualism.

In the struggle the Papacy possessed certain conspicuous advantages. Though the Empire was in conception extra-territorial, its power rested ultimately upon the German people; it could hope for little or no support from France or England or Spain. The Church, on the other hand, extra-territorial and cosmopolitan in its very essence, was able to draw strength from every nation in the West, and in the first stages of the quarrel the advantage thus possessed was increased by the piety or policy of Hildebrand. Celibacy was enforced upon all the clergy, who were thus converted into a species of papal army. Divided from the mass of mankind, freed as far as possible from those cares which served to distract the generality of the human race, the clergy were the more devoted to the cause of that institution to which they had given themselves so completely. And though hope of earthly honour, or a sincere conviction of the superiority of the imperial cause, gained some ecclesiastical support for the Emperor, the Popes had on the whole a remarkably loyal and single-minded body of adherents to carry on the struggle.

And the Popes of this period were themselves equally single-minded. Though both the imperial crown and the papal tiara were elective, there was a fundamental difference between the two cases. The Emperors laboured constantly to found a dynasty; family ambition distracted their policy; their partial success produced all the weakness and disorder practically inseparable from minorities in an age of personal rule. The Popes, on the other hand, succeeded as full-grown men, often well trained in the art of statesmanship prior to their accession. They had no natural heirs for whom they might labour to provide; they could found no dynasty. Consequently, each successive occupant of the papal chair was devoted only to the promotion of the interest of the Papacy; each was actuated by an unselfish and impersonal zeal for the cause of which he was the official champion.

A marked advantage also was derived by the Popes from the character of the age in which the struggle occurred. The Emperor was compelled to rely mainly on material strength. Only by gathering a powerful army could he win his way to Rome and to the imperial crown. His election at Aachen was but the first step towards the final goal of his ambition, and the reluctance of German princes to accord him their support was a less formidable obstacle than the mosquito-ridden Campagna. An army, laboriously collected in Germany after months of mingled cajolery and threats, as often as not dwindled to nothingness after a few weeks in the fever-stricken environs of Rome, and the Emperor, deprived of all compelling power, was driven to abandon the fruits of his arduous toil and to escape as best he might across the Alps.

The Popes, on the other hand, possessed no material strength. But the character of the age made the fact that they were driven to rely upon moral weapons almost a source of positive advantage to them. Spiritual censures, to which an earlier or a later generation would perhaps have been indifferent, constituted a very real menace to the superstitious mediæval mind; fear of excommunication constantly proved a far more effective means of persuasion or compulsion than the most formidable host. And whereas the Emperor had to rely on his ability to overawe or to persuade his vassals in order to gather together an army, the thunderbolts of the Lateran were at the free and absolute disposal of the Vicar of Christ.

All these factors contributed to secure the eventual success of the Papacy in its struggle with the Empire, but the greatest asset of the Popes was the fact that the Emperors were brought into more direct conflict with the growing spirit of Individualism. It has been already pointed out that the dominant characteristic of the internal organisation of states was at this period individualist. After the death of Charles the Great, his universalist ideas were abandoned so far as internal government was concerned, owing to the weakness of his successors. The *missi dominici* became counts;

they and the dukes of the more outlying districts asserted their local independence; offices which had been temporary became hereditary, and the authority of the central government was reduced to a mere shadow. And this decentralising process, of which the origin may be traced to the incapacity of Lewis the Pious, was accelerated by the peculiar conditions of the age.

Charles the Great was hardly dead before that system which he had so laboriously endeavoured to construct was shattered, and ample proof was afforded, if proof were needed, of how much his dominions had owed to his personal capacity and prestige. Issuing, as it were, from the Cimmerian darkness of Scandinavia, the Northmen swept, a devastating flood, over the lands of western Europe. Distracted by their private quarrels, the successors of Charles were rendered doubly incapable of combating a danger which their lack of ability utterly unfitted them to meet. From the Emperor the provinces had nothing to hope; as had been the case in the age of the barbarian invasions, they were driven to defend themselves or perish. The calamities of the period forced the individual man to care for himself rather than for the community; forced local districts to care for themselves rather than for the whole Empire. The distant central authority was forgotten or ignored; society, under compulsion, reorganised itself upon a feudal basis.

Feudalism was not a system. It originated rather from necessity than from choice; it expresses rather an attitude of mind than the calculated working of human wisdom. In its earliest form, it was the outcome of the spirit of internal Individualism. Men almost dissociated themselves from the state, which could do so little for them, to gather themselves into semi-isolated groups under the protection and leadership of some lord, who might at least save them from death. But the development of these small groups undermined the ascendancy of external Universalism. The theory of imperial or papal supremacy was not indeed denied; at no period, perhaps, was the conception of the common headship of the Christian world more lucidly or emphatically expressed; the ideal of a united Christendom received much lip-service. When, however, the crisis had passed and the Emperor attempted to reassert his universal lordship, it was remembered that in the time of trouble he had not come to the help of his people. The conduct of an Odo compared only too favourably with that of a Charles the Fat. The numerous cases in which some local magnate had driven off the invaders, or had at least died fighting for his men, were remembered to the prejudice of the imperial idea. And these local magnates themselves, having enjoyed a generous measure of independence when external help even if coupled with external control would have been most welcome, were more than reluctant to sacrifice anything of that independence at the very moment when they seemed likely to derive some profit from their liberty. They questioned, and were supported by their people in questioning, the validity of any claim made to their obedience by an external power; admitting the corporate character of human society in theory, in practice they denied it. They became external individualists.

It is clear that this new spirit must come into conflict with both Emperor and Pope. But at first it was against the former only that it struggled. The human mind, long accustomed to accept as axiomatic the existence of a divine vicegerent, could not immediately rid itself of the habit of obedience. Nor, indeed, were men altogether eager to be free; naturally they were less eager to deny moral than material obligations. Hence, the Emperor first suffered from the growth of Individualism. He was more obviously in opposition to it, since he demanded material sacrifices on the altar of external Universalism, whereas the Papacy demanded little more than a formal recognition of its authority. The Emperor required men and money; the Pope required only those men who would by inclination devote themselves to the service of the Church, and only those comparatively moderate contributions which in so pious an age seemed to be but the legitimate due of spiritual guides. In the quarrel between the Empire and the Papacy, therefore, the latter received for a while the support of the individualists. The newly developed kingdoms rejected the imperial claim to universal dominion; the princes of Germany unwillingly supplied the support which the Emperor demanded for the prosecution of the struggle to maintain that claim.

The history of the Middle Ages is in a great degree the history of this decline of external Universalism. Even at the height of the Holy Roman Empire, its authority had not been recognised in England, and after the death of Charles the Great it was equally disregarded in the rising Christian kingdoms of the Iberian Peninsula. Charles the Fat was the last Emperor to secure even nominal recognition in Gaul; Otto II was the last Emperor even to attempt to secure such recognition. The Capetian dynasty organised the French monarchy on a basis of external Individualism, and the explicit acceptance of imperial authority was early confined to the German and Italian lands.

Even in those countries, though explicit recognition was for some centuries longer accorded, the actual authority of the Emperor suffered constant diminution. As long as they were threatened by the aggression of the nobles in their districts, the Italian cities welcomed the presence of an imperial army in their midst. But when their growing wealth and importance had delivered them from this danger, they began to regard the passage of the Alps by their overlord with mingled anger and alarm; they became less and less ready to render obedience to him, less and less ready to assist him with either men or money. Frederic Barbarossa attempted to re-establish his authority over the republics of the Lombard plain; his attempt was finally defeated at Legnano. From that moment, if the Emperor could still count on some support from the Italian cities, he owed that support rather to the mutual jealousies of those cities than to any affection borne by them towards himself. If he gained the adherence of some former enemy, it was generally at the cost of the hostility of some old ally. Allies, not subjects, indeed, had the Italian cities become. Where Frederic Barbarossa had commanded, Frederic II entreated and cajoled. The spirit of external Universalism lingered still in Italy, but it was too weak to give effectual support to the Emperor in his quarrel with the Papacy.

Nor was the imperial position in Germany much more satisfactory. Otto the Great had crushed the rebellions of the dukes and had effected the temporary establishment of a strong monarchy. But his successors were speedily involved in difficulties more serious than those which had embarrassed the first Saxon Emperor. The existing spirit of internal Individualism was enhanced by the occurrence of minorities and by the quasi-elective character of the monarchy. The first resulted in feebleness of the executive. The second led each king to bid for the support of the nobles, the more so because he was concerned in an attempt to secure the establishment of his own dynasty. The permanent strength of the monarchy was sacrificed to the immediate interest of the monarch. And further concessions to local independence were occasioned by the fact that the German king was also Emperor; they were the price which he paid for the support of his vassals in those Italian expeditions which were essential for the actual attainment of the imperial crown, or which were undertaken in the hope of preserving imperial rights in the Peninsula.

Soon the princes of the Empire discovered a plausible justification for their turbulence. Theoretically, the Emperor was lord of the world; all kings were his vassals. The German magnates therefore claimed that the rights of their king had been extinguished by his accession to a higher office; that they, no less than the various rulers of western Europe, were tenants-in-chief of the Empire, and that it would diminish imperial dignity if they were degraded to any position lower than that occupied by, for example, a king of France. Such obedience as the Capetians rendered, they would render; and since the Capetians were entirely independent, the German princes claimed entire independence also. They laboured to exalt the Emperor into impotence. It is true that the strength of the Salian and Hohenstaufen dynasties prevented the magnates from realising their ambition, but they none the less possessed an argument which served to justify practical rebellion and which the universalists themselves found it hard to refute.

The Popes hastened to avail themselves of the advantages thus offered. As exponents of external Universalism, they could readily accept the theory put forward by the German princes of their relation to the Emperor. They encouraged the growth of local independence, supported insurrections, and urged the nobles to insist upon the alienation of crown lands. It gradually became habitual for the electors to demand such alienation as the price of their recognition; it was the design of the princes to secure that the king should not have demesnes sufficiently extensive to supply him with power to refuse their demands. If a Henry III or a Frederic Barbarossa proved equal to the task of curbing the turbulence of his vassals, it was still only at the cost of civil war; such civil war became the normal state of affairs in Germany. In short, the attempt to combine the Roman Empire and the German kingdom failed to give strength to the former and strangled the latter in its birth.

The Popes enjoyed a special advantage in their interference in the affairs of Germany. The archbishops of Mainz, Köln, and Trier were great territorial magnates; their influence, both as churchmen and as nobles, was considerable. But being ecclesiastics, though they might at times adopt an attitude of hostility towards the Papacy, they were ultimately its natural allies. The fact that the imperial crown was elective made their support doubly important, and assisted the Pope in the exaltation of rival Emperors. Claiming that it was part of the papal prerogative to supervise the conduct of the man upon whom the imperial crown had been conferred, the Papacy, from the time of Henry IV, frequently decreed the deposition of an Emperor hostile to it and the transference of his title to another. Nor did the German princes hesitate to transfer their allegiance to a papal nominee; from his weakness or from the consequent embarrassment of the legitimate Emperor, they might always win some new concessions, some fresh immunities. The spirit of internal Individualism ranged a large party in Germany on the side of the Pope.

At the same time, the Emperors were unable to

retaliate successfully by the creation of anti-popes. Originally, there had been an imperial veto on papal elections, but that veto was lost after the reign of Henry III, and soon even imperial recognition was no longer admitted to be essential. Whereas an imperial coronation could take place only at Rome, and the Popes were thus in a measure acknowledged to have at least some share in the choice of an Emperor, that Emperor had no similar share in the choice of a Pope. An anti-emperor was assured of a following among the princes of Germany; their Individualism impelled them to seize any opportunity for weakening the imperial position. But universalists and individualists alike tended to refuse recognition to an anti-pope. The clergy dreaded the possible disruption of the Church; those laity who were not actuated by the same dread feared the effects of an increase of imperial power, which threatened that liberty so dear to them as individualists.

It is small wonder, then, that the Papacy triumphed; its triumph was the first great victory gained by the forces of Individualism, little as that appeared at the time. With the death of Frederic II and the fall of the Hohenstaufen, the struggle came to an end. The Great Interregnum followed; the world learnt that it could dispense with an Emperor. On the other hand, papal supremacy was admitted by all; its recognition, indeed, seemed to be more complete than ever, since there was now no rival claimant to universal dominion. In reality, however, the ascendancy of external Universalism was impaired. During the contest between Empire and Papacy, mankind had been perplexed by the necessity of choosing between the two parties. If the verdict had been given for the Pope, this was the result largely of the fact that for the time the forces of Individualism were enlisted on his side. This did not prevent the casting of doubts upon that theory which had hitherto been almost unquestioningly accepted. And now when the Empire was practically suspended, further doubts arose; men began to ask whether there was indeed any human vicegerent of Christ. Serious resistance to papal claims followed immediately upon the too complete victory of the Papacy.

Once more, that victory was but the expression of the reaction which was occurring in the human mind. The theory of external Universalism had for centuries been generally accepted; now the contrary theory began to gain ground, and the closing stages of the quarrel between the Empire and the Papacy are marked by a growing disregard for the unity of Christendom. It is not a mere coincidence that the fall of the Hohenstaufen occurred at the very moment when the Crusades came to an end. There has never been a more remarkable expression of the corporate conception of human society than that which was supplied by the expeditions sent out for the rescue of the Holy Sepulchre. Western Europe poured out its blood and treasure for the attainment of an ideal; the early crusaders were inspired to forget all national and racial distinction, that they might combine to rescue Jerusalem from the infidel. Such was the spirit of the First Crusade; such was the chord in the human heart which responded to the appeal of Urban II at Clermont. Men forgot all, save the fact that they were Christians and brothers, that they must unite to avenge the wrongs of their Saviour.

But to the enthusiastic altruism of the First Crusade there presently succeeded a far different spirit. Philip Augustus, in the Third Crusade, pursued his own interest rather than that of Christendom; even Richard I was not above suspicion of selfishness. The Fourth Crusade was little more than a mercantile adventure;

it turned aside from Palestine, since there seemed to be greater profit to be gained from an attack on Constantinople. The expeditions, which still proceeded to the Holy Land, were principally dictated by a wish to keep open the eastern markets for the maritime republics of Italy; they resemble the expeditions of London merchants to the Iberian Peninsula rather than that which Godfrey of Bouillon had led to Jerusalem. The spirit of Universalism was gradually giving place to that of Individualism.

And it was both significant and appropriate that the last Crusade should have been led by Frederic II. In him the spirit of external Universalism found its true embodiment. Brilliant, cultured, brave, he was not unworthy to occupy the throne of the Cæsars. A lawgiver and a poet, the founder of a university, he possessed almost all the qualities which might fit a man to be the representative of the human race. By birth a German, by education an Italian, by policy almost a Saracen, he was essentially cosmopolitan; he would have been hampered by the possession of mere territorial sovereignty. He was veritably "the Wonder of the World," the last true mediæval Emperor. And it is equally significant that his Crusade should have been carried out despite a papal decree of excommunication against its leader; the Papacy, pursuing its apparent interest, had become almost individualist in spirit.

Henceforward a Crusade was an impossibility. External Individualism had gained too great a hold on mankind for them so to forget their private cares as to adventure their lives and money for the sake of establishing Christian rule over the grave of the Founder of the faith. The Papacy had shattered its rival, but it had done so only at the cost of shaking men's belief in that theory on which the papal, no less than the imperial, position rested. The world, so long desirous to be ruled, now conceived the desire to rule; excess, as always, brought its own retribution. And the effects of the reaction which they had encouraged were soon felt by the Popes; Frederic II was avenged by Philip the Fair, by Hus, and by Luther.

VIII

THE CONFLICT IN EUROPE: 3. FROM THE FALL OF THE HOHENSTAUFEN TO THE PEACE OF WESTPHALIA

THE fall of the Hohenstaufen marks an important epoch in the history of the world. To all seeming, a decisive victory had been secured by the Papacy, the supremacy of which appeared to be established beyond all dispute, since the Empire for a while practically ceased to exist. In reality, however, the victory was rather a defeat; it had been gained at the cost of weakening that sentiment upon which the power of the Papacy ultimately rested. For papal, no less than imperial, supremacy was only the expression of the corporate conception of human society; it depended for its vitality upon the strength of the desire to be ruled, upon the ascendancy of external Universalism. But in the course of the struggle the Popes had consciously or unconsciously availed themselves of the existence of the contrary sentiment. They had urged men to refuse obedience to the Emperor, had denied his claim to universal dominion, had reviled and degraded the imperial office. They failed to realise that by adopting this policy, though they might accomplish the defeat of their rivals, they were bound at the same time to inflict irreparable damage on themselves, to weaken permanently their own position. Once taught to gratify their desire to rule, men naturally proceeded to the rejection of all external authority, to the fullest satisfaction of that desire.

For a time, the spirit of external Individualism found a useful ally in the Pope; the Emperor was more obviously and immediately in a position of hostility to that spirit, since he demanded material and not merely moral obedience. But the alliance could only be temporary. When the Emperor had ceased to be a danger, Individualism found its enemy in the Pope, and the very completeness of the papal triumph made an attack upon papal supremacy both more inevitable and more vigorous. After the fall of the Hohenstaufen, not only did the intoxication of victory lead to the putting forward of exaggerated claims by the Papacy, but, further, the utter humiliation of their rivals led the Popes to appear clearly as the only barrier against the complete realisation of the ideal of external Individualism.

Even before the conclusion of the struggle between the Empire and the Papacy, the theory of papal supremacy had been at least tentatively called in question. The Roman populace never submitted readily to the rule of their bishops; seditions were frequent, and the authority of the Pope was constantly threatened. Among these seditions, that organised by Arnold of Brescia possesses a special significance. Not content with advocating the restoration of the Republic, he went further and denied the right of the Pope to intermeddle with secular affairs. This amounted to an assault on the doctrine of papal supremacy, since, though the Vicar of Christ was primarily the spiritual head of Christendom, he claimed also a definite superiority over all temporal rulers. On the authority of the alleged Donation of Constantine and of the Pseudo-Isidorian Decretals, it had been asserted that at the time of the foundation of Constantinople the government of the western provinces of the Roman Empire had been committed to the Pope, and if that grant had been a tribute to his ecclesiastical pre-eminence, it none the less conveyed with it some secular power. Arnold of Brescia, on the contrary, contended that a bishop should confine himself to the services of the Church, nor did he urge the maintenance of imperial government. Admitting that a formal recognition of the Emperor was either expedient or necessary, he supported the practical assertion of local independence; he denied in effect the existence of any human vicegerent of Christ.

Arnold had contented himself with attacking the secular side of papal supremacy. The Albigenses assailed the whole papal position. Politically, they denied the right of the Pope to interfere with the government and conduct of the count of Toulouse. Doctrinally, they asserted the right of private judgment, questioned the exceptional position of the priesthood, and even denied the vital dogma of transubstantiation. All the factors which eventually produced the Reformation may here be discerned, if only in embryo; the Albigenses resisted all the implications of that theory of the divine government of the world upon which papal authority depended. They failed in their revolt against external Universalism, but their importance cannot well be overestimated. That it was recognised at the time is sufficiently indicated by the fact that the expedition against them was described as a "crusade," a term hitherto applied only to the holy wars against the professed enemies of the Christian religion.

And the Friar movement itself, the most emphatic expression of the religious spirit during this period, contributed eventually to the decline of papal influence. At first, the devotion of the disciples of Dominic and Francis revived the waning reputation of the Church and riveted afresh its hold upon the human intellect. But this was only the immediate result of the work of the Friars. Themselves professing and preaching apostolic poverty, they rebuked by implication, and even explicitly, the wealth and luxury of the monks and of the episcopate. They crystallised a certain vague disapproval of ecclesiastical riches, and supplied arguments against abuses, the existence of which had long been deplored. In this way, they discredited all sections of the clergy except themselves. For the moment, their own popularity counterbalanced the unpopularity of the bishops and monks, and the Church as a whole gained rather than lost.

But the Friars themselves soon became guilty of the very vices which they had so eloquently denounced, and ecclesiastical credit was forthwith seriously impaired. Mankind had learnt to express its hatred of clerical abuses; open expression consolidated opinion, and a demand for reform was heard. The Pope, as head of western Christendom, was invited to satisfy this demand; he refused, and revealed plainly that apostolic poverty was an ideal unwelcome to the successor of the Prince of the Apostles. The Friars Observant, who held strictly to the original constitution of their Orders, were silenced, since they had insisted too strongly upon the original status of the founders of their Faith. But when once criticism had found expression, it could not be subdued by a papal *non possumus;* so far from ceasing, it turned to the theory of the supremacy of the Pope, which it had at first left unassailed. The abuses resultant from gratification of the desire to be ruled fostered the desire to rule. In existing circumstances, reform was impossible without papal sanction and support; since that sanction and support were not forthcoming, it appeared to be questionable whether a complete change in the whole scheme of ecclesiastical polity was not desirable.

The Friars, moreover, in face of the natural opposition

which their coming had aroused in the monastic orders, had been obliged to rely upon papal support against the clergy of those countries in which they laboured. They became an essentially international body, the very exemplar of external Universalism. So long as they retained their popularity, the Papacy benefited from this fact; it appeared as the champion of the only body of clergy which merited and received the respect and affection of mankind. But as soon as they had become corrupt, their very cosmopolitanism increased the dislike with which they came to be regarded. They found themselves in direct opposition to the spirit of external Individualism, and by their faults they fostered the growth of that spirit. They were considered as alien intruders; only by papal influence could they maintain themselves in any country. Consequently, a large measure of their unpopularity was transferred to their patron; the power of the Pope was held to be a bar to the accomplishment of salutary reforms, and the advantage of papal supremacy seemed more than ever dubious.

That doctrine of apostolic poverty which the Friars preached also reflected upon the Pope. Successive occupants of the papal chair found it necessary to rebuke the exuberant zeal of the Observants. The rigid asceticism of the early Dominicans and Franciscans, indeed, did no small disservice to the papal cause, since the Papacy had accumulated wealth from the piety and superstition of western Europe, and the continued possession of that wealth was threatened by the doctrine that true Christianity disdained or shunned all earthly things. The external individualists had already lamented the transference of so much wealth into alien hands. Now they seized eagerly on the arguments against ecclesiastical riches with which the Friars presented them, and their original regret was intensified or converted into anger when they had been taught that the holding of temporal property was incompatible with the sincere following of Christ.

The ultimate cause of the decline of papal ascendancy is to be found in the growth of individualist ideas, and in this period more especially in the development of external Individualism. Yet nothing more forcibly illustrates the complexity of the conflict of desire than the interaction of the two contrary emotions during the later Middle Ages. While external Individualism made progress, internal Universalism made progress also; the growth of the one assisted that of the other, nor is it too much to say that by the growth of the one that of the other was made possible. The western world tended towards internal Universalism because it was tending towards external Individualism also; the increase of internal Universalism in turn made that of external Individualism more rapid.

It has been pointed out already that in the period following the barbarian invasions the internal organisation of states was individualist. For this fact, the contemporary prevalence of external Universalism was largely responsible. Rulers were turned from the task of consolidating their immediate dominions by the hope of seizing the phantom of the imperial crown. Actuated by the same desire, they aspired to increase the area of their nominal possessions that they might thus appear more worthy of that higher dignity at which they aimed. And as the Emperor was content with bare recognition in a large part of the Empire, so kings tended to be satisfied with a similar position. Their states were large and loosely knit together; the exercise of control by the central government was negligible or spasmodic, and anarchy was the rule rather than the exception.

But this anarchy made resistance to external influences less possible, and if the Emperor failed to maintain his authority, that was due not so much to the strength of local resistance as to his own extreme weakness.

Presently, however, the ineffective character of the central government in each state produced an intolerable situation. Western Europe was exposed to and suffered from the attacks of Saracens and Northmen, and the reaction in favour of external Individualism was encouraged by experience of the practical evils resulting from the contrary system. But the individualists themselves, perhaps unconsciously, recognised that the most pressing necessity was a strengthening of the government to which they yielded immediate obedience; without such strengthening, there could be neither deliverance from anarchy nor salvation from foreign enemies. Society, therefore, was gradually reorganised in smaller units, internally universalist in character. Nobles who had undertaken the defence of their neighbours developed into kings of the districts in which they lived and which they protected; even if they did not assume the royal title, they at least enjoyed practically royal power. Cities, which had been compelled to work out their own political salvation, asserted their right to a measure of local self-government which amounted to independence; if they admitted the nominal overlordship of some external ruler, they became in reality free republics. Western Europe presented the spectacle of large states over which the authority of the ruler was almost non-existent, and smaller communities, often without definite legal status, in which the government was all-powerful.

This result was in a measure the outcome of the growth of feudal ideas, though those ideas were encouraged by the existing condition of society. Feudalism regarded the individual rather than the community; each man must have his lord, and to that lord the obedience of each man was due. A community might owe some service to its overlord, but that service was performed by a duke or count or bishop, the representative, as it were, of the people. It was not performed by all the members of the community. It was to a mediate, not to the ultimate, lord that the mass of the population rendered obedience; the vassals of a king of France admitted no direct obligations towards the Emperor, the vassals of a duke of Normandy admitted no direct obligation towards the king of France. All kingdoms were practically subdivided into extremely small units. This state of affairs was certainly the outcome of external Universalism; the organisation of the theoretical provinces of the Empire was modelled upon that of the whole. But it also gratified the external Individualism of the age. The central government was more powerful in the new small units than it had ever been in the old larger units, and with the strengthening of the central government, resistance to external interference was more possible. The growth of individualist ideas produced, as its initial result, a growth of internal Universalism.

That growth was, however, very slow. The conception of the unity of Christendom was too powerful to be destroyed readily, and that conception stood perpetually in the path of a national state, hampering its development at every turn. Abstinence from territorial aggrandisement has rarely been a characteristic of absolute rule; a despot will generally wage wars of aggression; what may be called political self-denial is the rarest virtue of a crowned head who not only reigns but also rules. And in the Middle Ages, this particular virtue was especially rare, especially difficult of attainment. The dream of the Empire hovered always before the fevered eyes of kings, the conception of world-wide dominion inflamed the coldest minds, and rulers and subjects alike were stirred to abandon the arduous toil of internal consolidation to pursue the dazzling prospect of extended dominion and an imperial crown. It seemed almost shameful to devote much attention to a mere national state, when the lordship of the world was the reward of successful ambition. So Otto the Great turned aside to visit Rome; so even the statesmanlike Henry II and the calculating Philip Augustus, both of whom listened unmoved to the story of the fall of Jerusalem, were credited with no slight longing to wear the crown of Constantine and of Charles.

And the result was that the natural development of mankind was impeded. External Universalism had enjoyed a long ascendancy; from that ascendancy the world had benefited. But the order of human life is conflict; the hour for a salutary reaction had now sounded; external Individualism was bound to displace the contrary theory. Men, however, would not or could not so easily forget their old ideals; they hesitated to enter that wilderness of doubt into which the casting away of the dominant theory seemed bound to lead them. Nations strive always to attain happiness; they grope for ever towards the Promised Land. They may be counted happy if they attain some Pisgah from which a glimpse of the distant plains may be secured; such glimpses, but no more, are at times vouchsafed to them. In the Middle Ages, at the very moment when the summit had been attained and the weary eyes of the traveller were refreshed by a sight of the Promised Land, a dark cloud ever arose to obscure the view; some force, the mighty influence of external Universalism, hurled mankind back into the Valley of Shadow from which they had so painfully emerged.

The history of the centuries following the death of Charles the Great is largely a history of lost opportunities, of a weary sacrifice of the real upon the altar of a vain ideal. Incalculable evils resulted from the fatal journey of Otto, since by it hope was revived that the Roman Empire might once more dominate and unify western Europe. Germany and Italy were condemned to centuries of disunion; endless wars were waged, countless lives sacrificed. The prestige of the Church was reduced, her reputation damaged, and the conception of Christian brotherhood degraded by use as a political asset by the Emperor or the Pope.

The history of France possibly affords even clearer evidence of the disasters resultant from the attempt to maintain external Universalism; there, if anywhere, may be seen the dreary cycle of misery to which mankind was condemned. The heirs of Chlodovech had enlarged their borders only to become *rois fainéants,* only to be driven to delegate all power to their Mayors of the Palace. Those Mayors had ascended the Frankish throne with Pippin, had attained the imperial crown with Charles. But forthwith delegation of power once more became necessary; the Carolingian Empire fell by its own weight. The Capetian dukes of France developed into "Mayors of the Palace," while their kings shrank trembling in the palace at Laon; Hugh Capet avenged the last Merovingian and accepted the dictum of Pope Zachary that "he who holds the power should possess the title of king." And at once Hugh's successors repeated the errors by which the Carolingians had been destroyed. The temptation of mere territorial increase overpowered them; the measure of their nominal authority grew, and they paid the price when they cowered before their overmighty subjects. William, duke of Normandy, might admit the legal suzerainty of the French king; he could afford to smile at the angry threats of his overlord, the harassed ruler of the Capetians' narrow patrimony.

And as good fortune or capacity united the great fiefs to the demesne, those fiefs were almost immediately granted away to cadets of the royal house; each king seemed to labour to undo the work of his predecessor. But this apparent anomaly is readily explained; it was the natural result of external Individualism. Such delegation of power as territorial expansion made inevitable would not have been incompatible with strong government if the sentiment of national identity had been widespread. But that sentiment was localised by difficulty of communication. An inhabitant of Blois regarded an inhabitant of Paris as a foreigner; the rule of a distant king was foreign rule, and by force of the spirit of external Individualism, it was therefore reduced to the merest shadow. A strong central government was really impossible except in small units; the permanent increase of those units could result only from a breaking down of the intense localism of the age. In short, just as in one period external Universalism had retarded the development of national states by keeping alive the conception of a world Empire, so in the next period external Individualism produced a similar result by hindering the recognition of real geographical and ethnical unity in large areas.

Nevertheless, the age was one of increasing internal Universalism, of the gradual formation of national states. Everywhere the power of government tended to grow, and the area accepting the real control of that government to grow also. The royal demesnes were slowly extended, though districts laboriously welded together seemed to separate almost before they had been united; the gathering of districts, geographically one, under a single ruler is a feature of the period. In France, the alien government of English kings was gradually extinguished; in Italy, the republics secured control of the districts lying round them. Even in Germany, the Hanseatic towns, the free imperial cities, practically escaped from the anarchical rule of the decaying Empire. But most significant of all, the Emperor and the Pope adopted a territorial policy; they cared less for their theoretical lordship of the world than for such measure of practical authority as they could gain over the territories more immediately under their control. Even Frederic II gave more attention to his Sicilian kingdom than to his imperial position; his quarrel with the Papacy partakes of the nature of a private war for the possession of southern Italy. After the Great Interregnum his successors became more and more unlike the earlier Holy Roman Emperors; they approximate more and more to the princes of Germany in their ambitions and policy. Henry VII was little moved by the eloquent appeal of Dante; the *De Monarchia* proved to be a vain attempt to revive in the Emperor a sense of his position as temporal head of Christendom and of the duties attaching to that position. Nor did the contemporary Popes escape the suspicion of caring more for their Italian interests than for the good of the Church. The bitterness of Gregory VII against Henry IV might be at least colourably attributed to zeal for the cause of spiritual power; the bitterness of Gregory IX against Frederic II was almost too obviously the result of fear of Sicilian aggression upon the temporal power of the Papacy.

It is clear that when an individualist policy was

pursued by those whose position made them the professed exponents of external Universalism, the ascendancy of that theory was necessarily imperilled. And the events which followed the death of Frederic II were at once an indication of the growth of external Individualism and an agency promoting that growth. Boniface VIII attempted to profit from the defeat of the Hohenstaufen to reassert and to advance to an extravagant point all the claims of the Papacy. He aspired to humble kings more effectually than even an Innocent III had done; to free the Church from all obligations to the state, to bring it under his own absolute and unfettered rule. But he had mistaken the temper of the age in which he lived. At all points the spirit of external Individualism rebuffed him; he failed in England and in France; he could not even dominate that creation of papal policy, the Angevin kingdom in Naples. It is an interesting commentary on his claim to be the lord of emperors and kings that he fell a victim to the inveterate hostility of a single Roman family, the Colonna. His death in a frenzy of impotent rage and cursing marks the fall of the universal dominion of the Papacy; henceforth no fictions of apostolic or imperial donations served to prevent states from pursuing a policy of external Individualism. It was no longer a question of complete papal domination; it had become a question whether any such domination should exist. The reaction had occurred; the history of the succeeding period was to determine the extent of that reaction.

At first it seemed probable that this reaction would be complete. The failure of Boniface VIII was something more than a mere defeat; it amounted to a positive disaster. For its direct consequence was the humiliation of the Papacy before Philip the Fair, the transference of the papal court to Avignon and the "Babylonish

Captivity." While one claimant to the lordship of the world had sunk almost to the level of his nominal vassals, the other now became little better than a servant of the French king. Nothing illustrates more graphically the result of the residence at Avignon than the attitude of England towards the Papacy during the Hundred Years' War. Hitherto in all disputes the Pope, as spiritual head of Christendom, was assured of a respectful hearing if he offered his mediation; now the English rejected such an offer with contempt, roundly declaring that they would not entrust the decision of their cause to the puppet of their enemies.

A severe blow, therefore, had been struck at external Universalism; presently that theory sustained a second and even more serious shock. Gregory XI had returned to Rome, to the great discontent of many of the cardinals who not unnaturally preferred the health and tranquillity of the Rhone valley to the malaria and turbulence of the Romagna. As a result, a double election occurred at the next papal vacancy; Urban VI at Rome, Clement VII at Avignon, alike claimed to be apostolic Pope. So weakened was the sentiment of external Universalism that neither party would give way; the Great Schism began, and the world was scandalised or amused by the vigorous anathemas of two Vicars of Christ. Attempts to heal the quarrel merely served to embitter it; the abortive Council of Pisa is more important as illustrating the callous disregard of the clergy for Christian unity than as a proof of any genuine desire to end the period of disunion.

Nor could it be expected that the growth of external Individualism should not have been encouraged by the troubles of the Papacy. It has been already pointed out that heresy is one of the most obvious expressions of individualist ideas, and the period of the Babylonish

Captivity and of the Great Schism is marked by heretical or quasi-heretical movements. The unity of Christendom became an ideal of ever-decreasing potency; in place of it, there is found the newer ideal of the liberty of national Churches. And this ideal secured the larger following because it gave expression to another phase of external Individualism, that conception of nationalism which had been slowly struggling to life through the ages.

Between heresy and nationalism there is an intimate, if not an inevitable, connection. To the ideal of authority, the heretic opposes the right of private judgment; to the Universalism of the orthodox, he opposes his individualist ideals. But inasmuch as the conception of the unity of Christendom implies some breaking down of the barriers between nations, it follows that this conception must make less appeal to those who regard such barriers as both necessary and admirable. The nationalist will tend in the direction of heresy, at least in so far as orthodoxy implies the admission of some measure of external control. And so it appears that in all the heretical movements of the Middle Ages the opponents of the orthodox faith were also champions of the political distinction of that district in which they lived. The schism between the Eastern and Western Churches owed its origin and permanence less to any enthusiasm for the *Filioque* Clause than to the antipathy existing between the Greeks and Latins. The Albigensian movement was less the result of sincere belief in and admiration for Paulician doctrines than of the racial and linguistic divergence between northern and southern France. Many, like the younger Bertrand de Born, whose religious views were at least obscure, showed bitter anger at the attack of the alien king of France upon the local independence of the country of Toulouse.

Nowhere, however, does this association of heresy with nationalism appear more clearly than in the Hussite movement. Before Hus began to preach, the University of Prague had been the scene of a violent controversy between the Slav and German students; the former objected vigorously and successfully to the academic domination of the latter. And when Prague had been converted from a centre of Germanising influence to a Slav stronghold, the teaching of the reformer won the more ready acceptance because it gratified the national spirit of Bohemia. The clergy of that land were largely aliens and considered to be representatives of the authority of an Italian prelate. They were placed in a position of admitted superiority by the doctrine of communion in one kind, which gave to the foreign priest a privilege denied to the native layman. It was this very doctrine that Hus most definitely assailed, and his attack upon it received the eager support of all who felt within them the stirring of Slav national spirit. It was less that the Bohemians were afflicted by the spiritual injustice of the denial of the wine, than that they deplored the temporal injustice of the stigma placed upon their race.

Nor was the resistance to papal supremacy confined entirely to heretics or nationalists, or even to advocates of external Individualism. Many universalists realised the abuses resultant from the uncontrolled authority of the Pope. They saw that the unity of Christendom was threatened by something far more serious than the mere occurrence of a temporary schism, and they imagined that they had found an effective solution of the crisis which they recognised. In the early days of Christianity the perils by which the infant creed was threatened had been successfully encountered by means of General Councils of the Church; the decisions of these

Councils had been accepted and had been regarded as of equal validity with the most definite pronouncements of the Fathers and even of the Apostles. Some of the most important dogmas had in this way secured their final recognition; to the Council of Nicæa was due the definite assertion of Christ's divinity; to that of Chalcedon the settlement of the momentous question of the two natures.

And when the Church, owing to the vices or incompetence of its temporal head, was once more threatened with imminent danger, it seemed to many ecclesiastics of indubitable doctrinal orthodoxy that the time had come to effect a constitutional revolution. The Pope appeared to them to have failed in his task, to require assistance in the spiritual government of mankind. And as in the past General Councils had successfully combated the assaults of heretics, so now a similar body might carry through certain necessary changes and defeat the attacks of those who were so vigorously assailing the position of the Church. The leaders of the so-called Conciliar Movement proposed to substitute for the absolute monarchy of the Pope a species of episcopal oligarchy. At regular intervals a General Council should meet; its decrees should have the force of law, and its power should extend, if necessary, to the deposition of its president, the Pope.

But this suggestion, though originating with those who believed in external Universalism and in the existence of a single authority over the whole Christian world, was in effect not only revolutionary but also evidently calculated to promote external Individualism. The basis of universalist ascendancy was the acceptance of the theory that Christ had committed the government of the world to some human vicegerent. The Pope might claim that position as the canonical successor of

St. Peter; it was difficult to contend that Christ had instituted a numerous council to be the inspired repository of His will. The Conciliar Movement could not fail to encourage the growth of external Individualism when it admitted in effect the falsity of the whole theory upon which the contrary doctrine was so largely based.

Throughout western Europe, then, the period of the Great Schism was marked by a tendency towards the complete rejection of external Universalism. But that theory, inevitably eternal because the expression of one of man's permanent impulses, was still powerful enough to make headway against the growing Individualism of the age. The meeting of the Council of Constance was greeted with unfeigned enthusiasm; its success in closing the Great Schism was heartily applauded. Even the probability that the reunited Papacy would in some measure recover an authority which had become unwelcome and distrusted did not greatly qualify the sense of relief and delight that the unity of Christendom had been restored. The election of Martin V was rather considered to be the dawn of a new golden age for the Church.

It did not herald any such dawn, but none the less the Council of Constance, like the death of Frederic II, marks an epoch in the history of mankind. Over its deliberations the Emperor Sigismund had presided. He had secured the rejection of John XXII and the acceptance of the Council's nominee, Martin V; he had appeared, if only for a moment, as the temporal head of Christendom. And the unexampled opportunity, which the Great Schism and the Council appeared to afford him, had moved Sigismund to attempt to recover something of the lost imperial power. He hoped that the revival of universalist ideas, resultant from the restoration of unity to the Church, might profit the Empire and lead to an equivalent restoration of prestige and authority to the Emperor.

But no sooner did he attempt to realise these hopes than he met with strenuous opposition. Any extension of secular power over the Church was anathema to the papal party; one section of the external universalists became his enemies. The external individualists were equally hostile. They would not admit the assertion of imperial authority within the borders of states which had gained independence since the days of Otto the Great. At Paris, Sigismund roused alarm and hostility by knighting a bastard on French soil. When he visited England, heralds rode into the sea and refused him permission to land, until he had disclaimed any intention of exercising jurisdiction in the island. Nor was Sigismund himself a single-minded universalist. Much of his attention was devoted to the creation of a territorial monarchy for the House of Luxemburg, and this design amounted to a tacit contradiction of his schemes for the revival of the Empire. His significance, indeed, lies really in his failure. He was the last Emperor to attempt the restoration of the old mediæval system, to attempt to base his power upon external Universalism. And he was the first Emperor to conceive the idea that his imperial position might be utilised to assist the formation of a territorial monarchy, of a dominion founded upon individualist principles. Sigismund emphasised the failure of the Hohenstaufen; he suggested the success of the Habsburgs.

At the same time, a decided modification appears in the policy of the Popes. Boniface VIII had deliberately attempted to make good his claim to universal dominion; he had proudly declared that he was Cæsar and Emperor. His successors, after the return from Avignon and still more after the Council of Constance, were content to pursue far humbler schemes. Martin V would perhaps have been well pleased if he could have imposed his authority upon the Romagna; to reduce the Patrimony to obedience became the primary object of every Pope. Papal policy assumed an increasingly Italian character; local territorial aggrandisement was its goal. But such territorialism was peculiarly injurious to the cause of papal supremacy. The field of action was limited, the interests at stake somewhat petty; success and failure appeared to be alike contemptible. An Innocent III, struggling for the mastery of Europe, the humiliator of Emperors and kings, extorted the admiration of those who most bitterly opposed him. There was a certain pathos even in the picture of Boniface VIII dashing his head against the narrow walls of his cell, bemoaning a fate which had made the rival of kings the victim of his own turbulent subjects. The spectacle of Martin V triumphant over an insignificant noble of the Romagna, the thought of the intrigues and plots in which he engaged to win some few acres of malarial desert, could arouse neither admiration nor sympathy. If some might be found to regret that a power which had humbled the mighty Hohenstaufen was so reduced, had fallen so low, more could be found to marvel that the world had so long trembled before the menaces of one who now seemed to be but an impotent Italian bishop.

And if the sentiment of external Universalism suffered from the mere territorialism of the Papacy, it suffered still more from a feature of that territorialism which excited anger as well as contempt. After the time of Martin V, nepotism became the keynote of papal policy. The exaltation of penurious relatives became the darling ambition of almost every Pope, and to that ambition were sacrificed the interest of the Church and the reputation of its temporal head. A cynical generation viewed sceptically the paternal affection with which Popes regarded their nephews; even before the days of Alexànder VI, the sons of celibate bishops afforded a source of scandalous amusement to the profane. If the pursuit of purely Italian interests had weakened the hold of the Papacy upon the imagination of mankind, the nepotism of successive Popes almost destroyed such respect for the papal office as had survived the degradation of the Babylonish Captivity and the calamitous disunion of the Great Schism.

It is clear that in such circumstances even the spiritual authority of Rome could hardly fail to suffer a certain diminution. As a matter of fact, the Popes themselves displayed a certain carelessness for the maintenance of that authority; the pressing need of defeating the Conciliar Movement led them to deviate still further from the universalist path. That movement owed such strength as it possessed to the growth of nationalism and to the desire for independence on the part of local Churches. English, French and German ecclesiastics hoped that the transference of nominal authority to an international General Council would secure to them practical liberty. They cared less for the projected reform of abuses, or for the theoretical limitation of papal power, than for the special and private advantages which they trusted would accrue to themselves from the permanent establishment of a Council as the ultimate sovereign of the Church.

At the same time, the Popes recognised that the creation of such a body would infallibly reduce them from an autocratic position to one of servitude to a probably hostile and certainly jealous tribunal; the conduct of the Council of Basle indicated what would be the outcome of a victory for the conciliar party. Eugenius IV therefore decided that at all costs a statutory limitation of papal supremacy must be avoided, and he adopted the obvious course of sowing dissensions among his enemies. While the Fathers of Basle pressed for the fulfilment of the pledges given, or alleged to have been given, by Martin V at Constance, Eugenius concluded separate agreements with the clergy of various countries. National Churches were induced to accept as a papal gift all that they had hoped to secure from the General Council. Immediate success crowned the efforts of the Pope. In a short while, the Conciliar Movement was not merely dead but damned, and no fear remained that unwelcome reforms would be imposed upon the Papacy, the absolute ultimate authority of which was definitely admitted.

But the policy of Eugenius was fraught with serious peril for the future. Practically it amounted to a partial abdication of that spiritual headship which had been so toilsomely created by the great Popes of the Middle Ages. The vast pretensions of a Boniface VIII could no more be asserted; it had been implicitly confessed that such pretensions were exaggerated. And ultimately the victory of Eugenius was still more disastrous to the Papacy. It was upon the desire to be ruled that papal power really rested; that desire had been weakened in mankind by the abuses attendant upon its gratification, and with the failure of external Universalism to produce a Utopia, external Individualism gained ground. This reaction in favour of the desire to rule could be checked only by proving that the abuses, to which objection was taken, could be remedied under a universalist system; that they were, in fact, not the necessary concomitants of gratification of the desire to be ruled. But the leaders of the Conciliar Movement were pledged to attempt reform, their opponents had denied the need for reform. When, therefore, the Pope had triumphed, he was unable or afraid to admit the justice of the complaints against the Church. All reform from within was prevented; the abuses continued, and the individualist reaction was proportionately hastened. The Reformation was an event bound to occur; the particular form which the Reformation assumed was due largely to the conduct and apparent success of Eugenius IV.

And even in the period which saw the supposed victory of Eugenius, the weakness of the Papacy was made apparent. Concessions to national Churches of unblemished doctrinal orthodoxy were followed by concessions to declared heretics. During the initial enthusiasm aroused by the Council of Constance, John Hus had been condemned and burned; the assertor of individualist ideas had paid the penalty of his daring; the accepted theory had been vindicated. But so far from being quelled by the death of its originator, the Hussite movement increased in vigour and its supporters became the more determined to resist coercion. The people of Bohemia rose in arms against the two custodians of external Universalism. They rejected alike the political claims of Sigismund and the spiritual claims of Martin; Ziska and Prokop, in a series of campaigns, successfully repelled the attacks of their orthodox and Teutonic enemies. So victorious were the Hussites that the Papacy was eventually reduced to the necessity of compromise; the demands of the Utraquists were conceded, and alone of all western Christians the Czechs were permitted to receive the cup. Nor was the grant of communion in both kinds to the laity of Bohemia a trivial event. It struck at the exceptional position of the priesthood; it declared that the right to rule did not rest with the clergy alone.

A further diminution of the influence of external Universalism thus characterised the epoch of the Council of Constance. Though reunited, the Papacy failed to regain the prestige and moral force lost during the Babylonish Captivity and the Great Schism; papal power was for ever reduced by the fact that the theory upon which it was ultimately based had sustained irreparable damage. Pius II, able and brilliant though he was, could not undo the work of the years previous to his accession. His solitary vigil at Ancona, as he waited for the crusaders to receive his blessing and set forth on their great mission, illustrates graphically the decline of the old conception of Christian unity.

Nor did the Empire profit from the efforts of Sigismund. If imperial leadership had for a moment been accepted, this was due to the accidental circumstance that the healing of schism was advantageous to the individualist cause. Churches which desired concessions to their local prejudices and interests naturally preferred that those concessions should be made by a universally acknowledged Pope rather than by a Pope of dubious catholicity. And the successors of Sigismund recognised the true explanation of that Emperor's brief triumph. They quietly abandoned all attempts to assert their imperial authority; they ceased even to believe in that external Universalism to which the Holy Roman Empire owed its being. With Frederic III, the last traces of mediæval imperialism disappear. It is true that he journeyed to Italy and was crowned at Rome. But his journey was hasty and apologetic; he seemed only too eager to renounce any possible claims, to abdicate any possible authority which he might still possess in the Peninsula. During his reign of half a century, his whole attention was absorbed in laying or strengthening the foundations of Habsburg power; he was, in fact, a typical statesman of the period, and by no means the least able.

It is significant that the most dangerous enemies of Frederic were neither Popes nor German princes, but national leaders. George Podiebrad and Matthias Corvinus almost succeeded in creating a powerful Slav state in Hungary and Bohemia; the Emperor was even driven from Vienna. But though Vladislav of Poland for a time asserted the cause of his race, he eventually made peace with Frederic, on terms which really sacrificed the Slavs to Teutonic supremacy. The aim of these leaders was national; they alike failed. Yet in their failure Europe still learned perhaps what was to be the basis of the new order of society. Mankind was slow to recognise the coming change; the human mind was reluctant to free itself from the domination of the desire to be ruled. The mediæval Empire died with Frederic II, the mediæval Papacy with Boniface VIII. Yet it was not until the Peace of Westphalia that either fact received explicit recognition; the victory of external Individualism at Constance was real rather than apparent.

The reluctance with which men permitted individualist ideas to gain control over them is abundantly illustrated in the career of Charles the Bold. Perhaps the most typical man of the age, his life reflects clearly the vigour of the mental conflict which absorbed mankind. Nothing could have been more entirely individualist than his conduct towards Louis XI; in his quarrel with the Valois he was disturbed by no scruples of duty. Yet, at the same time, Charles was largely universalist. He disregarded geographical and ethnical obstacles in his attempt to weld into a kingdom lands divided by race and language, historical associations and economic interest. It almost seemed as if he believed that because Lotharingia had once existed, it could exist again. And eagerly as he desired the kingly title, he was too much obsessed by universalist ideas to assume it without imperial sanction. He sought it at the hands of Frederic III, recognising that the lord of the world alone could create a legitimate king, and when the Habsburg cheated or deceived him, he still refrained from denying the rights of the Emperor. It is curious that Charles the Bold should have shown less independence of action than did Boso of Provence or Rudolf of Burgundy in the days of Charles the Fat; the fact may perhaps be explained as due to the stereotyping of human ideas during the long ascendancy of external Universalism.

Meanwhile, internal Individualism almost held its own. Difficulty of communication and the lack of compelling power in the central government still combined to maintain the strength of local feeling. Nor did the external individualists at first appreciate the necessity of making some concessions to internal Universalism if they were to preserve their liberty against foreign aggression. The two agencies from which such aggression might be expected were obviously powerless to coerce. The Emperor could no longer control even Germany and Italy, and if the Pope were still able to exercise spiritual authority, he had ceased to be a political danger. Those opposed to foreign influence therefore failed to realise that for the success of their opposition a measure of submission to authority was essential, while their intense localism led them to regard as foreigners all who were not inhabitants of their own immediate districts. The evils of invasion and conquest had to be experienced before the limitations upon gratification of the desire to rule could be understood. In no other way could men learn to adopt a wider view of national identity; in no other way could they learn that real independence was impossible in units too small to withstand foreign aggression.

The force of necessity, however, produced a gradual change of opinion. In every country the extreme of internal Individualism produced a condition of instability akin to anarchy; in many cases this semi-anarchy led to disastrous foreign wars. From the calamities which thus befell them, men learned to seek political salvation by entrusting greater power to the central government; their very external Individualism led them to become in a sense internal universalists. Hence it is that this period witnessed the establishment of despotism, open or veiled, in the Italian cities; the Visconti secured control of Milan, the Medici of Florence; Venice fell under the rule of the Council of Ten. In Spain, Castile and Aragon were united; Ferdinand and Isabella, having rescued their land from civil war and having conquered Granada, began the formation of a centralised monarchy. The Burgundian dukes laboured to destroy the liberties of the Flemish cities, repressing sedition with a firm hand. Even in Germany there were signs of consolidation; it was in this period that the various German states, such as Brandenburg, began to attain a measure of definition.

But the stages by which internal Universalism secured acceptance are nowhere so clearly discernible as in the history of France. That country had been handed over to the ravages of the English by the rivalry of the great feudatories; the Burgundians and Armagnacs forgot everything except their mutual hatred, and each felt that no price was too heavy to pay for the destruction of the other. The masses were as unwise as the nobles. Aiming at the removal of certain abuses, they failed to realise that the initial step must be a strengthening of the central government against external attack; the Jacquerie and the Cabochins, in effect, strove to remedy anarchy by increasing it.

The disasters of the Hundred Years' War, however, taught France the needed lesson. It was at length recognised that governance was necessary, and the French, with characteristic volatility, abandoned their excessive Individualism to fly to the contrary extreme. Not content with giving the king sufficient power to ensure the defeat of the foreign invader, the States General deliberately granted Charles VII a permanent revenue and army; they supplied him with the pre-requisites of despotism instead of the mere essentials for national defence. The English were expelled, and the king turned to the taming of those nobles whose turbulence had caused the disasters of their country; the defeat of the Praguerie may be regarded as the first step towards the accomplishment of that work which was eventually completed by Richelieu. Louis XI continued his father's policy, and though the end of his reign found his task unfinished, yet France by that date almost supplied Europe with an example of a unified state.

A series of notable victories had thus been gained by internal Universalism, though those victories were partially the result of the Individualism of the age. Submission to government had been recognised as necessary in every state, not so much because the desire to be ruled was predominant, as because such submission appeared to be the lesser of two evils to those who were filled with the desire to rule; the despotism of a fellow-countryman was preferable to that of an alien. While external Individualism constantly gained ground, internal Individualism was in reality only checked for a moment. Its power was great, and in the next age it contended vigorously with the universalist system which it had accepted from necessity.

And the Individualism of the period was soon forcibly illustrated in the Renaissance. At the time when the Papacy was sapping the foundations of its own power by destroying that of the Empire, there had been a revival of learning in Europe. By its very occurrence, the quarrel between Pope and Emperor imperilled the dominion of external Universalism. And as the two parties deliberately or accidentally encouraged the development of criticism, the resultant increase of mental activity produced political heresy. Growing independence of thought necessarily favoured the growth of Individualism. The exercise of the critical faculty was bound to lead some men to abandon the gratification of the desire to be ruled and to cause them to fall under the influence of the desire to rule.

But the so-called "First Renaissance" was not openly or entirely individualist in spirit. Dante, its most noted representative, was largely a universalist. He looked for the salvation of society in a revival of imperial power, and the *De Monarchia* is no more than an eloquent appeal to the Emperor to perform the higher duties of his office. Yet, if only subconsciously, Dante himself protested against the dominant theory, and aided the development of Individualism. Among the obstacles to any complete establishment of external Universalism, the lack of a common language is not the least important. During the golden age of mediæval Universalism, Latin was in a measure the general language of mankind; it was the medium of worship and of diplomacy. Any disuse of Latin was bound to emphasise the divergence between states, and thus to encourage men to regard their immediate or local interest rather than the general welfare of the human race. Hence the most noteworthy protests against papal supremacy came naturally from districts in which there was a vigorous and national language. The Albigensian movement flourished in the Provençal-speaking districts of France; the language of the Hussites was Czech.

Dante seems almost to have appreciated the importance of Latin as an agency for the maintenance of external Universalism. His *De Monarchia* was written in that language, the true medium in which to express conviction of the blessings of imperial rule. Nevertheless, he assisted to weaken still further the system for which he pleaded. The fragment *De Vulgari Eloquentia* praised the writings of the Provençal poets; it discussed and at least by implication advocated the creation of an Italian language from the dialects commonly spoken in the Peninsula. And the *Divina Commedia* was composed in the "vulgar tongue," thereby proving that the disuse of Latin would not render impossible the attainment of a high degree of literary excellence.

But the attack of the First Renaissance upon Universalism was negative rather than positive; the movement was not primarily individualist. The fifteenth-century Renaissance, however, was essentially individualist, alike in spirit and influence. The movement was not the result of the transference of manuscripts from Constantinople to the West, or of a wider diffusion of classical learning, or of the labours of a few scholars; even the invention of printing was an effect rather than a cause. The Renaissance was produced by the satiation following upon extreme gratification of the desire to be ruled; it was the first explicit declaration of a sentiment always existent in mankind, the expression of the desire to rule. It was the natural outcome of the palpable failure of external Universalism; it was a revolt against authority, literary, artistic, musical, religious and political. When Laurentius Valla doubted the authenticity of Livy, when Martin Luther denied the validity of papal indulgences, they alike expressed man's impatience of dogma, his resolve to test and to criticise. In a sense, a new epoch opened in the intellectual history of the world, and yet the Renaissance did no more than call into vigorous activity an emotion inherent in the human mind.

The movement necessarily threatened both external and internal Universalism. It was directed to free men from all submission not grounded upon conviction reached after the exercise of private judgment, and it could only be that from many no submission would be received. In some, the desire to be ruled would doubtless retain its ascendancy; in others, the desire to rule would destroy all inclination to accept any form of guidance. And since the tendency was in favour of a reaction against a hitherto dominant theory, the probability was that the majority of mankind would refuse obedience, would be profoundly influenced by the ideas of the Renaissance. Such was indeed the case, though the actual influence of the movement was limited by the divisions among its adherents.

For the Renaissance had two distinct sides. It was largely a literary and artistic movement, not concerned with the principles either of politics or of religion. So far as it did touch politics, it was conservative rather than revolutionary, universalist rather than individualist. Writers and painters profited from the munificence of princes; they inclined to accept and to praise the absolute rule of their patrons, from which such obvious benefits accrued to them. And the attitude of the Renaissance towards religion was, so far as its literary and artistic side was concerned, one of practical indifference. The Church had consistently condemned, or at least discouraged, the study of classical literature; it had attempted to divert art into purely religious channels. Moreover, the early Fathers, headed by Augustine, had declared that the divinities of Greece and Rome were real beings, dæmons employed by Satan to tempt and to perplex the elect. And if, in the course of ages, saints had found cause to regret the declining activity of their tempters, and if the belief in their existence had markedly declined, it was still existent. The result was that the literary and artistic side of the Renaissance tended almost to produce a revival of paganism. Polytheism has always attracted a section of mankind; the invocation of saints appeared to have given a polytheistic character to Christianity itself. When the discovery of classical manuscripts spread the knowledge of classical mythology, there were not wanting those who, in their admiration for Greece and Rome, inclined to revive the belief in the reality of the ancient divinities, to substitute Venus for the Virgin, the gods of Olympus for the apostles and saints. Their enthusiasm, however, was slight, and the chief result of this side of the Renaissance was not hostility, but indifference to the Church. Even so, a further spread of external Individualism resulted. Men who had become cold in their devotion to Christianity were not likely to be ardent in their support of the ideal of Christian unity; to them the continued existence of Christendom tended to appear as a matter of trivial importance. Few regrets were caused by the fall of Constantinople. The extinction of a Christian empire seemed to be a less momentous event than the recovery of some lost author or the printing of some classical work; the reverse sustained by religion was almost neutralised by the advantage to learning resultant from a still wider dispersion of classical manuscripts.

It is, however, perhaps true to say that the permanent importance of the Renaissance lies in the politico-religious revolution which, to a certain extent, it inaugurated. While many of the leaders of the movement were practically indifferent to religion, some were eager to utilise their increased knowledge in the service of Christianity. A fuller acquaintance with the original of the New Testament appeared to them to be the greatest and almost the sole benefit derivable from the new learning; Greek was the language of Paul rather than of Plato. And these men, though indubitably Christian, were yet out of sympathy with the Church as it then was. Their knowledge of the New Testament supplied them with grounds for an attack upon current abuses and with arguments in favour of the reforms which they suggested; they urged the adoption of measures similar to those which the leaders of the Conciliar Movement had advocated. And like the Friars of an earlier date, they gave expression to the general discontent felt towards the existing system. The criticism of Erasmus reflected the feelings of most laymen, and were far more dangerous to the Church as constituted than was the almost frankly avowed paganism of Laurentius Valla. It soon became clear to all who had eyes to see, that a religious revolution could only be avoided by the immediate removal of the more flagrant abuses.

To papal supremacy, this agitation for reform was fraught with grave peril. It was hardly consistent with the theory of the Papacy that guidance should be accepted from the general body of Christians, and that theory would therefore have been endangered, even if the Popes had been ready to reform, if they had been men of obvious sincerity and unblemished virtue. The danger was substantially increased by the actual character of the occupants of the papal chair. Since the time of Martin V, nepotism had steadily increased; each Pope seemed to make the exaltation of his family the keystone of his policy. And to this political error, grave faults of character had been added. Alexander VI has attained notoriety in the annals of vice; Julius II was greater as a general than as a bishop; Leo X was almost a typical product of the pagan Renaissance. From such men it was idle to expect the inauguration of reforms, and since the Holy Father would not hear the prayers of his children, those children were gradually driven to revolt. Criticism which had been friendly became hostile; a tendency to question dogmas appeared; a readiness to accept external Universalism in spiritual matters was replaced by advocacy of external Individualism. In short, the Christian Renaissance developed into a movement almost identical with the Reformation.

That identity, however, was by no means complete. Abuses of practice had been attacked by the leaders of the Christian Renaissance, but those same leaders had preserved the strictest doctrinal orthodoxy. Erasmus was disliked and possibly feared by the hierarchy whose errors he exposed, but he was in no sense a heretic; he has been regarded as the precursor of Luther, but he was more truly the original apostle of the Counter-Reformation. More pleaded for greater simplicity of worship and for the abandonment of ignorant superstition; but he died rather than deny the doctrine of papal supremacy. The leaders of the Reformation were more logical or less scrupulous. Luther was not content with denouncing the abuse of indulgences; he denied the doctrine upon which the issue of indulgences was based. Calvin was not content with indicating the vices and supporting the reform of episcopal government; he demanded the abolition of the institution. The religious sides of the Renaissance and the Reformation were indeed rather expressions of a particular sentiment than identical movements, nor did the one develop from the other, despite the interaction between them.

During the Middle Ages, authority had been generally admitted. It was not usual to doubt the written word; the dicta of Aristotle, of the Fathers, of St. Thomas Aquinas, were accepted almost without question. In art, literature and music, in politics and in religion, certain canons were held to be inviolable. As a result, though restriction and guidance at first made development possible, eventually that development was hampered; the desire to be ruled had been too fully gratified, and extreme gratification produced the evils inseparable from excess. Hence, the inevitable reaction occurred. Upon a readiness to submit to authority in all things, a refusal to submit at all followed; and of this reaction the Renaissance is one expression, the Reformation is another. The two movements are allied, but the occurrence of each was independent of the other. Between them there was even a certain hostility; the culture and moderation of the Renaissance were antipathetic to the relative crudity and violence of the Reformers.

To the Reformation there was a religious and a political side, both of which were essentially individualist. On its religious side, the movement consisted primarily in the assertion of the right of private judgment. Men had, during the Middle Ages, subordinated their judgment to that of the Church, which they regarded as infallible, upon which they relied to guide them and to determine their conduct. The doctrine of justification by works arose; the Church ordained what should be done to acquire eternal salvation. At first, this doctrine was readily accepted. But the Church lost the confidence of mankind, and implicit reverence turned to deep mistrust. Men no longer felt that the clergy could inform them with certainty what to believe and what to do. They regarded the Church as fallible in many respects; they suspected that the works ordained to be done might be either wholly inacceptable to God or at least insufficient to preserve from damnation. Another doctrine of justification became necessary; the right of private judgment, already applied to the practice of the Church, was still further exercised. And as there was no longer any body the guidance of which could be implicitly accepted, as the Bible itself could not be put forward, owing to its need of interpretation on some points and its silence upon others, the doctrine of justification by works was abandoned, and the doctrine of justification by faith introduced. The religious Reformation was thus wholly individualist. The individual was to judge for himself; he was to enter into direct, personal relationship with God. A freedom of opinion bordering upon anarchy was to be permitted; the desire to rule was to be gratified to the fullest extent.

Nor was the political side of the Reformation less individualist than the religious, of which it was partially the outcome. It was directed in the first instance towards the destruction of papal supremacy. The Popes had always insisted upon the infallibility of the Church. They had demanded complete submission, and were therefore altogether opposed to the exercise of private judgment and to the doctrine of justification by faith. The Papacy, moreover, appeared to have produced and to maintain ecclesiastical abuses. Its supremacy was essentially universalist, alien in conception and in spirit from that Individualism of which the Reformation was an expression.

But though the political side of the movement was at first directed against papal supremacy, its scope was soon extended. The rulers of many states were themselves ecclesiastics; they realised that their own authority was intimately associated with that of the Pope. Nor were secular princes without alarm as to the consequences of the rejection of papal supremacy. An individualist movement was not unlikely to lead to a revival of those centrifugal tendencies which had been suppressed in the previous age; it was noticeable that in France Protestantism secured most adherents in those districts which had displayed the greatest reluctance to submit to rule from Paris. Religious heresy was felt to be liable to produce political heresy. As unity of religion was a factor favouring unity of government, so religious disunion might be the prelude to political disunion. Rulers, therefore, came into conflict with the Reformation less on account of the orthodoxy of their own beliefs than from motives of policy; the resultant persecutions were in a majority of instances less religious than political. Francis I was hostile to the Huguenots; yet his dubious Catholicism was indicated by his alliance with the Turks, at a moment when the aggression of Suleiman threatened still further to limit the domain of Christianity in south-eastern Europe. Henry II inaugurated the era of persecution in France; he also allied with the German Protestants against the Catholic Habsburgs.

And the answer made by the Protestants to persecution was also political. Just as ecclesiastical opposition to the exercise of private judgment had produced the doctrine of justification by faith, so royal opposition to the same theory produced an attack upon the basis of political authority. It must, however, be admitted that an individualist movement was bound to lead to a questioning of internal Universalism. Even in those countries of which the rulers supported the Reformation, the reformers did not normally preach absolutist doctrines. They advocated obedience to the crown, but they tended to make that obedience depend on the continued goodwill of the king towards themselves, to substitute a species of limited monarchy for the prevalent despotic system.

The Reformation, therefore, inclined towards the attainment of a degree of Individualism productive of anarchy, intellectual and political; such anarchy was the logical result of the full exercise of the right of private judgment. This tendency of the movement appears clearly in the history of the period. In Germany the preaching of Luther was followed by the outbreak of the Peasants' War. That rising the reformer emphatically condemned, nor can it be contended that his teaching was directly responsible for it. Luther owed much to the friendship of the Elector of Saxony; his political theories reflected his sense of obligation, and he was the champion rather of absolutism than of anarchy in secular affairs. Nevertheless, the Peasants' War was closely associated with the Reformation. Those who had preached the rejection of papal authority could hardly be very convincing advocates of submission to royal authority; that which their teaching gained in practical merit, it lost in logical excellence. And as must always be the case, there were many who either could not or would not appreciate the limitations of a theory. Private judgment had been exalted; it was a refinement to limit its exercise to religion. So it was that the Reformation assisted to produce popular outbreaks, despite the efforts of its leaders to check such outbreaks. Even such extremists as the Anabaptists, preachers of a communistic republic and free love, were only the logical product of the theory that the individual was all-important, that he should submit to no restraint save that which he chose to impose upon himself.

Far more important than such occasional ebullitions as the Anabaptist outbreak and the Peasants' War was the new political theory put forward by the Huguenots. The idea had gradually arisen that kings held their office by divine right, that they were responsible to God alone, and that resistance to them partook of the nature of sin. But when the authority of government was employed against the right of private judgment and for the persecution of those who deviated from the orthodox path, the Protestants were driven to resist and to attempt a justification of their resistance; the desire to be ruled was quenched in them, and for a time the desire to rule gained an ascendancy over their minds. They produced a new theory of politics, basing the authority of kings not upon a divine commission, but upon a social contract. The king was regarded as being merely the lieutenant of his subjects, bound to perform certain functions, removable in event of failure. Monarchy was no longer considered as the sole legitimate type of government; a republic was equally admissible. And the judge of royal conduct was the people. The theory was thus individualist, since the people consisted of many individuals, each one of whom had the privilege of settling his own opinions. It was the application of the right of private judgment to politics, and its logical outcome was anarchy, an anarchy based upon a complete political theory.

The same individualist spirit appeared in most of the political movements of the age. Even the capture of Constantinople failed to unite the Christian powers; the foremost champion of Europe against Mohammed II was Scanderbeg, an obscure Albanian chieftain of dubious orthodoxy. At first sight, the policy of Venice may appear to have been directed to maintain the cause of Christendom, but this was due to the accidental identification of that cause with the economic interests of the Republic in the Levant. For the rest, an era of hitherto unparalleled selfishness dawned. The Emperor Maximilian I imitated his father, Frederic III, in his pursuit of the dynastic ambitions of the Habsburgs to the exclusion of all other considerations. Of the Popes, Pius II preached a crusade, to be beguiled by promises and to die broken-hearted at Ancona. His successors cared only for the establishment of their authority over the Patrimony and the exaltation of their families. If they advocated common action against the Turks, their appeals were heard with sceptical amusement, and the true motive for them sought in some project for the advantage of a papal nephew. France and Spain contended for the mastery of Italy, and such intermission of their hostility as occurred became the occasion for unscrupulous bargaining concerning the spoils of the Peninsula. The contemporary maxims of international morality are revealed by Machiavelli. For the first time, self-interest was openly admitted to be the true guiding principle determining the policy of a state. All idea of a commonwealth of Christian nations seemed to have disappeared; external Universalism seemed to be dead and buried.

Internally, a similar Individualism prevailed, if less completely. Centralised governments had developed from the necessities of national self-preservation, but such governments were now held to have fulfilled their function. The period was one in which anti-monarchical ideas gained a wide currency. Despite the praises lavished by the Renaissance writers on Lorenzo de Medici, and on other princely patrons of the arts, the "tyrannies," into which the city republics of Italy had been converted, were generally unpopular. The Medici were expelled from Florence. The Aragonese dynasty at Naples and the Sforzas at Milan owed their rapid fall before the French invader to the alienation of their subjects. In Spain, the rising of the Comuneros was a protest against the centralising policy of Ferdinand and Isabella, and somewhat similar unrest appears in the dominions of the House of Habsburg.

But the order of human life is conflict, and there was conflict in the age of the Reformation. The ascendancy of the desire to rule was not more, but rather less, complete than had been the previous ascendancy of the desire to be ruled. The leaders of the Reformation themselves were not wholly individualist. Luther's work, it is true, was little more than destructive; primarily the champion of private judgment, he was unable in any real sense to organise a Church. Admission of coercive power must be the ultimate basis of any ecclesiastical society, no less than of any political society; if the priesthood possesses no superiority over the laity, religious anarchy is the inevitable result. But logically the Reformation disclaimed coercion. By implication it advocated the destruction of every form of rule, since all men were equal in the sight of God, all equally fitted to judge of that which was requisite for salvation. Even Luther, however, was not entirely consistent. He frankly defended the theory of passive obedience in temporal matters. In things spiritual, his insistence upon the doctrine of justification by faith, his condemnation of papal supremacy and of papal dogmas, suggested a limitation of private judgment. He was, in fact, the victim of that necessity which compels thinkers to build where they have destroyed, to be positive as well as negative. No man can divest himself of one side of his nature. Those who most emphatically assert their desire to rule, who most strenuously urge others to gratify that desire, tend at the same time to limit its gratification. They demand authority over their fellows, since they claim to deny to others the right to submit. In the mind of every man, the two desires exist always side by side, engaged in an eternal conflict. The inconsistency of Martin Luther was little more than the measure of his humanity.

Yet he was, perhaps, the most logical of the reformers. In his hands, the movement was mainly negative, and as such, though it might win converts, it was unlikely long to retain their allegiance. This was realised to the full by John Calvin, and he forthwith supplied the needful constructive leadership. While accepting in theory the two great principles of the right of private judgment and justification by faith, in practice he denied both. The Bible was admitted to be the sole standard of human conduct, but it was the Bible as interpreted at Geneva. Faith alone was needed to save men from damnation, but it was the faith of Geneva. No Pope ever repressed heresy or silenced hostile opinion with greater vigour than did this champion of spiritual liberty. If the Catholic Church condemned to death those who rejected transubstantiation, Calvinism made life impossible for those who declined to believe that they were eternally predestined either for Heaven or for Hell. The Calvinists evolved the doctrine of the social contract. They were prepared to justify rebellion and even tyrannicide, if any ruler were unfavourable to them. But at the same time they showed that if possessed of authority, they would use it with vigour and effect. They realised that their own preservation depended upon some enforcement of discipline; they discovered that a high degree of internal Universalism was not incompatible with their individualist principles.

The Universalism of the reformers, however, may be regarded as accidental, the product of necessity and fear, and the universalist theory received far more positive and deliberate support. The growth of Individualism provoked earnest resistance. While Luther preached the right of private judgment and thundered against papal claims, Charles V stood forth as a new champion of authority and order. But he was a practical statesman. He realised that the mediæval system was a thing of the past, that it was impossible to revive the ascendancy of the old imperial ideal. Even a Frederic Barbarossa had been driven to rely upon material as well as upon moral force; such reliance was infinitely more necessary in the era of the Reformation. It was idle to hope that the outworn dogma of universal lordship would win acceptance when every theory was being subjected to the fiercest criticism.

No such idle hope inspired or deluded the Emperor Charles V. For him, the imperial position was only a means to an end. No doubt he did much to revive imperial power and prestige. He forced the German princes to show unwonted respect for their nominal overlord. During his expeditions to Tunis and Algiers, he did appear for a moment in the traditional rôle of his great namesake, as the champion of the Cross against the Crescent. Yet for the Empire in the truest sense, for the ideal of a united Christendom, he cared not at all. To extend the power of the Habsburgs was his ambition; Spanish military power was the means upon which he relied for the attainment of this ambition. He elaborated the tentative ideas of his predecessors; he almost evolved a new theory of empire. His authority was to be based, not upon mankind's acceptance of a political ideal, but upon their recognition of material necessity. If he aspired to be no less lord of the world than Charles the Great had been, if his success would have produced an actual unity of Christendom, yet his lordship would have been akin to that of territorial rulers, the unity dynastic rather than imperial.

The attitude of Charles towards the imperial office displayed his indifference to the formerly accepted theory of the Empire. In the Middle Ages, the title of Emperor had only been assumed after the imperial coronation at Rome. Maximilian I had supplied a precedent for disregarding the rite of coronation by assuming the title of Emperor-Elect. Charles, following this example, assumed the title of Emperor without qualification. And if he did eventually undergo the ceremony of coronation by the Pope, this was intended rather to signalise his Italian triumph than to be a tardy concession to the practice of his predecessors. Charles V was an external universalist, but his Universalism was not that of the mediæval Emperors. They had aspired to a moral supremacy; he relied upon force. They had conceived of themselves as the first servants of the Christian Church; he aimed at founding a European dominion in the House of Habsburg.

Charles V failed in his design. Certain causes of his failure may be readily discovered. France was inveterately hostile; other European states were extremely jealous. The dominions of the Habsburgs were heterogeneous in the extreme, and their ruler was embarrassed by Turkish attacks and by the disaffection of the German Protestants. Ferdinand, to whom the Emperor had handed over the immediate government of the Austrian provinces, hardly concealed his hostility and dislike towards his brother. And throughout his reign, Charles was constantly handicapped by lack of men and money; even the strongest armies which he raised suffered from that indiscipline which is the inevitable result of lack of pay.

But the real cause of Charles' failure lies in the Individualism of the period. The time had passed when nations would submit to alien rule without resistance; they refused to permit the sacrifice of their own interests to dynastic ambitions. Internally, the efforts of Charles to increase his authority and to produce a measure of centralisation met with opposition upon all sides. In earlier ages, the government of the Roman Empire had been accepted because the desire to be ruled dominated mankind, because that nationality which is the outcome of the desire to rule was hardly existent. By the time of Charles V, the desire to rule had gained strength. An acute observer of the age could have gauged from those events which had occurred and were occurring the impracticability of the Emperor's schemes.

Philip II of Spain was sufficiently acute partially to realise these facts. He understood that, in view of the determined external Individualism of a great part of Europe, the imposition of universal rule by force alone was impossible. It was his object, therefore, to discover means which would enable him to persuade where he could not compel, and he believed that in religious conformity he had discovered such means. During the Middle Ages, the general acceptance of external Universalism had been favoured by the existing identity of religious belief. Philip II argued that a restoration of such identity would produce a revival of external Universalism. To a certain extent his opinion was justifiable. But he failed to appreciate the fact that identity of opinion was itself the product of the desire to be ruled; he did not realise the interaction between that desire and its product; he tended to mistake the effect for the cause. Herein lay the secret of his failure. He laboured to produce a unity of Christendom based upon the material strength of Spain and the moral power of orthodoxy. But the former was unequal to the task of compulsion and the latter failed to command general assent in an individualist age. The desire to rule was stronger than the desire to be ruled.

Indeed, the very attempt to establish a moral basis for his dominion contributed to his defeat. Not content with the promotion of external Universalism, he strove also to establish internal Universalism. His system demanded that he should have power to coerce the opinions of his subjects. Hence he aroused the greater opposition; to foreign war, rebellion was added. In the path of his universalist policy abroad stood Elizabeth of England, the very incarnation of the spirit of external Individualism. In the path of his universalist policy at home arose the Dutch Republic. The movement which produced the revolt of the United Provinces aimed originally at local self-government. It gained strength from the circumstance that Philip's system was not confined to the enforcement of political conformity, but extended to the enforcement of mental conformity. Philip II did not fail because he was a bigot or a persecutor. His bigotry was not so intense as to prevent him from treating the Pope as cavalierly as any Protestant might have done. He could advocate toleration when persecution seemed likely to defeat his political ends. He failed because he was so well able to grasp the necessities of his age, so unable to grasp them fully. Essentially just in his belief that a moral basis for his dominion was necessary, he missed the truth that the greatest danger to that dominion lay in mankind's dislike of the particular moral basis which he projected.

The policy of Charles V and Philip II was universalist,

but its spirit was alien from that of mediæval Universalism; their efforts were directed to promote the interest of a particular dynasty. At the same time, there was a movement towards the restoration of something akin to the mediæval system. The Counter-Reformation may be described as an attempt by the more thoughtful universalists to rectify those evils which they deplored, and which afforded the best justification for Individualism. The leaders of the movement grasped the point which Philip II missed. They saw that if unity were to be given back to the Church, the desire to be ruled must be revived. They further appreciated two important facts. They realised that the desire to rule had been promoted by the internal disorder of the Church; that the restoration of unity and of ecclesiastical supremacy depended upon the effecting of certain requisite reforms in the practice of the Church. Moreover, they realised that the Reformation was largely the result of men's inclination to speculate upon all topics, that many had been led to indulge in speculation rather from ignorance of the orthodox view than from any actual heretical leanings. They saw that it was not enough to forbid debate; it was necessary to make it clear that those who debated were in grave danger of falling into heresy. In short, the leaders of universalist opinion wished to give the Church greater purity of life and practice, greater clarity of doctrine, that the rule of Universalism might be restored.

The Counter-Reformation was an attempt to supply these requisites. The Council of Trent, perhaps originally assembled with some faint hope of reconciling the Protestants with the Church, became an almost violently Catholic body. It proposed to effect the doctrinal extinction of Protestantism; for this purpose, it defined the fundamentals of orthodox belief in unmistakable terms. No one could any longer pretend that communion with Rome was compatible with the holding of Lutheran or Calvinistic doctrines; no one could excuse his heresy by pleading inability to discover the actual dogmas of the Church.

Simultaneously, the foundation of new religious orders, such as the Theatines and the Ursulines, converted the Church once more into an agency making for the uplifting of mankind. The clergy were brought again into close touch with the people. The lives of Popes and greater ecclesiastics ceased to be a source of scandal; they became models of Christian virtue. Moral turpitude could no longer be regarded, even by the most bigoted Protestants, as a necessary characteristic of Catholicism. It was incontestably proved that gratification of the desire to be ruled was consistent with the maintenance of the most lofty standards in private life. Virtue ceased to be the monopoly of Protestant reformers.

But the success of the Counter-Reformation was ultimately due less to the internal changes effected in the Church and to the definition of doctrine than to the labours of the Society of Jesus. The members of that Society fought the Protestants largely with their own weapons. The Reformation stood for personal service and devotion; it attracted many because it demanded a willingness to face peril, to bear all persecution for the sake of truth. The Jesuit missionaries set an example of hitherto unparalleled self-sacrifice; they gave their wealth, their lives, their very wills to the service of their Order and of the Catholic Church. In a measure, the Reformation was the outcome of the intellectual activity of the age; it attracted many by offering them the right to increase their knowledge. The Jesuits undertook the education of the world.

They gratified mankind's desire for knowledge, proving both by example and precept that a high measure of mental development could be attained within the Church no less than without it. They turned the learning of the age into channels which would make it flow to the profit of Catholicism. They inculcated the habit of submission to authority by the indirect method of secular instruction; they trained generations to find in them the best guides to every branch of knowledge.

The Reformation asserted the right of private judgment; many had welcomed it because they made their mental liberty an excuse for the freer gratification of their sensual desires. The Jesuits did not assert the right of private judgment; they did not burden men with the necessity of finding for themselves the true path to happiness in this world and in the world to come. But they eagerly accepted the work of hearing confessions, and in this capacity they emphasised rather the tolerance of the Church to her faithful children than her determination to dominate the minds of her subjects. Their penitents were impressed by the fact that reprobation of their sins did not preclude an easy pardon, that the punishment imposed upon them was duly proportioned to the frailty of their natures, that from the Catholic Church they could receive a complete absolution which elsewhere they might seek in vain. Luther bade sinners repent and make their own peace with an avenging God; the Society of Jesus also bade sinners repent, but would mediate their peace. The Jesuits were prepared to assure men of the acceptance of their repentance by Him Whose name the Society had adopted; the sinner was condemned only to perform some simple act in proof of his sincerity. And as the Jesuits became the most popular confessors, they were the more able to confirm the faith of waverers. They found themselves able to admit that those who remained within the Church and accepted her authority might be allowed much divergence of private opinion.

The Jesuits, indeed, turned Individualism itself to serve their own purposes. The most stalwart champions of Universalism, they yet enunciated a political theory hardly dissimilar from that of the Calvinists. They advocated resistance to heretical governments; they admitted the frequent legitimacy of tyrannicide. And their influence was the greater since their organisation was military, their obedience implicit; because the whole Society acted according to the will of one absolute general. And they had the additional advantage of believing themselves to be justified in the use of any means for the attainment of their ends.

In their skilful hands, the Counter-Reformation was largely successful. Their subtlety enabled them to avail themselves to the uttermost of man's attachment to the old. All those who desired to remain within the Church, but desired also some intellectual activity, were won back from heretical opinions. All those who had drifted rather than deliberately turned from the orthodox path were reclaimed.

But the Counter-Reformation was not entirely victorious. Its success was limited by the existence of the desire to rule. Individualism had attained definite expression; it could in no wise be entirely crushed or silenced. Many were not beguiled even by the ingenuity of the Jesuits; many peoples would in no case tolerate any reassertion of that external Universalism expressed in the theory of papal supremacy. If Ireland and southern Europe were held to their allegiance, if Poland, the Habsburg dominions and much of southern Germany returned to the communion of Rome, yet England, Scotland, Scandinavia and northern Germany remained obstinately Protestant. And in the presence of so great a hostile force, the supremacy of the Pope had of necessity to be exercised with moderation and discretion. Mediæval external Universalism was gone, never to return.

Internally, there was an equally bitter conflict between the two desires. Gradually and laboriously, during the later Middle Ages, the internal Individualism of most countries had been subdued; royal power had been extended, the triumph of centralised monarchy seemed to be assured. But, as ever, the moment of triumph was the moment of defeat. Men had, as it were, prepared to submit to governance, to acceptance of the existing order, when the Renaissance urged them to retain at least their mental liberty. And upon the Renaissance followed the Great Discoveries. During the Middle Ages, the unquestioning acceptance of certain supposed geographical facts had hampered private enterprise and had impeded the development of Individualism. But the growth of a critical spirit produced an inclination to dispute the truth of the oldest and apparently most proven beliefs. Men dared to doubt the validity of current theories of geography, and from this doubt resulted voyages of adventure culminating in the Great Discoveries.

Those discoveries in turn reacted upon the human mind. At this distance of time, and when the entire surface of the globe has been measured and mapped with approximate accuracy, it is impossible to realise the sensation caused by the sudden appearance of new continents, a sudden apparent increase in the area of the world. But the results of that sensation may be clearly discerned. Doubt, and the courage to act upon doubt, had led to the opening up of possibilities undreamt of in any previous age, to the acquisition of untold wealth in new lands of fabulous extent and fertility. It was not to be expected that men who had braved, and braved so successfully, the dangers of the physical unknown world would be readily terrified by the more remote dangers of the spiritual unknown. Among the causes productive of that rejection of ecclesiastical authority which was found in the Reformation, the encouragement to doubt afforded by the Great Discoveries must hold a foremost place. It is true that the pioneer explorers, the Portuguese and Spaniards, held to their original orthodoxy; they were absorbed in the pursuit of material wealth, and gold seemed to deaden their intellectual spirit. But those peoples who entered later into the field of adventure, the English and the Huguenots, the Dutch and the Scandinavians, became the natural champions of a new religious creed, the most zealous enemies of ecclesiastical domination. Nor were they more ready to accept without dispute the prevalent theories of government and politics. The Great Discoveries resulted from the Renaissance spirit; they aided that spirit in producing an atmosphere of unrest.

That unrest found expression in civil commotions in France, the Low Countries and Germany, in the so-called Wars of Religion. In those struggles, religion was certainly a factor; it was not the only or most potent factor. In France, it supplied the most obvious line of division between the two parties; it was probably responsible for much of the bitterness of the conflict. But other lines of division may be easily discovered. Between north and south there was a long-standing rivalry, born of divergence in race, language and tradition. Between the great families there were long-standing feuds. The Bourbons were jealous of the Guises; the older nobles hated the newer. The adoption of Huguenot opinions may in many cases be traced to personal antipathies.

None of these facts, however, supply the ultimate cause of the civil war. That cause is to be found in the growth of individualist ideas; the conflict was a phase in the eternal struggle between the desire to be ruled and the desire to rule. On the one hand, the supporters of Catherine de Medici, of the Guises and of the Politiques aimed at some increase in the control of the state over its subjects, though they advocated different means for the attainment of this end and though they desired the same end for different reasons. A wish to produce religious conformity played but a small part in the conflict. Catherine de Medici was prepared upon occasion to grant a wide toleration; the Politiques would gladly have shelved all religious questions in the interest of national unity. The massacre of St. Bartholomew was the result rather of jealousy than of religious conviction; the crime of Coligny was not his heresy but his ascendancy over the mind of Charles IX. If the Guises relied more definitely upon Catholicism, the explanation of this fact was that they were aliens and could find no other basis of power.

Nor were the Huguenots purer in their opinions or aims. They represented the centrifugal tendencies of the south; they were the champions of anti-monarchical, and even of republican, ideas. Their cities aimed at local independence; the essential principle of their conduct is to be found in their desire to be free from control. At a later date, when they came into conflict with the centralising policy of Richelieu, they were ready to ally with Spain, the supposed champion of Catholicism; they would not accept religious toleration unaccompanied by practical local independence. Throughout its history, the Huguenot movement was little more than the championship of internal Individualism against universalist tendencies in government. It found its chief support in those districts which were least French, which were traditionally opposed to the rule of Paris. The conflict culminated in the triumph of internal Universalism. The consolidation of despotism followed naturally upon the defeat of the advocates of an individualist political theory.

It is, indeed, a feature common to the conflicts of this period that while external Universalism was normally defeated, internal Universalism on the whole triumphed. No movement, perhaps, was more essentially directed against external Universalism than the rising of the Dutch; no movement was more clearly individualist in its internal aspect. It was a direct attack upon the centralising, despotic system of Philip II. It was produced by his destruction of municipal liberties, his attempted reform of the bishoprics, his employment of Spanish ministers, and his enforcement of religious conformity. It was no more an entirely religious movement than were the French Wars of Religion. The wish of the nobles to retain their position and the power to provide for their younger sons, the wish of the burghers to preserve their liberties and to avoid taxation, operated to combine in defence of Protestantism many who were Catholics by inclination and even by conviction. The enemies or victims of Spain were not invariably heretics. Egmont's orthodoxy was beyond dispute; William the Silent's heresy was long dubious. Had Philip been the very pattern of religious tolerance, the revolt of the United Provinces might have lost some of its bitterness; it would none the less have occurred. The Dutch were wedded to the idea of Individualism, external and internal.

Yet even here the triumph of Individualism was not complete. A republic, a loose federation, was theoretically created by the Union of Utrecht; the constituent states were theoretically granted as large a measure of local independence as was consistent with safety. They were, perhaps, theoretically granted more than was consistent either with safety or with the permanence of the state. But in practice the Union of Utrecht was revised. A single Stathalter was created in place of many; he secured a degree of power not contemplated in the framing of the original constitution. The wealth of the state of Holland, its control over foreign affairs, reduced the independence of the other provinces to little more than a shadow. The confederation became rather a veiled monarchy than a republic. Internal Universalism secured a notable triumph.

Internal Universalism, though perhaps to a lesser degree, triumphed also in the Thirty Years' War. There is a marked similarity between this conflict in Germany and the Wars of Religion in France. In each, religion appears as the most obvious cause of dispute; in each, there may be found the same strife between local and national interests, between Universalism and Individualism. Ferdinand II, Maximilian of Bavaria and Wallenstein were alike champions of centralised power rather than of religious uniformity. The Emperor aimed at the reassertion of almost obsolete imperial rights in the interest of his family; Germany was to be united in religion, that it might be united also under Austrian government. The same conception of unity appealed to Maximilian of Bavaria; it was to attain unity that the Catholic League was formed. But between Ferdinand and Maximilian there was one point of fundamental divergence. The latter proposed that the House of Wittelsbach should assume the position which the former assigned to the House of Habsburg.

Wallenstein was equally an exponent of unity, though he paid no regard to the dynastic interests either of Ferdinand or of Maximilian. He seems to have aimed at a restoration of imperial power. His desire was certainly to be the indispensable minister of the Emperor, but he did not care whether that Emperor was or was not a Habsburg. He would appear to have been actuated by a curious, almost altruistic, attachment to the abstract principle of imperialism. Yet, however greatly the three leaders of the Catholic party differed in their aims, they were agreed in championing German unity, in being exponents of internal Universalism.

On the other hand, the resistance offered to the Catholic League was largely the result of jealousy of the Habsburgs and of rivalry between the two branches of the Wittelsbachs. Maximilian of Bavaria regarded the attainment of the electoral dignity as a first step towards the establishment of his ascendancy in Germany. His relative, Frederic, Elector Palatine, feared that the victory of Bavaria would destroy his own position. And the Calvinist princes in general dreaded the result of Habsburg success. Their support of the Bohemian malcontents, their resistance to the exercise of the Bohemian vote in the imperial election, were alike due to their wish to maintain their local freedom.

To the same fear of domination may be attributed the hostility aroused by the Edict of Restitution; the right to secularise ecclesiastical lands implied an increase of princely independence. Nor were John George of Saxony and George William of Brandenburg, the apostles of the *status quo*, less opposed to any unitary schemes. They were resolved to prevent either an extension of imperial power or the entire overthrow of the Emperor. They wished to conserve a system under which they had acquired so large a measure of independence, and their vacillating attitude towards the struggle was the result of their determination to prevent any change in the existing Germanic constitution. They always opposed the party by which that constitution appeared to be threatened.

Even Gustavus Adolphus himself, the great protagonist of Protestantism, was actuated by individualist motives. Sweden needed above all things a field for expansion. The Polish war secured for her the control of the Baltic Provinces. The German expedition was necessary for the completion of the work begun in Poland. Wallenstein threatened to establish in Pomerania a new power which would threaten Swedish control of the Baltic, and Gustavus Adolphus invaded Germany to prevent the complete undoing of that which he had already half done. His policy was dictated rather by affection for Sweden than by any special love for his German co-religionists.

And after the death of Gustavus Adolphus, the decisive intervention of Richelieu was determined by the actual or supposed necessities of France. A Catholic and a cardinal saved German Protestantism from destruction, because a divided Germany was an advantage to the House of Bourbon. In short, the Thirty Years' War, rightly regarded, was but another phase in the secular conflict between Universalism and Individualism.

And as in the French Wars of Religion, so in the Thirty Years' War, the victory lay with internal Universalism, though the peculiar circumstances of Germany tend to obscure this fact. The attempt to secure unity, whether under the Habsburgs or under a branch of the Wittelsbachs, was defeated. But this defeat may be attributed to the traditional association of the Emperor with the mediæval idea of external Universalism, the day for which had passed, and to the fact that Germany was rather a conglomeration of states than in any real sense a single state. It was external Individualism which triumphed at Westphalia. The destruction of the last vestiges of the old imperial power facilitated and was followed by a development of internal Universalism in the constituent provinces of the Empire. The right of princes to pursue an independent foreign policy was recognised; their right to determine the religion of their subjects admitted. It was inevitable that such concessions should be followed by an increase of the power of the ruler in each state, since those rulers were no longer limited on two important points by theoretical subordination to the Emperor. The appearance of such sovereigns as the Great Elector was the natural result of the settlement reached in the Treaties of Westphalia.

Those treaties mark a definite epoch in the history of the world. The old type of external Universalism ceased to exist. The Holy Roman Empire had in reality died with Frederic II; its moribund condition was now recognised. The world-dominion of the Papacy had passed away with Boniface VIII; the recognition of this fact by Europe was emphasised in the contemptuous disregard of papal opposition to the terms of the Peace of Westphalia. And the old type of internal Individualism equally disappeared. The assertion of local independence by petty nobles was no longer possible. The day of centralised monarchies had dawned, and resistance to those monarchies, to be successful, had to be something more than the ambitious self-assertion of an individual or of a faction.

But the nature of man precluded all possibility of a permanent, or even of a temporary, cessation of conflict. Externally and internally, the struggle had of necessity to continue. Externally, men soon perceived the danger of perpetual war; the reaction towards a species of Universalism antedated the assurance of Individualism's victory. That reaction was foreshadowed by Grotius; his *De Jure Belli et Pacis* was an initial step towards the discovery of a new justification of external Universalism.

Internally, unrest was hardly stilled, though in a sense the victory of internal Universalism was more complete than that of external Individualism. In the Dutch Republic, the overthrow of the House of Orange marked a reaction against the growing strength of the central power. In France, Marie de Medici almost succumbed to the turbulence of the nobles; Richelieu was forced to reduce La Rochelle before he could pursue his designs abroad. After his death, Mazarin was faced by the outbreak of the Fronde, an expression not only of the unwillingness of the nobles to submit to control, but also of the more widespread feeling that despotism was an imperfect type of government. The pretensions of the Parliament of Paris to exercise the powers of a representative body were crushed by Louis XIV, but though his reign was marked by almost complete political silence, discontent still muttered. At rare intervals, signs of resistance appeared, even during the height of the *ancien régime*; Vauban found that system imperfect. Generally speaking, however, the limitations upon internal Universalism were more real than apparent. Such expressions of unrest as the hostility to Christina in Sweden and the rebellion of Massaniello at Naples only served to emphasise the almost universal existence of superficial peace. The Treaties of Westphalia, in short, may be described as marking the triumph of external Individualism and internal Universalism.

IX

THE CONFLICT IN EUROPE: 4. FROM THE PEACE OF WESTPHALIA TO THE FRENCH REVOLUTION

AT first sight, the conflict ended by the Peace of Westphalia appears to have lain between those who desired to restore the lost doctrinal unity of Christendom and those who desired to perpetuate the work accomplished by the Reformation. But a further consideration of the character of the period makes it clear that divergence of religious opinion was not the sole cause of the struggle, that it does not afford a complete explanation of the divisions of western Europe. Catholic France allied with Protestant Sweden; her policy, which had favoured the growth, secured the permanence of Lutheranism and of Calvinism in Germany. In the foreign policy of Richelieu, there is little trace of devotion to the Papacy; the cardinal never forgot that he was a Frenchman, he seems never to have remembered that he was a prince of the Church. Nor were the great protagonists of the rival faith more single-minded. William the Silent accepted the reformed creed with apparent reluctance. Gustavus Adolphus was perhaps a paladin of Protestantism, but he was far more obviously the exponent of a short-sighted conception of Swedish imperialism.

Indeed, to explain the so-called Wars of Religion in France or the Thirty Years' War as being a strife of creeds is to omit all explanation. It is still necessary to account for the fact that any given nation was Catholic or Protestant; to discover, in fact, the ultimate cause which leads an individual or a people to accept and to adhere to a particular form of religious belief. That cause lies in human nature. It is to be found in the secular conflict between the two fundamental emotions of man, the desire to be ruled and the desire to rule. Of these two desires, the first is gratified by Catholicism, which in its true conception is no more than the religious aspect of Universalism; the second is equally gratified by Protestantism, the religious aspect of Individualism. Catholicism is cosmopolitan in essence, Protestantism is national. Catholicism urges submission to authority, Protestantism urges the assertion of the right of private judgment. The one is the creed of law and order, tending towards despotism; the other of independence, tending towards anarchy. And both possess a permanent place in the intellectual life of the world; each gratifies to the fullest extent one paramount emotion; neither can ever cease to exist.

The Wars of Religion and the Thirty Years' War, therefore, were not struggles in which the existence of Catholicism or of Protestantism was at stake. It would be idle to pretend that the spiritual power of the Papacy was not imperilled, that the creeds born of the Reformation were not in danger of extinction. The immediate success of the movement inaugurated by Luther did threaten the withdrawal of all Europe from papal allegiance; the progress of the Counter-Reformation did promise the restoration of all the lands lost to that allegiance. But Catholicism was not created by the Papacy nor Protestantism by Martin Luther, and the preservation of neither depended upon the fate of the Vicar of Christ or of believers in the Augsburg Confession. The Pope might have been destroyed; Lutherans, Calvinists, Zwinglians, might have been exterminated. But Catholicism and Protestantism were bound to endure while man retained his fundamental characteristics; their extinction could not have been accomplished without the simultaneous accomplishment of a complete revolution in human nature. Universalists must always be Catholics; individualists Protestants. That some universalists have rejected papal supremacy, that some individualists profess adherence to the Roman communion, is merely accidental, the result either of past training or of real religious indifference. It is impossible that a true believer in the desire to be ruled should be also a sincere advocate of the right of private judgment. It is certain that those who desire to rule cannot sincerely assent to that surrender of their power of initiative which the Catholic Church demands from her faithful children.

And it follows that the attitude adopted by any individual or nation towards religion has always been and always must be determined by their attitude towards the conflict of which religion is one expression. The true conflict in the sixteenth and seventeenth centuries was something much more permanent than any mere quarrel as to the way of salvation; it was part of the eternal struggle between Universalism and Individualism. Where internal or external Universalism prevailed, Catholicism retained or recovered its ascendancy; where internal or external Individualism prevailed, Protestantism was victorious. Spain, aiming at the headship of Europe and inclined to accept despotism at home, was loyal to the Papacy. The Dutch, eager to free themselves from the Spanish yoke, turned to the new national creeds. Paris aspired to dominate France; the south resented the dictation of the capital; the former was Catholic, the latter Protestant. During this period, the mediæval conception that Europe might be united as a Christian confederation, that a government must be in close accord with the Church and control the religious beliefs of its subjects, continued. Philip II pursued the policy which Charles the Great had pursued; he persecuted as a political necessity, because, alike in his external and internal policy, he believed Protestantism to be an obstacle to the realisation of his aims. And in general, those who were externally wedded to the old idea of political organisation, those who internally wished to consolidate their power, were Catholics; those who believed in national and local independence were Protestants.

Nor are the apparent exceptions true exceptions to this rule. It may be admitted that the Lutheran princes of Germany were aiming at strengthening their authority, but they aimed also at freeing themselves from imperial control, and at first their external Individualism was a greater passion than their internal Universalism. The natural result was that deliverance from the Emperor should be followed by a reversion to Catholicism. In some cases, as in that of Saxony, this reversion occurred. In those cases in which it did not occur, the permanence of Protestantism may be explained either by the existence of such difficulties as that of Polish suzerainty presented in the case of Brandenburg, or by the danger of absorption by larger, Catholic neighbours which was feared by the smaller states. In the history of Sweden, the determination of religion by political considerations appears clearly. Christina, aiming at absolutism, abandoned the Lutheranism of her father; the Swedes, always hostile to despotic rule, clung to the reformed faith and secured the abdication of their crypto-Catholic queen.

But the Peace of Westphalia proved that the old mediæval conception of external Universalism and internal Individualism required revision. Imperial power was reduced to less than a shadow. The princes of the Empire, already practically independent within their own territories, received the right to conduct their foreign affairs without regard to the Emperor. Germany became a collection of sovereign states united only by the most formal tie. And for the first time, the limits of the Holy Roman Empire were specifically circumscribed in a public document; the Swiss and Dutch Republics were declared to be beyond its borders. At the same time, the Papacy lost both influence and prestige. It entered a protest against the signature of the Treaty of Westphalia by Catholic rulers; its protest was ignored, and Europe thereby declared its rejection of the papal claim to intervene authoritatively in temporal matters. The recognition of the doctrine *cujus regio, ejus religio* further struck at the root of that conception of Christian unity upon which the supremacy of the Pope ultimately rested.

Nor did mediæval internal Individualism survive the period of stress. The evils of the civil wars convinced men of the necessity of law and order. They realised that the attempt of each town and village to assert its practical independence would lead to a paralysis of government, which could culminate only in anarchy or in subjection to some foreign power. To avoid these evils, not only the internal universalists but also the external individualists permitted or assisted the development of royal authority. The calamities which had resulted or which were expected to result from lack of governance produced centralised monarchies. The epoch of the Peace of Westphalia saw the abandonment of the mediæval conception of external Universalism and internal Individualism. In this fact lies its interpretation and its importance.

But the order of human life is conflict; the struggle

between Universalism and Individualism is eternal. The Peace of Westphalia, therefore, was not and could not be followed by a cessation of strife. It was, perhaps, no longer possible to advocate the union of Europe into a Christian commonwealth, based upon religious orthodoxy, or the subdivision of kingdoms into minute particles. But neither the external universalists nor the internal individualists abandoned their ultimate beliefs, because a particular expression of those beliefs happened to have been discredited. Advocacy of some form of international unity, of some limitation on absolute power, persisted; the change was merely that of the basis of this advocacy. Mediæval conceptions were abandoned, but in the inevitable reaction against the too complete domination of external Individualism and internal Universalism, new conceptions were discovered.

Externally, just as the triumph of Individualism was the more complete, so the reaction was the more rapid. And it was hastened by the character of the new centralised monarchies. Universalist at home, their foreign policy was intensely individualist. That disregard for the claim of the Emperor or Pope to exercise European authority, which had prevailed since the days of Frederic II and Boniface VIII, was accentuated and developed into a disregard of the claims of any state even to its own national existence. But just as the extreme of internal Individualism would produce anarchy at home, so the extreme of external Individualism threatened to produce perpetual war. Some curb on the foreign policy of states had to be discovered, some principle devised to replace that which had been lost in the fall of the mediæval Empire and Papacy, if the world were not to pass into practical barbarism by the path of international anarchy.

The need for some such curb had been felt ever since

the mediæval system had begun to break up, and the search for an expedient antedates the Peace of Westphalia. But the search had been spasmodic and had produced no very tangible result. In the first place, the world was as yet unconvinced of the futility of the older expedient. There was a possibility that the Pope or some sovereign, representing the temporal power of Christ's Vicar, might win acceptance as an international arbiter. Such had been the hope of Philip II, the dream of Ferdinand II. But the end of the Thirty Years' War saw the determination of two problems in such a manner that the creation of an arbiter of this kind became an impossibility. It was then decided that the work of the Reformation was to be permanent, and, as a corollary to this, that Europe should henceforward be divided between Catholics and Protestants.

In the second place, the duration of warfare and its intensity had been alike increased. During the Middle Ages, the existence of feudal relationships between king and king, and between the vassals of different kings, tended to hamper all hostile operations, while the short period of service owed by feudal hosts led to constant interruption of such operations. Even when the use of mercenary troops had become general, a lengthy campaign was still often rendered impossible by the mere poverty of rulers. The Italian Wars afford abundant illustration of the difficulties to which sovereigns were reduced by their inability to pay their armies with anything approaching regularity. But in the period following the Peace of Westphalia, two causes contributed to extend the duration of war and to increase its frequency and bitterness. All those bonds which had united states during the Middle Ages were swept away or were at least disregarded. In place of feudal relationship there was now only such unity as might result from interest; even the closest ties of blood between rulers did not contribute to maintain international peace. And the sovereigns of the new centralised monarchies, possessing absolute or almost absolute power, were able to raise supplies according to their will; the only limit upon their expenditure was the entire exhaustion of all sources of revenue. Hence, the search for an expedient by which hostile feelings might be controlled, the search for a new basis for external Universalism, became vigorous and produced definite results.

That the expedient when found was accepted may perhaps be attributed principally to the character of French policy at this time. Both in his own and at the present day, Louis XIV has given his name to the age in which he lived, and justly, since he was the very embodiment of its spirit. Internally, the last traces of opposition seemed to have vanished. Henry IV had defeated the Catholic League; Richelieu crushed the political independence of the Huguenots and limited the power of the nobles. Mazarin completed the work of Richelieu, the defeat of the Fronde marking at once the extinction of the political power of the nobility and the silencing for half a century of the Parliament of Paris. Louis XIV assumed the government of an absolute monarchy. The States-General had ceased to meet; their very existence was hardly remembered. There were no more chief ministers. Colbert and Louvois were little more than efficient clerks, owing their position solely to the king, acting entirely according to his will, referring to him the minutest details. The lack of real centralisation was concealed; diversity of law, taxation and administration passed unnoticed. Internal Universalism appeared to have attained its apotheosis in the France of Louis XIV.

On the other hand, the foreign policy of Louis affords

a perfect example of external Individualism. At first sight, indeed, his desire to dominate Europe recalls the ambitions of the great mediæval rulers. But between them and Louis there is an essential difference. Charles the Great, the Hohenstaufen, Innocent III or Boniface VIII aimed not so much at the union of the continent into a single state, as into a confederation inspired by the ideal of maintaining Christian fellowship and extending the borders of Christendom. They were cosmopolitan, extra-territorial in their ideas. Even Philip II had something of this same spirit; typically Spanish in many respects, he was in others the political heir of the mediæval Emperors. Louis XIV was essentially French; the first, perhaps the greatest, nationalist. He possessed, and even in double measure, all the ambition which had actuated the great rulers of earlier ages. He would have extended the borders of France on every side. He dreamed of uniting the Spanish dominions with his own kingdom, of the creation of an empire in comparison with which that of Charles V should fade into insignificance. And over and above such extension of his direct rule, he aspired to control England, Sweden, Poland and Turkey, as subordinate allies. But in his ambitions and in his policy there was nothing either cosmopolitan or Christian; there was no ideal beyond that of the glory of France and of her king. Louis was no external universalist. He was rather so complete an individualist as to forget the very existence of any people save his own subjects.

It is, indeed, in the opponents of Louis XIV that the contemporary external universalists are to be found. There was a very real danger of French domination, and that danger could be met only by a combination of states, no one power being capable unaided of offering prolonged and successful opposition. But the creation of a durable and effective alliance has always been a matter of extreme difficulty. With no ostensible object, beyond self-interest, it is really impossible, and it was therefore necessary to discover some theoretic basis upon which an anti-French league might be founded. During the Middle Ages, such a basis had been supplied by Christianity; states had combined against the unbeliever or to effect the overthrow of an excommunicate. But the failure of the Crusades had illustrated the inefficacy of this principle; Macchiavelli had given a distinctly secular character to all political relations, and the Reformation, by perpetuating and intensifying religious disunion, had made it entirely impossible to found any European league upon the defence of orthodoxy. Religion could not afford even a colourable pretext for joint political action by the powers against France.

Opportunely, however, a new basis for external Universalism was discovered in international law. At the very moment when the complete breakdown of the imperial and papal system threatened to dissolve the last slender ties which bound together those units of which the continent was composed, the value of certain broad rules for regulating interstate relations was suggested. It was felt that nations were "in a state of nature towards each other"; that they could not be subjected to the rule of any external power, but that they might without derogation of their entire independence accept as the guide of their conduct propositions which might be regarded as "natural." Though anticipated in many respects by such writers as Oldendorp and Winkler, Grotius was really the first to draw these propositions together into a species of code, and his *De Jure Belli et Pacis* may be regarded as the primary exposition of international law. It consists, perhaps, of little more than a number of common-sense suggestions for the regulation of intercourse between state and state, and since all positive sanction was absent, the acceptance of these suggestions, the validity of international law, could depend only upon the public opinion of the continent. Acceptance, however, was secured, and a new basis for external Universalism constructed.

That this occurred was ultimately the result of the permanence of universalist ideas in the human race, and of nothing else; it was impossible that external Individualism should enjoy unquestioned supremacy. But the immediate occasion of the acceptance of the new basis may be found in the need for some principle of resistance to French aggression. Resistance to that aggression was intensified by the very prevalence of external Individualism; every nation was eager to maintain its independence, and that desire was all the stronger owing to the recent defeat of the original claimants to universal lordship. The theory of Grotius at once justified this prevalent desire and supplied a principle upon which resistance, and united resistance, to aggression could be based. It was laid down that every state had an inalienable right to preserve its integrity and its freedom from foreign control, and from this it followed that opposition to such states as might infringe the liberty of others was fundamentally justified.

At the same time, however, it was generally admitted that within very wide limits a state ought to have absolute control over its own foreign relations, that its abstinence from war should be entirely voluntary, that its alliance should be of its own making. Only if the policy of a state should become so aggressive as to threaten the denial to others of that liberty which it claimed for itself, was coercion justified in the view of the exponents of international law. It still remained to define that degree of aggression which should pass the limit of legitimate pursuit of self-interest, and in that age no exact definition applicable to all cases could be discovered. But a working definition was found in the conception of a balance of power. The new external universalist declared, explicitly or implicitly, that any disturbance of the existing ratio of strength among the states of Europe was an infringement of the rights of nations, a breach of international law.

Traces of this conception may be found at a much earlier date. During the period of the Italian Wars, occasional leagues had been formed to counteract the overwhelming preponderance of French or of Spanish influence in the Peninsula. The apparent strength of Charles V had led to the conclusion of alliances having for their object the imposition of some restraint upon that Emperor. But all these earlier leagues referred to little more than a single district; they were not inspired by any theory of a balance of power as the permanent basis of the political organisation of Europe. It was in the age of Louis XIV that the originally vague idea of union among the weak against the strong developed into a clear policy of preventing any one state from acquiring a predominant position on the continent. This policy then took the place left vacant by the failure of the mediæval conception of the Christian commonwealth; it became the expression of external Universalism.

Such, then, was that new theory of external Universalism through which the secular conflict against external Individualism was continued. To those states which claimed entire liberty of action in foreign affairs were opposed other states which desired to curtail that liberty in the interest of Europe. Alliances were formed to enforce observance of international law, the acceptance of a *modus vivendi* which should prevent the occurrence of international anarchy, a condition of perpetual war. Only accidentally were those alliances directed against France. Louis XIV happened to be the prime disturber of the *status quo;* he alone appeared reluctant to accept some theory of a balance of power. But the ultimate aim of the allies was to coerce, not the king of France or of Spain or of any given state, but the troubler of the world. No power should be allowed to infringe the liberty of its fellows.

And the new external Universalism, therefore, up to a certain point, afforded a guarantee of external Individualism; the reaction of which it was the outcome was gradual, not violent. Louis XIV came into conflict with the individualist tendencies of his age, because he was so typical of that age, because his own intense Individualism denied to others that liberty which he claimed for himself. In other words, the extreme of Individualism touches the border of Universalism; there can never be proselytism without a tendency to coercion. Nevertheless, the opposition to France was primarily universalist. It was based on the assumption that the various states of Europe had certain common interests, that they must admit a measure of control, that the concern of each was to a certain extent the concern of all. If France were permitted to destroy the independence of the Dutch, the safety of other states would be endangered. Europe was no congeries of isolated units. It was in a sense a unit in itself, however impalpable might be the bond drawing its component parts together.

Hence the new theory, while according liberty to all states, qualified its grant with the proviso that the freedom of action admitted in the case of one state should not be used to curtail the same freedom in other states. But it is clear that here a certain difficulty at once arose. It was necessary to define what should be the limit of liberty in each case. At first, and in a somewhat broad sense, it was held that the Peace of Westphalia had created a balance of power which should be maintained. That treaty became, as it were, the basis of international law, and the aim of the universalists was to preserve the *status quo* therein established.

Even so, the exponents of the theory were doubtful as to the exact interpretation of their own doctrine. They hesitated between an attempt to preserve the actual balance ordained by the Peace of Westphalia, and an attempt to preserve a vaguer balance, readjustable if necessary. Of these two possible interpretations, the first implied the maintenance of existing territorial arrangements, the prevention of all aggression, and logically the prohibition even of any rectification of frontiers. The second regarded the balance of power as indefinite rather than exact. The inevitability of territorial changes was admitted; a certain degree of aggression was almost tolerated. But at the same time, the disproportionate strengthening of any state was to be prevented; the balance was not to be destroyed, and even the existing balance was not to be unduly disturbed by the self-interest of one member of the European comity. From this desire to prevent the disproportionate strengthening of any state, the idea of compensation arose. If any country increased its power, and more especially if it increased its territory, all other countries affected by such an occurrence were held to be legitimately entitled to secure a compensating increase. An aggressor was only to profit by his aggression in a limited sense; all other states were, so to speak, to profit from their abstention from aggression. The acquisitions made by war were to be equalled by those of diplomacy and of peace. War was to be rendered decreasingly advantageous to the power which should first take up arms. The original balance was ultimately to be preserved, perpetual strife to be prevented.

This new theory of external Universalism was gradually evolved during the age of Louis XIV. At first, universalist efforts were directed to the preservation of the existing balance in its entirety. But such efforts were foredoomed to failure. Externally, the spirit of the age was individualist, and into conflict with that spirit came the exponents of the new theory. For while it was certainly true that the states of Europe were ready to combine against France and to prevent such aggression as might be detrimental to their own interests, this was the limit of their Universalism. That which was regarded as aggression in the case of others, they held to be merely lawful expansion in their own case. They were externally individualist, quite unprepared to sacrifice one iota of the advantage which they trusted that they might reap by breaking the Peace of Westphalia, by destroying the *status quo* which that peace had established. That curious altruism which appeared from time to time during the Middle Ages had now vanished almost entirely from the domain of high policy. John Sobieski of Poland supplies a possible exception. Regardless of the injuries which the Habsburgs had inflicted, or had attempted to inflict, upon him, he saved the Emperor from the Turks, and the relief of Vienna recalled to mind those achievements of the earlier crusaders by which the mediæval world had been thrilled, its imagination excited. But Sobieski was an anachronism. If he saved the Austrian capital, it was at the expense of Poland. The energy and genius which protected Leopold would have been far more profitably expended upon the reconstruction of his own kingdom. His heroism was certainly greeted with due applause, but diplomatists smiled in secret at the folly which dissipated too scanty resources upon an exploit rather detrimental than advantageous to the hero and to his state. The day when the reputation derived from such an achievement would have produced a commensurate political benefit had already passed. Every state was prepared to preach altruism to its actual or potential rivals; no state was prepared to practise such altruism. Sobieski was born out of due season.

And the prevalent selfishness of international policy ensured the failure of any attempt to maintain the settlement reached at Westphalia. Individualist states were in no case really prepared to sacrifice themselves in order to deliver Europe from the spectre of continual strife. The history of the wars of Louis XIV, and of the alliances which those wars produced, illustrates the failure of the first form of the new theory of external Universalism, and in the record of that failure gradual progress towards the evolution of the second form may be traced. The alliances were the direct product of the determination of France not to be hampered by any external considerations in her pursuit of territorial expansion. Europe was first roused to a sense of the real danger of French domination by the enunciation of the doctrine of "devolution," by which Louis attempted to apply to the whole Spanish Netherlands that law of inheritance which determined the succession to private estates in Brabant. The legal pretence under which his aggression was masked deceived no one; the Triple Alliance was created to hold France in check, to assert the interest of Europe in the maintenance of a balance of power. The allies, however, were really united in defence of an indefensible position. It was possibly feasible to attempt the restraint of France, if a certain measure of expansion were allowed to her. It was assuredly not feasible to attempt to retain within limits already reached, a state possessing great military power and instinct with the spirit of external Individualism.

Accordingly, the Triple Alliance, though it secured apparent success, in reality failed completely. Louis made peace, but he did so less from compulsion than from deep motives of policy. The formation of a league against him gave warning of the possibility of an effective European concert; he saw how valuable a reputation for moderation might be to him. Still more, he was determined to crush the Dutch who had stood in his path; to have a free hand, untrammelled by the existence of any anti-French alliance, when Charles II of Spain should die and the fate of his dominions become a question of practical politics. The authors of the alliance might congratulate themselves on an apparent victory; the short duration of the league put a period on those rejoicings, and if an attempt be made to discover the ultimate importance of the alliance, it will perhaps be found in the fact that its ostensible success aided Louis XIV by encouraging his opponents to devote themselves to the pursuit of an impracticable ideal.

That no lesson had been learned from the failure of the Triple Alliance appears in the history of the league formed for the defence of the Dutch Republic which Louis presently assailed. The root idea of that league, as it ultimately found expression in the Treaty of Nimeguen, was still the maintenance of the exact *status quo*. The Peace of Westphalia was regarded as part of the fundamental public law of Europe; theoretically, no modification of its terms was to be permitted, and the purport of the Treaty of Nimeguen was merely the interpretation of the earlier agreement. It is true that in practice certain changes, not authorised at Westphalia, were permitted, but such apparent acceptance of the inevitable was rendered nugatory by the determination, emphasised at Nimeguen, that the limit of change had been reached, that there should be no further alteration in the future.

Such a determination was rendered futile by the character of Louis XIV, and of the French people, who were as resolved as their ruler not to submit to any dictation by foreign powers. France was intensely individualist so far as her external policy was concerned. Though indubitably Catholic, she was at one with her king in resisting not merely papal aggression, but even the attempt of Innocent XI to preserve that minimum of independence, the loss of which would have been inconsistent with his position as a sovereign prince. And it was obvious that a people who would not agree to accord a reasonable measure of deference to the acknowledged Head of the Church would be even more unwilling to admit the right of any temporal ruler, or combination of temporal rulers, to set bounds upon the extension of French territory or of French glory and prestige.

It was the existence of this pronounced external Individualism which led Louis XIV to disregard the terms of the Treaty of Nimeguen. That disregard was not indeed expressed deliberately; it was cloaked under a pretence of giving effect to the very document to which his opponents made most frequent appeal. A clause in the Peace of Westphalia had transferred to France the bishoprics of Metz, Toul and Verdun, "with the lands belonging to them"; the vagueness of the phrase afforded Louis the excuse which he desired, and the Chambers of Reunion were created, ostensibly to determine what districts were lawfully attached to the three sees. No one credited the French king with any sincere wish to secure a just interpretation of the treaty. No one doubted that the Chambers were merely an excuse for aggression, and if there had been any doubt, it would have been speedily dispelled by the decisions of those bodies. In short, the experience of the fate of the Treaty of Nimeguen served to prove it was at least extremely difficult to draft any document so accurately as to leave no loophole for those who wished still to pursue an individualist policy. A state which desired to be aggressive would be restrained from aggression only by *force majeure*.

From this it followed that the maintenance of the exact *status quo* could hardly be secured unless the powers of Europe were ready to face perpetual war. There was no nation, possessed of military strength, which was prepared voluntarily to forego any reasonable chance of extending its territory and its influence. Only by positive proof that the chance was not reasonable, that any attempt to gain something would in all probability lead to the loss of that already possessed, could a state be restrained from attacking the *status quo*. But such proof could be supplied in no other way than by the hazardous experiment of an appeal to arms; so long as a state was undefeated in the field, it could not be convinced that victory in war was an impossibility for it. It was, therefore, necessary to sacrifice the actual *status quo*; to discover some alternative method by which peace might be maintained, the aspirations of an aggressive or progressive country sufficiently gratified to induce that country to refrain from war, by which and at the same time the balance of power might also be preserved.

Such an alternative was found in the theory of compensation. The origin of that theory may be traced back at least as far as the period of the Italian Wars, when Louis XII and Ferdinand the Catholic arranged the partition of Naples, when the League of Cambrai was formed for the despoiling of Venice. Practically, however, it developed in the years following the Triple Alliance, and was first expressed in the agreement concluded between Louis XIV and Leopold for the eventual division of the spoils expected to accrue from the proximate extinction of the male line of the Spanish Habsburgs. But the theory did not immediately secure acceptance. Louis was too thorough an external individualist to admit the effecting of any real compromise. After the Treaty of Nimeguen, he speedily revealed his resolve to profit to the uttermost from his military power and from the distraction of his enemies, and his continued aggression produced the League of Augsburg.

That League marks a distinct advance towards the second interpretation of the new external Universalism. It was a definite attempt to compel France to agree to a permanent settlement of Europe; it was a European combination, and no mere alliance of two or three powers specially affected by the policy of Louis. The allies recognised that it was futile to attempt the maintenance of the Peace of Westphalia, except in the most general sense. Though they appealed to that document, though it was professedly taken as the basis of the Treaty of Ryswick, yet the aim of the powers was really to secure the safeguarding of their own interests. In other words, they admitted the impossibility of preventing some advance on the part of France. They were determined that they would ensure that this advance should not imperil their own safety, that they should receive practical compensation for any concessions which they made. Thus, though Louis retained Strassburg, he had also to recognise William III; he was forced to forego his design of including England within the orbit of Bourbon influence, and thereby forced also to concede political and economic security to the Dutch. These limitations compensated Europe for the increase of French power recognised in the treaty.

The idea of compensation, however, and the attempt to discover a satisfactory and permanent *modus vivendi*, appear less clearly in the actual terms of the Treaty of Ryswick than in the circumstances in which that treaty was concluded. Its signature was hastened by the posture of affairs in Spain. Charles II was dying; the problem of the Spanish succession held the deepest interest for France and for the allies. Both parties wished to be free to deal with the question, to be able to devise a settlement unhampered by other considerations. At the same time, the conflicting claims to the Spanish inheritance put forward by Louis XIV and the Emperor made it clear that renewed war would result from the death of Charles II, unless means were found by which each claimant should secure reasonable satisfaction. The diplomatic energies of Europe were directed to the task of inducing France and Austria to accept something less than they demanded and desired, to the discovery of adequate compensation for both parties.

More especially, William III devoted his attention to this problem. He has frequently been described as the inveterate enemy of Louis XIV; the humiliation of the Bourbons has been regarded as the keynote of his policy. But his efforts were directed less to the depression of France than to the maintenance of a balance of power between her and the other states of Europe. He was, indeed, the first clear exponent of the doctrine of compensation. He interpreted the new external Universalism as being directed to secure, not the preservation of any given distribution of territory, but the preservation of a balance of power, by ensuring that the development of any one state should be accompanied by a similar development on the part of those states whose interests would otherwise be endangered. And nowhere does this aim of William appear more clearly than in his treatment of the Spanish question. He rejected at once the idea of ignoring French claims and aspirations; he recognised at once that the integrity of the Spanish monarchy could not be maintained. In place of putting himself into a position of hostility towards France, he hastened the conclusion of the Treaty of Ryswick that he might act in conjunction with Louis XIV for the preservation of European peace. To attain this end, he formulated the two Partition Treaties. Austria and France were to make substantial gains in consideration of the abandonment of their claims to the whole Spanish inheritance. That inheritance was to be divided as equally as possible, and the powers of Europe were to combine to secure the general acceptance of the division. In short, the idea of compensation was to prevail, and by prevailing to ensure the maintenance of the balance of power.

It is not impossible that the scheme contained in the Partition Treaties would in any case have proved abortive, but it was accidental circumstances that forced Europe into a new war. The death of the Electoral Prince removed a candidate for the actual throne of Spain whom Louis and Leopold were alike ready to accept. The second Treaty gave a certain preference to the Austrian claim, and secured only a reluctant assent from the French king. In Spain, it secured no assent at all. Charles II's will forced Louis, even if he had been unwilling, to accept the crown offered to his grandson, and the struggle for the Spanish inheritance followed inevitably. But the ideas of William III bore fruit. They supplied the basis upon which the Grand Alliance was founded.

That Alliance may be regarded as a definite expression of the new external Universalism. It admitted, as the Partition Treaties had admitted, that France had a prescriptive right to pursue her own interest; so far it admitted a measure of external Individualism. But it was directed to prevent the danger of excessive Individualism, the danger of international anarchy. No state was to promote its own interest in such a way as to impair the position of other states; all reasonable aspirations should be gratified, but the measure of gratification was to be determined by a species of European concert, was to be such that the balance of power would be preserved. In event of a refusal to accept the decisions of Europe, force might be used to coerce the recalcitrant state. Yet force was not the primary idea of the Grand Alliance. France was rather to be persuaded by a display of military strength, than coerced by the use of that strength And in the view of its inceptors, the aim of the Alliance, and hence of any war which it might undertake, was the establishment of a durable peace.

The Grand Alliance led to war. Louis had reluctantly accepted an arrangement to which he had been a party; he was entirely unwilling to endure the dictation of a European confederacy. To induce him to abandon his extreme external Individualism, it was necessary to resort to arms, and when the war had once begun, the Individualism of the allies reasserted itself. If Louis was prepared to sacrifice Europe upon the altar of French prestige and power, Charles VI was equally regardless of all interests save his own. He aimed at the reunion of the Habsburg dominions, at an overthrow of the balance of power hardly less complete than that which the Alliance had been formed to prevent. The Dutch, moreover, were concerned with the prosecution of their economic interests, no less than with the original purpose of the league. Hence the war was needlessly prolonged. From a sincere attempt to attain a *modus vivendi*, it became an attempt to humiliate France and to secure the special interests of certain members of the confederacy. But in the Treaty of Utrecht, the original aim of the Alliance reappears. The doctrine of compensation gained its first great triumph. France accepted, while the allies granted, some satisfaction in return for the abandonment of her full claims, and at the same time each confederate secured some advantage which might serve to counterbalance the possible increase of French power. At Utrecht, the idea of an adjustable balance was clearly put forward; the new external Universalism received definitely the second of the two possible interpretations, and that creed which was in general to prevail during the succeeding period was now really formulated.

This fact, however, was not immediately realised. Up to the time of the Treaty of Utrecht, it so happened that European leagues had been formed only against France, and from this circumstance arose the idea, countenanced by some historians, that the object of these leagues was the humiliation of the Bourbons. It was supposed that France was a permanent menace to European peace, that the welfare of the continent required her coercion and restraint, that some intrinsic qualities in the French people made it essential to watch every action of the French government with suspicious jealousy, and precluded any possibility of an amicable agreement with it. The history of the Partition Treaties might have indicated that this was not the opinion of William III. An impartial study of the circumstances in which those treaties had been disregarded by Louis XIV might have suggested that France was not permanently or necessarily irreconcilable. Yet it was only with great difficulty that Stanhope secured the acceptance of a French *entente* in England, so convinced were many that France was the one source of danger. In reality, however, the inspiration of the Grand Alliance was drawn from a far deeper source than mere antipathy to a particular king or a particular dynasty. Louis XIV typified the external Individualism of the age; France was the state at once most ready and most able to disregard the interest and the will of Europe. But this was merely an accidental circumstance. The history of the period following the Treaty of Utrecht reveals the true spirit of the Grand Alliance. From that history, it becomes clear that the powers which united against France were actuated less by fear of subjection than by the conviction that the concern of each is the concern of all, by external Universalism.

For no sooner was Louis XIV dead than there ceased to be any anti-French alliances. It would be absurd to contend that the character of the French people suddenly changed. It cannot be asserted with even a suspicion of truth that the king coerced his people or that after the death of Louis there was so strong a popular influence on government that at last, and for the first time, the court of Versailles was driven to modify its policy in deference to the will of the nation. No ruler, however despotic, however able, can compel his subjects to sacrifice their lives and fortunes in a cause of which those subjects really disapprove; the wars of Louis XIV were made possible by the external Individualism of the French nation, and the unparalleled exertions which France made were the result of the fact that royal policy commanded popular approval, were the proof of that fact.

But there is a limit to exertion, and the long wars of

the seventeenth century produced exhaustion. France began to desire peace; Louis himself, ever the most typical Frenchman of his age, showed a new spirit of conciliation in the last years of his reign. At the moment of his death, the individualist tendencies of France were curbed by exhaustion; for the remainder of the eighteenth century, France undertook no positive war of aggression. Orléans and Dubois have been credited with the successful revolutionising of French foreign policy; in actual fact, they merely gave expression, as Louis XIV had done, to the dominant feeling of the French people. For a time France ceased to be externally individualist; she became content to satisfy her reasonable claims in concert with the powers of Europe. If she engaged in wars, it was only that she might defend her legitimate interests and secure adequate compensation.

And the result of this modification in French policy was that the Universalism underlying the leagues formed ceased to be partially obscured; the practical supremacy of the idea of compensation became apparent. It was realised that the ultimate aim of every European alliance was to prevent the occurrence of perpetual war by creating a *modus vivendi*. Thus, immediately after the conclusion of the Treaty of Utrecht, the attention of the powers was directed to Spain. There was certainly no danger of a Spanish domination of Europe; the Triple Alliance was formed, not to prevent such domination, but to secure that the external Individualism of a single state should not be permitted to disturb the balance of power. At the same time, the alliance was not intended to preserve the exact *status quo*, as it had been established at Utrecht. Had they so desired, England, France and Holland could have coerced Spain, could have entirely ignored her aspirations. But they attempted nothing of the kind. Alberoni, and after him Ripperdà, was driven from office; they had endeavoured to act independently of the will of Europe. Yet the allies who had secured their downfall proceeded to grant almost all for which the ministers had schemed. The question of the Italian duchies was settled with at least a due regard for the interests and claims of Spain. In other words, the right of a sovereign state to attempt expansion and the gratification of its ambitions was admitted. Spain was dissatisfied with the settlement effected at Utrecht; attention was paid to her complaints and the settlement was so far as possible revised to meet those complaints. But she was not permitted to take what she would or could; she was not permitted to act without reference to the equally recognised interests of the rest of Europe. She was given something with, as it were, the proviso that she should acknowledge the right of the powers to determine the nature and extent of the gift.

In the decision of this question, the working of the theory of compensation is to be seen. The states of Europe were primarily individualist in their external policy, and they felt that every country had in a measure the right to act independently of all other countries. But the danger of extreme Individualism was also recognised; to a certain extent, external Universalism prevailed. This fact led to the demand that the degree of satisfaction accorded to any given state should be determined by a concert. Such was the principle underlying the Treaties of London, Seville and Vienna, by which the claims of Spain were met; such was the principle which appears in the Wars of the Polish and of the Austrian Succession.

In the case of Poland, France was admitted to possess a legitimate interest in the disposition of the crown;

Austria and Russia were held to have an equally legitimate interest. Hence at the end of the war, while the candidate of the eastern powers secured the disputed throne, France, defeated on the ostensible point at issue, received compensation in the shape of the reversion of Lorraine. In the whole history of the Austrian Succession question, the same conception of national interests appears. Charles VI desired to secure the whole Habsburg inheritance for his daughter, Maria Theresa, and to that end promulgated the Pragmatic Sanction. Yet he recognised that the claim of other states to a voice in the settlement of the problem was not to be ignored, and admitted this by seeking to obtain beforehand the assent of Europe to the scheme which he had devised. In this he was apparently successful; guarantees of the Pragmatic Sanction were given in return for more or less substantial concessions. But as soon as Charles VI was dead, Frederic the Great deliberately set aside the undertaking into which his father had entered, invading Silesia and openly attempting to partition the Austrian dominions. His conduct was not really susceptible of even a colourable justification; he acted as an extreme individualist, careless of all rights and interests save his own. Nevertheless, Europe recognised that he had a certain liberty permitting him to act as he did. The efforts of the peacemakers, both during the War of the Austrian Succession and at the Conference of Aix-la-Chapelle, were directed, not to punish Prussia for her aggression, but to induce her to accept in full satisfaction some part of that which she had at first implicitly or explicitly demanded. Frederic stole Silesia; Europe condoned, applauded, envied the theft. The external Individualism of the age had asserted itself. The external universalists recognised that though the independent action of states might be alien from their own principles, yet it could only be restrained and minimised, not entirely prevented.

And it was this prevalent external Individualism which led in large measure to the failure of the new Universalism, limiting its ascendancy, making its complete success impossible. It was admitted that every state had a certain inherent right to expand, a certain inherent right to receive compensation for the gains of its rivals. But a problem arose as to the true limits of expansion, the degree of compensation which was to be regarded as adequate. It was clear that the satisfaction to which the powers would in any given case assent would be too slight to satisfy the state seeking such satisfaction, too great to be acceptable to the state compelled to grant it. Both parties, therefore, tended to be so aggrieved that they were prepared to enter upon war rather than accept the decision given; acceptance was generally the outcome of compulsion rather than of voluntary consent. Spain agreed to the Treaty of London only when her fleet had been crushed at Cape Passaro and her territory entered by a French army. It was the imminent danger of a hopeless struggle against a European coalition that led to the abandonment of the schemes of Ripperdà and to the acceptance of the Treaty of Seville by Spain and of the Second Treaty of Vienna by Austria. France would not give up her support of Stanislas Leszczyński until she had been defeated in the War of the Polish Succession. Austria only relinquished Silesia after Frederic had inflicted crushing reverses upon her.

And even after the Treaty of Aix-la-Chapelle she remained a malcontent. The Diplomatic Revolution was merely the expression of Austrian and French dissatisfaction at the terms which that treaty had imposed upon them. Maria Theresa would not accept a decision which deprived her of a great province. France, offended by the treachery of Frederic on the continent, was further discontented because her efforts had neither secured to her the Austrian Netherlands nor effected the destruction of English power in North America and India. It was found necessary to fight the Seven Years' War before the conclusions reached at Aix-la-Chapelle were accepted by the two malcontent powers, nor when the Treaties of Paris and Hubertsburg had been signed did the Habsburgs cease to seek compensation for the loss of Silesia, the Bourbons to desire vengeance upon the country which had destroyed their colonial empire. Wars of aggression were not prevented by the new external Universalism; the attempt to curb the prevalent external Individualism of Europe did not achieve complete success. Something was certainly done to limit the duration and extent of conflicts; the aftermath of hostility between belligerents was reduced. But the universalists, on the whole, failed really to attain their end.

Nor was this true only of their efforts to preserve peace. The basis of the new theory was the doctrine of the balance of power and the meeting of legitimate claims by means of compensation. But the compensation sought was generally, if not invariably, territorial, and land is not susceptible of indefinite increase. It therefore followed that it was not every state which could receive even a limited satisfaction; that the moderate satisfaction of one state was liable to involve the serious dissatisfaction of another. It was probable that the wishes of the greater powers of Europe would be gratified, and that this gratification would be at the expense of the lesser powers. Such, indeed, was the case. In order to meet the demands of Spain, the independence of Parma was practically extinguished; to compensate France and Austria, the exchange of Lorraine for Tuscany inflicted a similar fate upon the latter district, while the former was soon incorporated in the Bourbon monarchy.

And probably the most characteristic feature of the new external Universalism was that while the interests of the larger states were almost scrupulously regarded, those of the petty states were almost as generally ignored. To some extent, this was the natural result of the dominance of internal Universalism, which made consistently for the increase of the area under any one government, for an ever greater departure from mediæval heterogeneity. To some extent, it was due to the fact that the danger to European peace from the malcontent of a small state was really negligible; complaints unsupported by adequate military force could be and were disregarded with impunity.

But the prime cause of the neglect of the weak and the consideration for the strong is to be found in the change of conditions since the Middle Ages. Then, there had existed a convenient mean between complete independence and complete subjection, the relationship of feudal subordination. Few European states had actually possessed entire freedom; a feudal tie generally bound them to some other state. Thus the external Universalism of the Middle Ages, of which feudalism was a product or expression, really saved both the greater powers from humiliation and the lesser from extinction. The cities of Italy and the Swiss cantons secured a large measure of liberty, but they were content formally to recognise imperial supremacy. But in the period after the Peace of Westphalia such variation between actual and nominal conditions became impossible. No state would any longer admit even theoretical limitations on its independence; the reign of mediæval fictions ended; the very continuance of the Holy Roman Empire itself was in the nature of an accident, the result of the entire absence of any vitality in the institution.

It is true that for their own sake the larger states became partially universalist in their external policy. They sought to discover a *modus vivendi ;* they admitted that they were to some extent bound to observe the rules of international law. But they applied those rules to themselves alone. The sacrifice of smaller states was in no wise precluded; rather, the doctrine of compensation further imperilled their safety. For only at their expense could the great powers secure any reward for their abstention from war; only at their expense could the great powers make the acquisitions necessary for the maintenance of the balance. And this same doctrine of compensation led also to the formation among the strong of alliances having for their purpose the despoiling of the weak.

Of such an alliance the fall of Poland was the result. Russia desired primarily to regain the provinces of which she had been despoiled during the "Time of the Troubles," even if she ultimately desired also to absorb the whole Polish state. But, in any case, Austria and Prussia would not agree to any extension of Russian territory without securing adequate compensation for themselves. Therefore Catherine II, who might have been content to leave the really Polish lands untouched, was driven to accept the idea of partition. In the interest of the balance of power, in deference to the new external Universalism, Poland was gradually divided between her neighbours. Her right to a national existence was denied; her independence was extinguished. And in this period, if independence were extinguished, it was extinguished completely. No feudal superiority, no mere suzerainty, would content aggressive states. Over lands united to their dominions, the eighteenth-century rulers demanded and secured entire control. The sacrifice of small states was one outcome of the new external Universalism. Power to resist constituted the sole right to resist; might was the only measure of the right to be externally individualist.

In the century which elapsed between the conclusion of the Peace of Westphalia and the outbreak of the French Revolution, there was a certain reaction against that extreme of external Individualism which had prevailed at the beginning of the period. There was, indeed, no return to the mediæval conception of a Europe united under Emperor or Pope, but there was an acceptance of the principle which had formed the ultimate basis of that conception. To Grotius, nations had been in a state of nature towards each other: by the close of the eighteenth century they had come to be regarded as members of a more or less definite corporation. In the Middle Ages, they had also been regarded as united, not isolated; as members of an essentially Christian society, to be tended and guided by the paternal care of the temporal or spiritual representative of Christ on earth. After the Peace of Westphalia, even formal religious unity ceased to exist. The Christian commonwealth was dissolved; all things seemed to be fast degenerating into a condition of international anarchy. In the new union, devised during the following century, all thought of Christian brotherhood and of paternal authority passed away. Whereas the liberty of nations had been theoretically restricted by their obligations to their common Church, and limited as that of children by a father, now the only recognised restraint was the minimum essential for the preservation of any order of society. Into the complete external Universalism of mediæval theory an individualist element was intruded. Each state was essentially individualist in its foreign policy, though an enlightened self-interest dictated a limitation of that Individualism. The reaction was incomplete; the wheel had not swung full circle.

Though more slowly and less definitely, a similar internal reaction occurred during this period. At the time of the Peace of Westphalia, there had been an apparent triumph of Universalism in every European state; mediæval internal Individualism disappeared. And universalist ascendancy was strengthened and maintained owing to the recent experience of the evils resulting from weak government and civil strife. Men were ready to endure much that they might escape calamities such as had befallen France during the Wars of Religion, such as caused a large part of Germany to lie waste for two centuries after the Thirty Years' War. And the inevitable reaction against the gratification of the desire to be ruled was hindered by other circumstances. The extreme external Individualism of the age induced most countries to pursue an aggressive foreign policy, which served to distract attention from internal affairs. Rulers did not devote their energy to the further consolidation of their authority at home; subjects were generally content to commit a large measure of power to sovereigns who waged successful wars.

But before all, the reaction was delayed because the necessity for it was hardly acute. Though most states appeared to possess centralised governments, their centralisation was incomplete; the supremacy of internal Universalism was rather apparent than real. France under Louis XIV has often been regarded as a typical despotism. Yet, while there is an element of truth in this view, the element of error is far greater. At no time during the *ancien régime* was France a truly centralised state or her king a truly absolute monarch. Some

Frenchmen lived under the *droit écrit*, others under the *droit coutumier*. Some provinces were ruled directly by royal intendants, others were *pays d'états*, possessing local estates and parliaments. The method of taxation varied from province to province; internal free trade was unknown. It was not until the time of Colbert that state regulation of economic conditions was really introduced. Religious conformity was not enforced until after the Revocation of the Edict of Nantes.

And that which was true of France was true of other countries. Prussia long remained merely a loose aggregation of lands, happening to own a common ruler. The Austrian dominions were anything except a centralised monarchy. Even in Spain, remnants of old mediæval liberties were to be found in Catalonia and in the Basque Provinces. Indeed, the majority of European states presented a somewhat curious contradiction. The king was absolute in theory, almost absolute in practice. He could dispose at will of the public revenue; he possessed the right of peace and war; he could even legislate by prerogative. He might sell his subjects to their death, as did the landgrave of Hesse, or by condemning them untried to perpetual imprisonment make their lives a veritable hell. Yet, on every side, he was hampered by a mass of local customs and privileges, by rights which he might theoretically disregard and which he was practically bound to respect. Not even a Louis XIV could dare to impose direct taxation upon the nobles. No Habsburg could with impunity ignore the liberties of the Magyars; no Spanish king could defy the Holy Office or deprive ecclesiastics of the right to indulge their inhumanity.

This incomplete centralisation makes the history of the internal conflict during the period following the Peace of Westphalia more than usually complex. In it a dual movement may be discerned; to a certain extent, Universalism and Individualism make progress simultaneously. On the other hand, governmental authority was gradually extended and consolidated. On the other hand, there was a growing tendency to advocate some limitation of the ruling power. And of these two movements, the first was for a while impeded by the prevalent external Individualism. Attention was distracted from internal affairs by its concentration upon foreign policy; frequent wars and crises threatening war served to hinder changes at home. Generally speaking, the progress towards more complete centralisation was very slow. It was not until the new theory of external Universalism had gained a measure of supremacy that the work was resumed, and on the very eve of the French Revolution there was still a distinct movement in many countries towards a greater degree of absolutism.

The gradual progress of the universalist movement may be attributed in a measure to the belief that despotism had already been established by the end of the first half of the seventeenth century. The limitations on royal authority were rather real than apparent; rulers seemed to dispose at will of the lives and fortunes of their subjects, and the absence of resistance created an idea that resistance, or at least successful resistance, was impossible. This appears very clearly in the history of France. The overthrow of the Fronde seemed to have completed the centralising work begun by Louis XI and resumed after a long interval by Henry IV, Richelieu and Mazarin. Both by his own subjects and by foreign observers, Louis XIV was regarded as an absolute monarch. He himself held the same idea; his well-known remark, "*L'état, c'est moi,*" indicates his mistaken belief. And to this circumstance may perhaps be attributed the fact that, during his reign, no advance was made towards the real establishment of despotism, save in the domain of economics by Colbert and of religion by the Revocation of the Edict of Nantes. The infinitely more vital checks upon the power of government, diversity in administration, taxation and law, remained untouched until the removal of an able, and the substitution of a weak or incompetent, ruler made their existence both apparent and a menace to royal authority. Even the economic centralisation of Colbert was less a conscious extension of the province of government than the adoption of certain means to attain an end. It was necessary to make France prosperous that she might pursue an aggressive foreign policy; Colbert held the mercantile theory, and therefore regulated industry and commerce in order to secure the wealth needed for the prosecution of war. And the Edict of Nantes was revoked, the Huguenots persecuted, less as the result of a settled scheme of policy than as the result of the influence of an immoral pietist upon her superstitious and egoistical paramour or husband.

Egoistical to a degree, Louis XIV failed to realise that there were in France any elements of successful opposition to the royal will. Their existence became very apparent after his death, and in the reign of Louis XV some attempt was made to effect the real consolidation of the French monarchy. The Regent Orléans, while posing as an admirer of limited monarchy, endeavoured to create a more uniform administration. He was thwarted by a combination of circumstances, the incapacity of the nobles, the failure of Law, and, above all, by the resistance of the Parliament of Paris. That body came more and more frequently into opposition to the king during the reign of Louis XV. *Lits de justice*, and the banishment of the offending lawyers, served rather to discredit the monarchy than to enhance its power, and eventually Maupeou made a positive attempt to secure that uniformity of justice without which centralisation was a mere name. The Parliament, which he established, failed to achieve its dual purpose of popularising despotism and providing an improved legal system; Louis XVI restored the old order, and when the Revolution broke upon France, she was still a decentralised state.

Nor was the supposed absolutism which reigned in other states any more complete than that of France. Spain possibly affords the best example of a highly centralised monarchy. After the War of the Spanish Succession, the work of Charles V and Philip II was resumed, and almost the last vestiges of mediæval liberty were destroyed. Catalonia had always been a seat of internal Individualism; its inhabitants had been led to support Charles of Austria against Philip of Anjou, feeling that they had more to hope or less to fear from a king brought up in the atmosphere of Vienna than from one educated in that of Versailles. The one was a member of a dynasty ruling a motley conglomeration of loosely-united territories, and might be expected to regard leniently the existence of local independence. The other was a Bourbon, a member of the supposedly most despotic reigning family in Europe; his grandfather had but recently torn up an agreement, sworn to by his predecessor, merely because it guaranteed to some of his subjects the right to worship God as they would. The Catalans, however, supported the losing cause; the majority of the Spanish people loved intolerance and was prone to submit to authority, social and political. And the triumph of the internal universalists sounded the death-knell of the liberties of Catalonia; the first care of Philip V was to sweep away the privileges of his rival's most loyal supporters. Yet even so, the centralisation of Spain was incomplete. The Basque Provinces preserved traces of their old local self-government, and despite the prevalence of the desire to be ruled among the people, royal power was subjected to very real limitations. It was found impossible to destroy the Inquisition. The efforts of Charles III to modify the national dress and to provide adequate street lighting for his capital almost produced a revolution in the most conservative and loyal country in Europe.

And if signs of internal Individualism are not wanting in Spain, they may be found far more abundantly in other lands. Prussia was hardly united at all until the reign of the Great Elector, whose work it was practically to provide a common government for his dominions. Though centralisation and despotism made progress under Frederic William I and Frederic the Great, there was still a lack of real cohesion in the Prussian state; that lack of cohesion largely accounts for Prussia's overthrow by the arms of France and of Napoleon.

Russia, at the time of the Peace of Westphalia, had hardly emerged from barbarism; she had not emerged at all from mediæval decentralisation. So far from being absolute, the Tsar had a spiritual colleague, until Peter the Great abolished the Patriarchate of Moscow. Even at the close of Catherine II's reign, the wide extent of the Russian Empire, and the extreme difficulty of communication between its different parts, left a large measure of local self-government to the provinces. Not only were the nobles almost independent princes on their estates, but in the remoter districts unnoticed city republics preserved their existence.

But it was in the Austrian dominions that the absence of real despotism was most marked. The Habsburgs ruled over races singularly tenacious of their local privileges; they long failed to create even a single, unified administration for their empire. Maria Theresa, it is true, did something to remedy this defect, but when Joseph II went further and attempted to destroy the liberties of the Magyars and of the Austrian Netherlands, he aroused a storm of opposition. In Belgium, an actual revolt took place; Hungary was on the verge of rebellion; before his death, the reforming Emperor was driven to attempt concessions. Leopold II has been regarded as a statesman largely because he admitted the futility of his predecessor's dream of a united Germanised monarchy.

Nevertheless, though consolidation was nowhere really achieved and despotism was thus everywhere imperfect, there was yet a general movement towards both centralisation and absolutism. Even the so-called republics participated in this movement. Venice, for centuries controlled by the Council of Ten, became an extremely narrow oligarchy. Holland accepted the practical sovereignty of the House of Orange. Sweden, long a veiled republic, was temporarily converted into an absolute monarchy by Gustavus III. Only in Poland did internal Individualism hold its own, and Poland paid for this by passing through a period of anarchy into a state of subjection to her universalist neighbours. On the eve of her dissolution, she had recognised the errors of her past; the reformed constitution, annulled at the Second Partition, endowed the executive with powers greater than those which any Polish king had possessed since the extinction of the House of Jagiello.

When, therefore, the French Revolution occurred, Europe presented no picture of uniform absolutism, but rather one of countries in almost every stage of centralisation and decentralisation. Spain was, perhaps, as near a complete despotism as possible; Poland was as near complete anarchy as a state can be and yet continue to exist at all. Between these two extremes, most varieties of government were to be found; monarchies masquerading as republics, republics masquerading as monarchies; countries possessing a mediævally nebulous unity, countries recalling the Greek city-states in the extension of the functions of government.

And this peculiarity of eighteenth-century Europe must be attributed to the fact that at this time a dual process was occurring. While internal Universalism was labouring to complete its triumph, a new theory of internal Individualism was being painfully evolved. Just as there was no return to the external Universalism of the Middle Ages, so there was no return to the internal Individualism of that time. But each dominant emotion found a new mode of expression, as was bound to be the case unless human nature changed. And just as the new external Universalism made some concession to the individualist spirit, so the new internal Individualism made allowance for the prevalent Universalism.

This reaction against the supremacy of the desire to be ruled first appeared in the gradual evolution of the new theory of monarchy. During the Middle Ages, as soon as kingship ceased to be tribal, it became essentially territorial; the king was, above all, a great landowner, and his duties were held to be equivalent to those of a good landlord. His title to rule was similar to the title of every possessor of property; it was divine in origin, based ultimately upon the distinction made in the Decalogue between *meum* and *tuum*. But at the time of the Reformation, this idea of monarchy was necessarily and seriously assailed. Forced to find a ground for resistance to government, the Protestants, not daring to refuse obedience to a divine institution, were driven to discover some human foundation for royal authority. The Huguenots therefore produced the Social Contract, formulating a theory that government is based upon an original agreement between ruler and subject. Kings, as one writer expressed it, were made by men for their own convenience, " for quietness' sake, as one member of a family is appointed to buy the meat." The idea of contract, however, failed to secure ascendancy, partly because it could be turned to support extreme tyranny, partly because kings were reluctant to permit debate concerning the origins of their authority, partly because subjects were generally disinclined to enter upon such debates.

On the other hand, the idea of convenience as a basis of government developed and bore abundant fruit. It became a recognised idea that royal authority was a trust, that power was given to kings, not that they might gratify their own inclination, but that they might promote the welfare of their subjects. That welfare was commonly interpreted as consisting in the maintenance of prestige abroad and the promotion of material prosperity at home. The external influence and interests of the state were to be safeguarded; public works were to be undertaken; everything possible was to be done to improve the lot of the people. Kings, no less than their subjects, accepted this theory of monarchy. Frederic the Great was only voicing the opinion of contemporary rulers when he professed himself to be " the first servant of his people." The sovereigns of the eighteenth century were almost morbidly eager to recognise and to fulfil their obligations.

But those obligations did not, nor were they in any wise intended to, limit the absolute power of the king. Monarchy was to be benevolent; it was at the same time to be despotic. Frederic the Great crystallised the contemporary conception of the royal office in his well-known phrase, " Everything for the people, nothing by the people "; rule was to be autocratic, no less than paternal. The governed were not to be permitted any voice in determining the conduct of the governor; they were held to be incapable of deciding what was and what was not for their own good. No sovereigns, perhaps, were so entirely resolved to disregard adverse expressions of public opinion as were the benevolent despots of the eighteenth century. They seemed to feel that they could secure the welfare of their subjects; they laboured conscientiously towards that end. They seemed at the same time to be determined that no one else should undertake that task which they conceived it to be their duty to perform and to appropriate to themselves.

In these circumstances, it is hardly matter for surprise that the enlightened despots engaged in undertakings not obviously fraught with advantage to their subjects, and of which those subjects disapproved. Generally speaking, they were warlike, and if some of the wars which they waged resulted in benefits to their people commensurate with their cost, others had no such merit. Frederic the Great's long struggle for the possession of Silesia may be defended on the ground that it gave Prussia a valuable and even necessary province, and that it raised her to the rank of a first-class power. The wars of Catherine II have a similar justification. Swedish rivalry in the Baltic was economically dangerous; victory over the Ottoman Turks served to give Russia an outlet to the south, and was valuable as supplying a community of sentiment, promoting a patriotic enthusiasm, by which the empire of the Tsars was welded into a single state. But the intervention of Charles III in the Seven Years' War and in the War of American Independence produced nothing but evil for Spain; the attack of Joseph II on Turkey merely served to accelerate the advance of Russia and to embarrass the Emperor still further in the prosecution of internal reforms. Few, if any, of the wars undertaken by Louis XIV and Louis XV were conceived in the best interests of France, nor did they result in any advantage to her sufficient to excuse the expenditure which they necessitated. None of the Bourbons, however, can be with any real justice included among the enlightened despots; the selfishness of their foreign policy supplies a fair indication of the whole tenor of their conduct. Even the great public works, completed under the *ancien régime*, were designed largely to gratify the ostentatious vanity of the French kings; on the testimony of Arthur Young, they served no very useful purpose.

And if the wars undertaken by the enlightened despots were not always advantageous to their subjects, their internal policy was frequently still less advantageous, still less in accord with the wishes of their people. Frederic the Great deliberately organised his kingdom as a camp, and if military strength was essential to Prussia, the exaggeration of that strength was largely responsible for the failure to cope with the many social and economic evils eventually remedied by Stein and his collaborators. But it is in the case of Joseph II that the faults of enlightened despotism are best discerned. His measures achieved so little popularity that the agitation aroused by them shook the Habsburg throne. Himself indubitably intelligent and sincere, he lacked that patience in face of stupidity and prejudice which is one of the most necessary qualities in a statesman. Enthusiastic to a degree, he attempted to impose his will upon his reluctant subjects, to accomplish by means of a few edicts the laborious work of centuries. And the methods and errors of Joseph were those of his contemporaries; his haste was really typical of the working of that system of which he was perhaps the truest representative. The enlightened despots were alike in their impatience of opposition, in their conviction that they possessed a practical monopoly of political wisdom. Catherine II abandoned the duma which she had called into existence, when she found that even a tentative representation might produce the expression of hostile public opinion. Pombal in Portugal, Charles III in Spain, forced through the suppression of the Jesuits, with little regard for the feelings of the people.

Such disregard for the real wishes of their subjects on the part of the benevolent despots produced important results. It was admitted that government should be for the good of the governed. The despots claimed to be the sole judges of what constituted that good. But their claim was soon disputed; Joseph II received practical proof of the fact that his views were unacceptable to his subjects. And even when no such dispute occurred, when the ruled were content to receive without questioning the verdict of the ruler, a difficulty still arose. If the majority of sovereigns sought, to the best of their ability and knowledge, to promote the welfare of their people, all did not do so. The benevolence of the government of Louis XV was at least dubious; the malevolence of that of Hesse, whose landgrave sold his subjects to fight in wars in which they had not the least interest, was beyond doubt. And the existence of unenlightened despots produced a corollary to the original thesis. If government was to be for the good of the governed, there must be some sanction by which such an employment of authority might be secured. A ruler who misused his position must be liable to adverse criticism and eventually to deposition, as having failed to fulfil the duties imposed upon him by his office.

But though this corollary seems to follow logically from the original hypothesis, it did not secure immediate enunciation. The theory of benevolent despotism also implied submission by the ruled, and upon this aspect emphasis was laid owing to the prevalence of internal Universalism. Mankind was in general inclined to obedience; it was necessary to destroy or at least to impair the ascendancy of the desire to be ruled before men could be led to consider either the possibility or the advisability of resistance to constituted authority. And it is in the gradual growth of criticism of the established order that the second stage of the reaction against internal Universalism is to be found, in the intellectual movement which characterised the latter half of the eighteenth century.

The inclination to accept authority, to bow to the decisions of all established powers, extended not only over the realm of politics, but also over those of religion and economics. In every direction the human intellect was cramped and confined to certain recognised channels. The task of the internal individualists was therefore the harder; they were forced to induce the minds of their contemporaries to break the shackles of convention, as well as to brave the anger of governments and to convince the world that the supposed danger of anarchy was unreal. They were obliged to run counter to all accepted theories; it was their task to convert mankind to a new mode of thought. And their success was the more difficult since the agencies created by the prevailing desire to be ruled were powerful, the defences of internal Universalism strong. Those defences would indeed have been impregnable if it had not been that the human mind is easily satiated by gratification of one or other of the two paramount emotions. As it was, the triumph of the individualist reaction might be delayed; it could not be permanently prevented.

A certain weakness in the universalist position

facilitated the individualist victory. During the Middle Ages, the bondage of the human intellect had been well-nigh complete, because men upon one important topic dared only to debate even with themselves in secret, in fear and in trembling. Dogmatic religion possessed a strong hold upon the world; men were hardly unorthodox in their own minds. Kings might be powerful and impious, powerful and clear-headed; they still shuddered before the prospect of excommunication, of condemnation by the Church. Nor was it merely that they dreaded the political consequences of such an event, calculated as those consequences were to give pause to the boldest statesman. They trembled also, and sincerely, for their eternal welfare; the flames of Hell blazed brightly before the minds of mediæval rulers. And their subjects lived in a condition of equal dread of ecclesiastical censures; they held fast in terror to a body which claimed to control the only path to Heaven.

That there were sceptics in the Middle Ages is indeed certain. Agnosticism is no less permanent than Catholicism, nor has there been any period in which all men have been ready to modify their conduct merely because a given course of action might be displeasing to a distant and unseen Being. But mediæval heretics could with difficulty discover those who thought with them; they were not strengthened in their hostility to the existing system by the knowledge that this opposition enlisted wide sympathy. The Church had secured a practical monopoly of the written word; her censorship was severe and effective. Only by public preaching could heterodox views be popularised, and it was no very arduous task to silence a few preachers. Hence the heretical movements of the Middle Ages always failed; the Albigenses, the Hussites, and all other assertors of individualist religious opinion were crushed more or less effectively by the dominant Church.

The invention of printing, however, made the dissemination of any opinion infinitely easier, and from that moment heresy grew apace, until its progress culminated in the Reformation. Individualism was at last generally preached; the enunciation of the doctrine of private judgment marks an important stage in the assertion of the desire to rule against the desire to be ruled. Religious bodies, other than the Catholic Church, sprang into existence. Those whom fear of excommunication had deterred from the expression of their secret convictions were now able to console themselves with the hope that there might be byways to Heaven, even if the road which they had been taught to follow was closed to them. A critical spirit developed; a tendency appeared to reject the accepted because it was accepted. But the individualist triumph was wholly incomplete. Universalism had enjoyed a prolonged ascendancy; its influence remained extremely powerful. Not only did Catholicism regain much of the ground which it had lost, but Protestant Churches proved to be, or became, equally universalist in their principles and their organisation.

Indeed, it was not until the latter half of the eighteenth century that the work of the Reformation was completed. At that time the internal individualists realised the prevalence of superstition and of dogmatic opinion. They saw how this hampered them in every way; they came to appreciate the fact that they could not hope to attain their object unless and until they succeeded in training the human intellect to question accepted ideas. Above all, they grasped the necessity of combating dominant religious creeds, and especially of combating the Roman Church. Catholicism has always been primarily logical. It has offered consistent opposition to all free expression of opinion, realising that if liberty of thought were conceded in one direction, a first and probably a fatal step would be taken towards the admission of a similar liberty in the domain of theology. The condemnation of Galileo was not due to any special ecclesiastical objection to the rotation of the earth round the sun; it was a measure necessary for the safeguarding of the theory of St. Peter's keys and the dogma of transubstantiation. And while the Catholic Church controlled education and possessed a practical censorship over profane literature, the cause of Individualism could make but little progress; the association between the extreme of dogmatic religion and the maintenance of universalist ascendancy over the human mind was at once intimate and inevitable, since dogmatic religion is nothing but one expression of the desire to be ruled.

Hence, it was against dogmatic religion in general, and against the Catholic Church in particular, that the first efforts of the eighteenth-century individualists were directed. Two circumstances combined to encourage their attack. In the first place, the age was rather superstitious than religious. Obedience to the Church was the product of fear, not the outcome of love; the tendency to follow the promptings of fear was sedulously encouraged by the clergy. The more influential laymen were retained in communion with the Church largely by the extreme tact of their confessors. The indulgence of an inclination to infringe every provision of the Decalogue was punished by the most moderate penalties; the most profligate princes and nobles were never refused the consolations of religion, and their mistresses were often among the most favoured daughters of the Church. Towards the masses, no doubt, the attitude of ecclesiastics was more severe, but even the God of the Many was found to be most tolerant of any specially popular vice. Nor were the Protestant clergy more sincere in their obedience to the creed which they professed. In England, courtly bishops were ready to compliment the reigning beauty without regard to her morality; a drunken clergy were prepared to laugh with appreciation at the broad jests of the local squirearchy, and to marry the discarded mistresses of their patrons.

In the second place, the Catholic Church was characterised by grave faults both of theory and of practice. As education and learning increased, men abandoned many beliefs countenanced by ecclesiastical authority; the universal deluge and the Biblical account of the creation were questioned, while the Copernican view of the solar system was accepted. If such unorthodox opinions were at first not openly proclaimed, this was only because a superstitious and cynical age deemed it to be expedient as well as possible, to hoodwink the Deity, if indeed He existed, and His ministers, if indeed those ministers were not themselves equally heretical.

The faults in practice were still graver. The richer benefices were practically the perquisites of the cadets of noble families; pluralities abounded, non-residence was rather the rule than the exception. The higher clergy were commonly unfitted for spiritual office; the lower clergy were frequently too uneducated to minister effectively to the needs of their flocks. All the ill-consequences of enforced celibacy were apparent among ecclesiastics, whose serious employment was politics and whose recreation was vice. The undoubted devotion of the few was forgotten in the irreligion of the many.

But the degeneracy of the Society of Jesus most of all contributed to facilitate the individualist assault upon the Church; and upon that Society it fell to bear the first brunt of the attack. The Jesuits had been missionaries of noteworthy zeal and efficiency, educationists of marked capacity; they had deserved and had secured a wide popularity. But corruption is the fate of most religious orders; they generally decline from their original perfection, and the Society of Jesus afforded no exception to this rule. They came into contact with politics at home, entering with zest into every intrigue; abroad they developed into merchants of dubious honesty. As a result, their dictum that the end justifies the means, which had been pardoned or overlooked while their work was full of benefit to the human race, began to provoke more or less vigorous criticism. As long as they had conscientiously fulfilled their purpose they had been forgiven much; when they had ceased to do so they were credited with faults of which they were guiltless. The Jansenist movement was directed primarily against the Jesuits, nor did the Society ever recover entirely from the attack made upon it in the *Provincial Letters* of Pascal.

And the teaching of Port Royal prepared the way for the final assault, which was based upon the political and economic conduct of the Order, but which would have failed if that Order's reputation had not been already undermined in other respects. As it was, Pombal was enabled to set the example of expelling the Jesuits. They had interfered with his foreign and internal policy; they were therefore driven from Portugal. And his example was followed in other Catholic lands. The bankruptcy of La Valette afforded the occasion for the suppression of the Order in France: in Spain, Austria and the Italian principalities, the welfare of the state supplied the formal justification. Eventually, Clement XIV, by the Bull, *Dominus et Redemptor*, declared the dissolution of the Society, and the growing Individualism of the age achieved a remarkable victory.

For the suppression of the Jesuits was an event of no

ordinary importance in the history of the world. Whatever emotion may from time to time be ascendant in the human mind leads to the creation of agencies to secure and to maintain its ascendancy, and of the agencies so produced by the universalist spirit the Society of Jesus was one of the most notable and effective. Its members had undertaken the education of the world; they had been successful in this work and had trained their pupils in habits of obedience. Hence, they had also done much to ensure the supremacy of that emotion to which they really owed their origin. It was their success in inducing submission which secured them a welcome from Frederic the Great and from Catherine II, when Catholic rulers had expelled them; those who were endeavouring to establish autocracy could wish for no better helpers than the Jesuits. But this very fact made their formal suppression all the more valuable to the cause of Individualism. Their place as educationists had to be supplied; it was supplied by men inspired rather by the desire to rule than by the desire to be ruled. It is no mere coincidence that the French Revolution, in one aspect an individualist movement, found its most typical leaders in men of that generation which had received its education after schools had ceased to be controlled by the Society of Jesus.

Nor was this the only importance of the fall of the Jesuits. The event involved a defeat for the Pope, the great exponent of Universalism; the prestige of the Papacy almost reached its nadir at the moment when Clement XIV was compelled to abandon the most able defenders of the Holy See. And the victory which Individualism had achieved in this case encouraged the opponents of the constituted ecclesiastical system; the first success in the reaction against Universalism led to further efforts. Accepted theories were generally attacked. Montesquieu by implication criticised the government of France in his *Persian Letters;* the Encyclopædists questioned almost every recognised belief, Diderot, in particular, preaching a practical agnosticism.

But it was Voltaire who really expounded that gospel of disbelief which inspired the individualists to break away from the past entirely. He was by nature devoted to the desire to rule. He hated all dogmas, save those which he himself propounded; he was the enemy of all intolerance, save intolerance of intolerance; he was the opponent of all superstition, save the superstition that the human intellect is perfect. He was eager to subject all things to the cold light of reason, and his great literary gifts, his wit and his satirical power, made him a peculiarly formidable opponent of prevailing beliefs. In him, the work of the Reformation reached its logical conclusion. Luther had asserted the right of private judgment, but had anathematised those who dared to exercise it upon such questions as the authenticity of the Bible or the dogma of justification by faith only. Voltaire asserted the same right, and to him nothing was too profound, nothing too sacred, to be submitted to the test of human reason. Himself a deist, he taught his contemporaries to dare to deny the existence of God, necessary as he supposed the Deity to be; he taught them, in short, to dare to be complete individualists.

Voltaire appealed to a relatively limited audience; his chief importance lies in the fact that he made it the fashion to attack the Church, to question dogmas and to despise superstition. It was the work of Rousseau to popularise anti-clericalism; he appealed to a wider public, and brought his ideas home to the many by the very exaggeration of his language. Upon that exaggeration, upon the self-contradiction of which he was guilty, his opponents seized eagerly; they hastened to apply exact meanings to phrases probably inexact by intention, nor, when arguments failed them, did they refrain from descending to more or less scurrilous abuse. His success may be gauged from the violence of the opposition to him. The anger which he aroused in the minds of the universalists is evidence that they realised how vital a force the individualist creed had become in his hands.

And the fact that Rousseau compelled an answer, compelled a counter-attack, was of no slight assistance to his cause. Voltaire, though he had not entirely escaped persecution, had yet found admirers among those who rejected his opinions, and the resultant hushing of controversy really subserved the interest of the dominant theory. By provoking debate, Rousseau extended the knowledge of his views, and increased knowledge of the individualist theory meant an increase in the number of those who adhered to that theory. For though Individualism, no less than Universalism, is a passion inherent in man, it is less susceptible of clear expression than the contrary ideal, and hence for it to make progress, to come as near as may be towards attaining an ascendancy, there is almost need for some written, and even for some graphically written, exposition of its nature. But no sooner has such an exposition been secured than many who had merely felt a vague discontent with things as they were, a vague distrust of Universalism, realise that Individualism is the creed which they have subconsciously professed. Voltaire and Rousseau together, therefore, did much to hasten the reaction which, though it could not have been prevented, might yet have been longer delayed. Much as they differed from each other, they were alike individualists, and as such contributed to undermine the ascendancy of the Church, to make irreligion both fashionable and popular, to encourage the rejection of all hitherto accepted ideas, to ensure the emphatic assertion of the desire to rule.

In this weakening of the Church, a definite advance towards a complete reaction is to be found. Education had been altogether in the interests of dogmatic religion; its spirit had been wholly universalist. If it did not become less dogmatic, the dogma was changed; it was no longer the duty of obedience that was taught, but the obligation to rebel. Whereas in the past men had learned that certain things were beyond criticism and beyond question, now they learned to reject every standard save that of their own reason, to hold nothing too profound or too sacred to be debated. And the removal of the long-standing barrier against free discussion of religion paved the way for the free discussion of all topics, and more especially, for the free discussion of politics. The Church was closely allied with the crown in every state; the power of priest and king went hand in hand; ecclesiastical political theory was almost always monarchical. The decline of the Church therefore led to a decline of royal prestige; the growth of free thought tended to produce the limitation or destruction of monarchy.

Nor was it the ascendancy of dogmatic religion alone that the individualists attacked, though it was into that channel that their first efforts were really directed. Economic and political, no less than religious, liberty was denied by the prevalent Universalism. The mercantile theory had been everywhere adopted; the government claimed the right and professed the duty of regulating the industrial life of the community in the real or supposed political interest of the state. But this doctrine was called in question during the eighteenth century. The Physiocrats preached the freedom of industry; their ideas were elaborated by later political economists, who taught a completely individualist creed. All restraints upon trade were condemned; freedom of contract between man and man, whether citizens of the same state or no, was applauded; the dogma of *laissez-faire* was promulgated. A definite individualist reaction occurred in the sphere of economics, or at least of economic thought.

That same reaction eventually extended to the region of political theory. Absolute monarchy was criticised at first by implication. Montesquieu and Voltaire admitted their admiration of the English constitution, and such admiration could only be construed as a tentative condemnation of unrepresentative government. Rousseau went further. *The Social Contract* declared in vivid phrases the inalienable right of peoples to choose and to remove their rulers; the divine basis of royal authority was ridiculed rather than seriously attacked. And the immense popularity which Rousseau's essay secured armed individualist opinion for the contest against internal Universalism. It became, so to speak, the gospel of the desire to rule.

But the theory of internal Individualism, evolved in the eighteenth century, differed widely from that which may be found in the Middle Ages. Mediæval Individualism lacked systematisation. It amounted to little more than a claim by every district to exist in a state of anarchy, a denial of the right of the central government to perform the elementary function of preserving law and order. The internal Individualism of the eighteenth century was a clear theory, carefully based upon certain fundamental facts or assertions. It declared the excellence of human reason, denying entirely the theory of a divine moral code and the idea that any person or class was specially qualified or empowered to teach morality. Man had a right to order his intellectual life as he saw fit; he possessed an identical right so to order his economic and political life. The relationship between the state and the individual could be legitimately determined only by those individuals of whom the state was composed. No one had any prescriptive right to rule; all sovereigns were limited by the inclination of their subjects. To the thesis that government is for the good of the governed, the new internal Individualism added the corollary that rulers who failed so to rule as to promote the welfare of their people might be and should be removed from their office.

On the eve of the French Revolution, then, there was a general reaction against the conclusions which had been reached in the Peace of Westphalia. Externally, Individualism was losing ground. A new Universalism, based upon the conception of a balance of power, had been evolved, and the maintenance of that balance was to be secured by the combination of such states as individualist aggression might threaten. Expressions of this idea are to be found in the alliances formed from time to time to resist the isolated expansion of a single state. The theory underlay the Armed Neutrality, designed to oppose the claim of England to disturb the commerce of the world in her own interest. It produced the intervention of France, Spain and Holland in the War of American Independence, a league which proposed to readjust the balance held to have been disturbed by the colonial successes of Great Britain in the Seven Years' War. It led to the Fürstenbund, a union of the smaller German states under the auspices of Frederic the Great, to defend the *status quo* in the Holy Roman Empire from the danger to which it was exposed by the ambition of Joseph II.

But perhaps the most complete expression of the new

external Universalism is to be found in the Triple Alliance of England, Holland and Prussia. Originating from the restoration of the House of Orange to the stathaltership by a Prussian army, this alliance attempted to secure a preponderating influence on all European affairs. It imposed an armistice upon Sweden and Russia, when the former seemed to be threatened with conquest. When Catherine II and Joseph II combined to inflict upon Turkey the recent fate of Poland, the allies intervened with effect, and it was the mobilisation of a Prussian army in Silesia, the imminent threat of war, which led Austria and Russia to conclude the treaties of Sistova and Jassy. And it was the Triple Alliance which determined the conditions upon which Leopold II should be permitted to restore his authority in Belgium. It had, indeed, become clear that any deliberate aggression would cause the formation of a European league, that external Individualism was limited by compulsory regard for the interests of at least the greater powers. The Universalism of the last years of the eighteenth century recalled the ordering of Europe by mediæval Emperors and Popes; the reaction would have been complete, if the alliances had been permanent instead of occasional, if a definite concert had been created.

Internally, there was an equivalent reaction against that Universalism which had been established at and after the time of the Peace of Westphalia. Absolutism and centralisation had never been perfectly secured; throughout the eighteenth century, rulers were endeavouring to consolidate their power while subjects were evolving a new principle of resistance. But, at the end of the period, it had almost become clear that the ultimate victory would not lie with the universalists, that they had already attained the highest point of their success. Joseph II failed to impose his reforms upon his dominions; the Belgian Revolution indicated that there was a definite limit to the submission of peoples to their sovereigns. Gustavus III, who had been handicapped by the individualist predilections of his subjects, established a despotism; his triumph was brief, and after his assassination Sweden became once more a limited monarchy. In France, Louis XVI found himself obliged to restore the Parliament of Paris, and was forthwith handicapped in his support of Turgot's reforms by the factious opposition of a privileged bureaucracy.

In general, the reaction was evident, though incomplete. Nothing appears more clearly in the history of the eighteenth century than the permanence of the secular conflict between Universalism and Individualism. The triumph which one or other of the two seems to have gained proves to be essentially unreal; the reaction ever anticipates the completion of the victory. At the time of the Peace of Westphalia, the destruction of imperial and papal authority promised the beginning of an era in which nations should be unimpeded in the pursuit of their own interests; the crushing of internal disorders promised the consolidation of every state, the end of all resistance to government. At the outbreak of the French Revolution, the general acceptance of the balance of power as the ultimate basis of international relations evidenced the vitality of external Universalism; the growth of criticism and of resistance to government evidenced the vitality of internal Individualism. All expectations were falsified save that of the enduring nature of the struggle between the desire to rule and the desire to be ruled.

X

THE CONFLICT IN EUROPE: 5. FROM THE FRENCH REVOLUTION TO THE PRESENT DAY

No great event in history is susceptible of and has received so many different and contradictory interpretations as has the French Revolution. Some have regarded the movement as being essentially directed against absolutism; some have held that it was designed to secure unity and centralisation. But it is easy to show that the French government under Louis XVI was less, rather than more, autocratic than had been the government at any other time during the *ancien régime*. The Parliament of Paris successfully resisted the royal will; Turgot and Brienne were alike thwarted by its opposition. And the Revolution did not develop until the king, by summoning the States-General, had implicitly abdicated any claim to dispose at his pleasure of the lives and fortunes of his subjects. Nor does the fact that the Revolution culminated in a highly-centralised and despotic system prove that to create such a system was the original design of the movement or of its leaders. On the contrary, the weakening of the executive by the Constitution of 1791, the subsequent disappearance of the king, the delegation of power to the commune, the reluctance with which the republican legislature consented to part with its absolute control over the administration, and, above all, the definitive assertion of popular rights, indicate that the Revolution was not wholly a unitary and centralising movement.

Objection may equally be taken to the view that it was intended only to sweep away intolerable political, religious, social and economic abuses. The government of Louis XVI had displayed its anxiety to remedy all that called for remedy; the nobles and clergy voluntarily surrendered the privileges which had been cause for complaint, and the way had already been prepared for a thorough reform before the Revolution had finally developed, since not until after the flight to Varennes was the cause of limited monarchy irretrievably lost.

Nor, again, was the Revolution an uprising of the masses against the classes. Only for a brief moment did it create a franchise without a property qualification; universal manhood suffrage was hardly advocated even by the most extreme revolutionaries. The leaders of the movement were drawn from various walks of life. Mirabeau was a noble, Sieyès was an ecclesiastic; Robespierre, Danton, Marat, can hardly be described with any justice as men of the people. And finally, the Revolution is not to be degraded into a mere disturbance organised by a dissatisfied middle class anxious to appropriate to themselves that political power from which they had been excluded under the *ancien régime*. Apart from the inherent improbability that an event fraught with such tremendous and enduring consequences should have been the work of selfishly discontented politicians, it is clear that the people at large favoured the Revolution, that at no time did they really withdraw that favour. And the dictum of Abraham Lincoln is true: "You cannot fool all of the people all of the time."

The truth is that no one of these explanations is satisfactory. In each of them there is an element of justice; each, as a complete interpretation, is unjust. The French Revolution was all these things, all and more also. To appreciate it, the true nature of History must be realised, the true character of man and of nations. Men are both individualist and universalist; their life is made up of an endless conflict between their two paramount emotions. One or other may attain a momentary ascendancy; that ascendancy is ever momentary, the reaction always inevitable. The most human man, perhaps, is one in whom the desire to be ruled and the desire to rule are most evenly balanced, and in such a man's life periods of reaction are most frequent and most violent; he turns most readily from one extreme to the other. And nations resemble individuals. There is always and must always be an opposition to the existing system in every state, be that system what it may. Reaction from Universalism to Individualism, or from Individualism to Universalism, will occur with more or less frequency, and it will occur most frequently in the least stolid race, the most human race.

Of all nations upon earth, the French is the most essentially human. They embrace with enthusiasm; they spurn with equal enthusiasm; they are almost feminine in their moods. " A dancing nation, fickle and untrue," characterises them from a hostile standpoint. More friendly criticism recognises their generous temperament, their idealism, their gifts of imaginative construction, their sense of the poetry of politics. During the period of the Revolution, the French people acted more typically than ever before or since. Under the *ancien régime* there had been too large a measure of Universalism to satisfy the individualists, too large a measure of Individualism to satisfy the universalists. Both parties were therefore eager to alter the existing system; each in turn secured a passing ascendancy. The movement thus became complex in character; its variations of aim and attainment were numerous. So violent, indeed, were those variations that France during the Revolution resembles some passionate maiden, storm-tossed by alternating gusts of love and hate.

This interaction of Universalism and Individualism, the momentary triumph of each, appears alike in the external and internal history of the French Revolution. At the outset of the period, and in their attitude towards foreign affairs, the French people were captivated by the idealism of the desire to be ruled. They disclaimed, and disclaimed sincerely, any wish to break the peace; they would not imitate the vices of the *ancien régime* by waging wars of aggression. They were rather inspired by love for their fellow-men, even though their love was somewhat impatient and this impatience at times produced a violence of affection closely resembling hatred, at least in its results. The Revolution would perhaps not have led to war at all if it had not been for the unconciliatory attitude adopted by the powers of Europe.

That attitude was partly the result of the reaction towards external Universalism which had marked the eighteenth century. It had become a political postulate that the concern of each was the concern of all, and in accordance with this supposition the internal changes in France were held to be matter for the attention of other states. In particular, Austria and Prussia claimed that the French should not be allowed to settle their government without reference to Europe. They were led to take up this attitude partly by the prevalence of internal Universalism, since the individualist tendency of the Revolution appeared dangerous to such as were actuated by the desire to be ruled. France was thus, in a sense, driven to defend her existence as a sovereign state, her right to determine her own internal concerns. Excuses were certainly put forward by the allies to justify their intervention; the Habsburgs became suddenly solicitous for the welfare of the imperial princes, the Hohenzollerns for the safety of the Bourbons. But such excuses were too unreal to hide the underlying motive of the two powers. Just as the Triple Alliance had vetoed Joseph II's Belgian policy, so the new coalition proposed to veto the Constitution of 1791, to annul the work of the National Assembly, to restore the *ancien régime.*

Even so, the revolutionaries were eager to preserve peace. Their determination to do so was explicitly announced in an article of the Constitution, and when war had broken out, it did not at first become aggressive on the side of France. The cosmopolitan view of foreign politics still held sway. If France proclaimed her willingness to assist all nations striving to be free, she equally proclaimed her resolve to exact no recompense for the good which she proposed to do. The revolutionaries repudiated all idea of hostility towards the inhabitants of the lands invaded by their armies. They warred with rulers, not with subjects. They adopted a self-denying ordinance, prohibiting them from doing anything which might offend the sacred brotherhood of man. They would annex no territory, they would reap no profit save the abstract reward of virtue, the consciousness of probity. Even the Girondists, who advocated war from less pure and more political motives, did not attempt to reinforce that advocacy by any proposal to secure the territorial prizes of victory. Revolutionary France at first held fast to external Universalism.

But not all Frenchmen were altruists, not all external universalists. Though few, if any, dared dispute the dogma of international fraternity, an individualist view of foreign policy gradually secured adherents. The allies were defeated, the war proved costly. These two facts combined to assist the development of an external

Individualism in France. Adopting the Pauline dictum, that "those who preach the gospel should live of the gospel," the revolutionary armies proceeded to levy contributions on the lands in which they had sown the spiritual things of liberty. The French Republic permitted or persuaded, and eventually compelled, the districts occupied by its troops to desire incorporation with it. When some of these districts declined to receive so great a benefit, an excuse for their annexation was speedily found. Louis XIV had established the Chambers of Reunion to cloak or to facilitate his aggression. The external individualists of the Revolution produced the doctrine of the natural frontiers. They claimed that they were doing no more than giving to France that which Nature herself had accorded.

The natural frontiers, however, were partially unnatural. The Rhine proved to be less a boundary and a barrier than an ever-open door into Germany, the existence of which encouraged advance in place of producing the satisfaction of achievement. When the projected goal had been attained, it was found that it was of necessity merely the prelude to further effort. The frontiers had to be defended. Such defence was susceptible of facile justification, and the idea of buffer states for the protection of the frontiers was easily adopted even by those who had viewed with apprehension the original annexation of territory. But from the formation of such artificial barriers it was but a small step to proceed to open aggression. By degrees, all pretence of an appeal to natural rights was abandoned. As under the *ancien régime*, the interest, real or supposed, of France became the sole determining principle of French foreign policy.

Napoleon, in effect, resumed the work of Louis XIV. He completed it and went further; at the height of his power, his empire recalled that of Charles the Great, to whose example he made a conscious or subconscious appeal. The annexation of the Illyrian Provinces marks the entire rejection of the original principles of revolutionary policy. It could not be contended that lands beyond the Adriatic Sea were attached to France by any natural right, that France had indeed any title to possess them other than that conferred upon her by victory in war, the right of the strong to despoil and to oppress the weak. At the same time, the substitution in the client states of monarchical for professedly republican government marked the abandonment of the revolutionary crusade for the spread of liberty, for the delivery of mankind from the tyrant's yoke. Spain may have been ruled badly by her Bourbon kings. The attitude of the Spanish people, when Joseph Bonaparte was substituted for Charles IV, shows that the change of ruler was not in accord with their wishes, suggests that it was not conceived in a spirit of anxious consideration for their good. And Napoleon's cynical repudiation of his original championship of Italian unity, his treatment of Germany and his entirely political attitude towards the Poles, were only the logical development of his adoption of French nationality and interests as the keynote of his conduct. At the time of the Preliminaries of Leoben, he had rejected revolutionary idealism by arranging the partition of Venice. His later policy fulfilled the promise given at the close of his first Italian campaign. And that policy was popular in France. The nation had soon wearied of unselfishness; having wearied, she became more entirely selfish than any other state had ever been. From the extreme of external Universalism, she reverted to that of external Individualism; the wheel swung full circle.

An equivalent variation appears in the internal policy

of the French Revolution. At the outset of the period, though France was imperfectly centralised, though despotism was qualified, yet the executive was powerful and irresponsible, the king at least theoretically absolute. Nor was this absolute power at first very antipathetic to those who became the later revolutionaries. When the States-General met, men were ready to commit the leadership of the nation to Louis XVI; it was to his beneficence that they trusted to secure such changes and reforms as they desired. They believed implicitly that the king would judge rightly as to what constituted the good of his people; their spirit was universalist. Even the preaching of liberty, equality and fraternity was primarily little more than an assertion of the brotherhood of all Frenchmen under a paternal ruler. Republican or democratic doctrines were hardly known; Individualism was almost silent.

But among the most marked characteristics of the French people is love of logical conclusions. The internal universalists of the revolutionary period were typically French, and therefore were lacking in moderation. They aimed at the preservation of the *ancien régime;* they regretted the most necessary and salutary changes. And this fact enabled internal Individualism to gain converts; it hastened the reaction. Many who would have been content to support a reasonable measure of Universalism were forced or induced to embrace the contrary creed, and the folly or blindness of the king, the lack of organisation of the conservative elements in France, completed the work which the violence of the internal universalists had begun. The demand for a definite constitution was an initial victory for the forces of Individualism; the Constitution of 1791 was a triumph. Logical, because French, it adopted the extreme contrary to that which had prevailed under the *ancien régime.* Prefaced by a declaration of the Rights of Man, itself an assertion of the privileges of the individual, the Constitution established a weak executive, reducing the king to the position of a shadowy figurehead for an almost anarchical state. In place of a theoretical right to legislate by prerogative, Louis XVI was granted merely a suspensive veto. Election everywhere took the place of royal appointment or hereditary succession. The ministers of the crown ceased to be able to impose their will on the nation; they were instead forced to attempt the carrying out of laws in the making of which they had no voice.

Even so, the internal individualists were not satisfied. They pushed forward to the logical conclusion of their theory, and the destruction of kingship was followed by an attempted establishment of anarchy under the guise of a pure republic. The Constitution of 1793 did more than sweep away the few remaining vestiges of the *ancien régime.* Executive power shared the fate of monarchy. The popular assembly itself was distrusted; though permitted to suggest laws, it was prohibited from enacting them. The right of legislation was given to the people at large, and, that no regulations of which they disapproved might possess validity, they were discouraged from obeying even the laws which they had themselves ordained. A clause of the Constitution insisted not merely upon the right, but also upon the duty, of rebellion; every Frenchman was urged to determine for himself the degree of obedience which he would render to constituted authority. Not even in Poland had legalised anarchy been more completely proclaimed, had internal Individualism approached more nearly its logical conclusion. The Constitution of 1793 established the private judgment of every man as the sole standard of his political conduct.

It is, however, in the relations between the Revolution and the Church that the effects of the individualist side of the movement can be most clearly seen. Dogmatic religion is based upon the desire to be ruled; Catholicism gratifying that desire more completely than does any other creed, is essentially the creed of the universalist. The Roman Church denies to its members the right to criticise the Vicar of Christ, or even to judge the priesthood. The conscience of the individual is in the care of his spiritual father; to that father he must yield implicit obedience. But whatever else popular government may imply, it implies a certain exercise of private judgment. The individual must possess the right of security from oppression, the right to criticise the conduct of his rulers. Without the existence of such rights, liberty is a mere idle name, a mere phrase coined the better to conceal the reality of tyranny. And for this reason it is in truth impossible for a sincere Catholic to be also a sincere believer in democratic rule, or for popular government to exist in any sincerely Catholic land.

So far, therefore, as the French Revolution was directed against absolutism, so far as it involved championship of the right of the people to govern themselves, championship of the desire to rule, it was bound to come into conflict with the Catholic Church. The disciples of an Ignatius Loyola and those of a Rousseau were fundamentally in disagreement. Conviction of the merit of entire submission and conviction of the iniquity of such submission could not exist in harmony; conflict between the two theories of happiness and right-doing was inevitable. And the intensity of the necessary conflict was bound to increase in exact ratio to the increase in the strength of the individualist side of the movement; its bitterness afforded a satisfactory index of the degree of ascendancy possessed by the apostles of the desire to rule.

At the beginning of the French Revolution, this conflict was rather real than apparent. All, save such as battened on corruption, were ready to agree that the regulation of the Church was a necessary measure. The abuses of the existing system were too patent to be ignored, too great to admit any real apology. No one could conscientiously defend clerical privilege, the gross inequalities between the incomes of the higher and those of the lower clergy, the faulty character of ecclesiastical appointments, the prevalence of non-residence and pluralities. The most sincere adherents of the Church and her bitterest enemies united to effect certain reforms.

And, indeed, the Civil Constitution of the Clergy was, up to a certain point, in the nature of a compromise. Those who wished to maintain the institution assented readily to the destruction of certain obvious abuses in it; even the establishment of state control over the Church was hardly a measure antipathetic to the Gallican Catholics. But the Civil Constitution went further. The elective principle was applied to ecclesiastical, no less than to civil, offices; the clergy were brought directly or indirectly under the control of the laity. Whereas the Catholic Church had always insisted that the priesthood was responsible to God and to His earthly representative alone, a certain responsibility to the people was now introduced. This change was alien from the historical attitude of the Church; it struck at the desire to be ruled. And it was followed by the establishment of toleration for all creeds, the state refusing to declare an absolute preference for any particular form of religious belief.

But such toleration was insufficient to satisfy the individualists. All religious creeds are universalist to a greater or less degree; all insist upon a measure of submission to authority; all depend for their vitality upon the degree to which they gratify the desire to be ruled. Dogmatic religion, in its very essence, is hostile to Individualism. That theory rejects authority and upholds the right of every man to work out his own salvation or damnation. Logically, it declines to admit the control of a Deity, no less than it declines to admit the control of any man or of any human institution. And to this logical conclusion the French individualists tended. They regarded the recognition of mere equality between the various creeds as at best a half-hearted step towards the recognition of the truth. They were ill-content that the state should professedly admit the existence of a Deity Whose wisdom transcended that of man; that the Declaration of the Rights of Man, prefixed to the Constitution of 1791, should be said to have been drawn up "in the presence and under the auspices of the Supreme Being."

The individualists, therefore, continued to expound the cult of Reason. They advocated the doctrine that there was no external power to which the will of the individual should, or indeed could, be subordinated. And just as they secured the legal establishment of practical anarchy in civil affairs, so they secured a momentary triumph in ecclesiastical affairs. Christianity, and thereby all dogmatic religion, was abolished. The Feast of the Goddess of Reason was the final victory of those who, pushing their theory to the uttermost, denied the existence of any moral code other than that which each individual might devise for himself. There was a certain significance in the selection of a beautiful and abandoned actress to personify the presiding genius of the human intellect; such a goddess would never be likely to enjoin restraint of inclination. In worshipping the embodiment of beauty and of vice, men were accepting slavery only to their own passions, and such slavery has, perhaps, never been regarded as impairing perfect liberty. The identification of human reason and human appetite marked the climax of the individualist triumph.

But such an orgy of gratification of the desire to rule as appeared in the Constitution of 1793 and in the Feast of Reason necessarily produced an early reaction. The very completeness of the individualist triumph hastened the revival of the contrary theory, and the more rapidly because the logical character of the French people induced revulsion from one extreme to the other. In face of grave external dangers, the Constitution of 1793 was never actually put into operation; government was entrusted to Committees of Public Safety, and the rule of these committees tended to become increasingly autocratic. The period of the Convention was not one of a weak executive. Nor did the victory of Individualism in the Feast of Reason fail to produce its retribution. Immorality became almost a political offence, at least in theory. The Hébertists were guillotined, and the Festival of the Supreme Being announced to the world that the governing party in the French Republic was convinced that unrestrained licence was incompatible with the existence of civilised society.

Indeed, the constitutional and religious history of France, from the fall of the Hébertists to the establishment of Napoleonic despotism, is a record of the gradual revival of internal Universalism. Executive power was restored in the Committee of Public Safety; the Constitution of 1793 was annulled almost at the moment of its creation. The idea of direct popular control over legislation was abandoned in the Constitution of the Year III. A second chamber was created; an executive of five was established to secure freedom from sudden change such as had resulted from the caprice of a despot or of a despotic assembly. The Directory failed, but its failure was due to the fact that the reversion to the old order was incomplete, not to the fact that there was a certain reversion.

At an earlier date, the statesmanlike warnings of Mirabeau had been disregarded by the dominant individualist party. The French people had declined to admit the possible fallibility of their chosen representatives; the doctrines of Rousseau had prevailed. The result had been anarchy, from which the nation had painfully emerged by passing through the nightmare of the Terror. And the lessons of the period of the guillotine had been learned if anything too thoroughly. The complaint against the Directory was that it did not approach more nearly to the old order, that it was a compromise between monarchy and a pure republic, that it therefore offended the French love of logical conclusions. Nor were the framers of the constitution blind to their lack of popular support. They insisted on the re-election of a percentage of their own party sufficient to secure their control of the new legislative bodies; they declined to submit the system which they created to the verdict of the nation. But though they were possibly able to hinder the reaction they were unable to prevent it. The Directory was a period of incessant disturbance, of frequent *coups d'état.* It culminated in the most complete victory ever gained by internal Universalism in France.

The results of that victory were crystallised in the Constitutions of the Year VIII and of the Empire, the latter of which merely emphasised the absolutism established by the former. Alike in religious and in secular affairs, there was a definite return to the past. Catholicism was declared to be the religion of the majority of

Frenchmen under the Consulate; under the Empire, the conclusion of the Concordat marked the definite restoration of the Roman Church. Napoleon rightly interpreted the opinion of France; his government was made possible by the new prevalence of the desire to be ruled, and to that desire the fullest possible rein was given. Legislative power was entrusted to a nominated body; if the forms of popular government were retained, popular influence on the administration was reduced to a minimum. The First Consul was exalted to the position of a king; the Emperor was more powerful than any king of France had ever been. The advocate of centralisation triumphed; the universalist side of the revolutionary movement gained the ascendancy. If it had not been that the abuses of the *ancien régime* were finally swept away, the Revolution might seem to have been effected in vain. But equality before the law was established, even though it was an equality of subjection; uniformity of administration and of law was secured, privilege died for ever. The internal Universalism which had secured the victory was inspired by a different spirit from that which had inspired the Universalism of the Bourbon monarchy. If it gratified the desire to be ruled, and gratified it to the fullest extent, it had in it also an individualist element; it accepted the doctrine that government should be for the good of the governed.

Externally and internally, therefore, there was a universalist and an individualist aspect of the French Revolution. Robespierre and Napoleon were alike typical products of the movement; each embodied the spirit of the Revolution. In his attitude towards foreign affairs, the former represented the extreme of Universalism. A firm believer in the essential brotherhood of man, he was an earnest and sincere opponent of war. Even when the conflict had begun he deprecated the idea that France should profit from victory to promote her private interest. He refused to gain such advantage as might have been derived by giving assistance to the Polish revolt, because the private and political character of the Poles, in his opinion, debarred them from the privilege of alliance with a pure republic.

In his attitude towards internal affairs there was an identical spirit of idealism. Robespierre was a pronounced individualist, the champion of decentralisation, the advocate of direct popular government. His apparent inconsistencies were nothing more than the measure of his intense conviction. His share in the establishment of the Reign of Terror, his restoration of religion in the Festival of the Supreme Being, only illustrate his Individualism. In his view, and in that of the party which he led, the French people had been crushed under a tyranny, stupefied by long gratification of the desire to be ruled. They were to be roused from their stupor, taught to be free. But some, like Circe's swine, loved their degradation and gloried in their shame. Such must learn the error of their ways, or die, lest their evil example should corrupt the very elect. Nor were any to be permitted to degrade their freedom by abandoning themselves to licence; such must learn the perfect liberty of self-control, and recognise their obligation to obey the divine instinct of their individual consciences. The guillotine was set up, a régime of compulsion applied to the recalcitrant. Those who refused to accept the blessings of liberty should be threatened with, and in the last resort should suffer, the utmost penalty that human government can inflict. Yet it was not that France might learn to obey that Frenchmen were put to death. They died that by their death their brothers might learn to live, to live the only true life, the life of liberty; that the desire to rule might triumph. It was true that the extreme Individualism of Robespierre tended to become extreme Universalism. Such, however, must always be the case. The strongest advocates of the gratification of the desire to rule must always tend to deny to others the right to gratify the desire to be ruled.

And, owing to this connection between the two extremes, between the logical conclusions of the two theories, a curious apparent kinship exists between the ideas and methods of Robespierre and those of Napoleon, the exponent of the external Individualism and internal Universalism of the Revolution. In reality, however, they were entirely divorced. If, at the outset of his career, Napoleon preached nationality in Italy, if he could later urge the "Illyrians" to be free, he was nevertheless essentially an external individualist. His appeal to the altruistic sentiments, which the idealism of the Revolution had invoked, was insincere, designed to cloak or to support selfish, non-altruistic designs. He was the political heir of Louis XIV. He aimed at the establishment of a French dictatorship over Europe. He would have revived the territorial empire of Charles the Great, but the inspiration of that dominion would have been no conception of a Christian commonwealth; it would have been the Bourbon conception of the glory and interest of France.

Internally, Napoleon was as determined as Robespierre had been to destroy all who differed from his views, as determined to crush all opposition. But his motive was no ideal of a pure state, no resolve to make men virtuous whether they would or no. Rather, he recalled the memory of Louis XIV, was actuated by the same principles and carried out the same ideas with greater success. He established that centralised absolutism towards which the Bourbon kings had striven and to which they had failed to attain. His word was law, since the legislative body was composed of his pliant nominees. He attempted even to mould literature and art according to his will. The press was severely censored; no one might write anything, no one might say anything, which should detract from, or even fail to exalt, the glory and reputation of the Emperor. The Church was restored that it might promote the desire to be ruled and thereby support the imperial system. By the Concordat, France was reconciled with the Papacy, but the reconciliation lasted only so long as the Pope subserved or appeared to subserve the interests of Napoleon. The clergy were to preach Bonapartism rather than Christianity; the Napoleonic Catechism was to supply the matter of their sermons. They might direct men's consciences and save their souls, provided always that they taught their disciples to place their lives at the disposal of the Emperor. Nothing was to exist in France which did not contribute to the maintenance of Napoleonic imperialism.

That interaction of Universalism and Individualism which appears so clearly in the French Revolution appears also in every episode in the secular conflict between the two desires; to every episode there is a dual aspect. But in other cases the interaction is less evident. The sixteenth-century Reformation appears, at first sight, to have been individualist throughout; above all things, it was the assertion of the right of private judgment. But the episode of the Reformation is only completed in the Counter-Reformation, in the reaction from the ascendancy of the desire to rule towards a revival of the desire to be ruled. And the same is true of all the great movements of History. It is not in the fact that it possessed this dual aspect that the interest of the French Revolution lies, or that its peculiarity is to be found. It is rather in the rapidity of transition from extreme to extreme. Violent reaction produced an equally violent counter-reaction. Externally, France passed from Individualism through a period of Universalism to Individualism once more. Internally, she had been universalist when the States-General met; she became intensely individualist, bordering upon the extreme of anarchy. And when the movement culminated in the Napoleonic empire, she was universalist once more. Into the space of a single generation the changes of centuries were concentrated. The French Revolution is a veritable epitome of History.

Nor was the French Revolution really an isolated event. Though it actually occurred in France, it might, but for accidental circumstances, have occurred in almost any European country; the ideas from which it was born were current throughout the continent. And the history of other countries during the revolutionary period displays a series of reactions, external and internal, similar to those which appeared in France. At the beginning of the epoch, Europe was possessed by the spirit of Universalism. Externally, the ascendancy of that spirit had been exemplified in the Triple Alliance; England, Prussia and Holland had attempted to regulate the affairs of the continent. And consequently, when the Revolution occurred, the affairs of France were held to be of international importance; a change in the internal organisation of the French monarchy might disturb the peace of Europe and overthrow the balance of power. Austria and Prussia allied to watch over their own interests and to secure that there should be no undue interference with the political welfare of other states. The exponents of external Universalism regarded the altruism of the revolutionaries with suspicion. They refused to accept their professions of disinterestedness, and by this refusal they gradually produced an individualist reaction in France, enabling those who disbelieved in cosmopolitanism as the basis of foreign policy to emphasise their objections. The revolutionary war thus early became a contest between French Individualism and the Universalism of the allies, between a nation resolved to shape its own destiny and nations resolved that the affairs of Europe should be settled by some species of European concert. The coalitions formed against France were all directed primarily to maintain the balance of power, and ultimately to compel the acceptance of the doctrine of compensation.

The coalitions failed. French victories broke up league after league, and this ill-success of external Universalism prepared the way for a revival of external Individualism. The reaction was begun by Prussia when she concluded the Treaty of Basle; under practical compulsion, her example was followed by other states. And the resultant Individualism was more extreme than had been that of any other age. Institutions which had survived the conflicts of centuries fell to the ground; a complete breach with the Middle Ages was effected. The Holy Roman Empire, which had prolonged its moribund existence despite the Reformation and despite the Peace of Westphalia, finally passed away. The venerable character of the Venetian Republic did not suffice to save it from extinction. The temporal power of the Papacy, after having escaped unscathed the many revolutions of Italy, was for a while extinguished. Nothing was sacred from the destroying hand of the new Individualism; nothing was permitted to stand in the way of the gratification of self-interest.

But the failure of the European concert, and the growth of external Individualism, consequent upon that failure, produced no cessation of opposition to France. It rather led to the evolution of a new and individualist principle of resistance. Nationality is primarily the claim of a nation to exist; alike in its internal and in its external aspect, it is individualist. It opposes any attempt to subject a nation to foreign rule; it opposes also any attempt at the exercise of control over a nation by a concert of states. During the revolutionary period, France set the example of championing the idea of nationality. She refused to order her internal affairs according to the will of foreign powers; she asserted the right of all peoples to freedom. She declared that she herself would not impair that freedom, would not coerce or repress nationalities. Thus, even when her foreign policy was most emphatically universalist, it had an individualist basis; her very cosmopolitanism, the very theory of international fraternity, was the outcome of the desire to rule. And the actual conversion of her external attitude from one of Universalism to one of Individualism was a triumph for the national idea. It was the result of her enthusiastic championship of French nationality.

And when the coalitions had been dissolved, when the attempt of the concert to dictate to France, or even to restrain her Individualism, had failed, nationality became, for a time, the governing factor in the policy of the powers. That policy became externally individualist, partly because Universalism had achieved no success, partly because the danger of subjection to France had become both evident and acute. In most lands, this fear of conquest produced a spirit of resistance; the extreme of Universalism led to the natural reaction. It was no longer merely a case of preventing the destruction of the balance of power. External and internal affairs became inextricably blended; countries adopted an attitude of hostility to France, lest the continued success of French arms should effect their annihilation. However illegitimate the aggression of Napoleon may have been, the struggle against him partook of the nature of rebellion rather than of that of war.

France, therefore, was successively attacked by states, acting upon individualist principles. After concluding the Treaty of Basle, Prussia had deliberately dissociated herself from the other powers. She had declined to join any coalition; she had preserved the strictest neutrality. But the very Individualism which had inspired her to adopt a neutral attitude led her to resent the cynical contempt with which she was treated by Napoleon. At the time of Austerlitz, she had threatened France; her indecision exposed her to renewed insults. Eventually her patience was exhausted. Without waiting for Russian aid, she entered upon war, and her precipitancy, the measure of her Individualism, involved her in the disaster of Jena.

Though the fact is somewhat obscured, it was outraged Individualism which moved Prussia to attempt her deliverance from the thrall of Napoleon; the spirit of nationality inspired her policy. But it is in the later resistance of Austria and Spain to France that the new individualist principle appears most clearly. The Habsburgs had consistently opposed the Revolution, had consistently championed the balance of power. Their external Universalism, however, had brought upon them nothing but disaster; provinces had been torn from their rule, and the position to which they had been reduced by the Peace of Pressburg was one in which the very existence of their empire was imperilled. Fear of subjection produced its inevitable result; the individualist element was aroused. Stadion, the exponent of this reaction, preached the gospel of nationality; he appealed to the desire to rule, that his country might be delivered from the French. But his preaching was necessarily ineffective. The Habsburg dominions were united only by political bonds; Individualism was so far weak within them. Conquest seemed to mean nothing but a change of masters; to peoples impregnated with the desire to be ruled, freedom was an idle word. The very circumstances which made the existence of the Habsburg monarchy a possibility ensured the failure of Stadion's crusade. The desire to be ruled was at once the salvation and the temporary destruction of the Austrian Empire.

Nor was the national resistance in Spain much more successful. It may be admitted that it did, in a measure, prevent the complete reduction of the country by Napoleon. But the resistance to the French was only that of guerilla bands; such resistance has never attained permanent success, and, unaided, the Spaniards would have been defeated. As it happened, at the critical moment, an English army landed, and if, indeed, it did not turn the scale against the invaders, it at least served to readjust the balance. Nationality inspired the original resistance of Spain to Napoleon; it saved Spain from immediate conquest. But having achieved such negative results, it proved to be incapable of securing positive results also; it could not drive the French across the Pyrenees. The individualist movement in Spain was only rendered successful by the introduction into it of a universalist element.

It was this general failure of the national wars, of isolated resistance to Napoleon, that enabled Universalism to regain its influence, and that influence was all the greater since the need of coalition was so clearly realised. The defeat of external Individualism produced a solidarity of Europe. In face of the common danger, the powers reconciled their differences; by a true European concert Napoleon was eventually overcome. Victory, even in the War of Liberation, that imagined triumph of nationalism, was really the result of universalist ideas and policy. The French were at least holding their own when the intervention of Austria proved decisive. But that intervention was secured at the price of the abandonment of the national crusade. The treaties between the powers were conceived in a universalist spirit; their inspiration was the desire to maintain the balance of power, not to further nationalism. As in Spain, so in Germany, nationality, an assertion of internal Individualism, supplied the motive for the original resistance and gave the will to oppose subjection. But the current universalist ideas afforded the necessary material strength to them, the power to prevail was due. Stein led his countrymen to dream of possible deliverance; the decisive intervention of Metternich secured the realisation of this dream. At the time of Leipsic, Europe resumed that devotion to the balance of power from which she had momentarily strayed; her devotion was increased by the emphatic Individualism of the supposed arch-disturber of peace, the alleged enemy of the human race. A temporary alliance between the forces of external Universalism and internal Individualism effected the downfall of Napoleon; the fruits of victory were garnered by the exponents of the desire to be ruled.

And the domestic history of European states during this period reveals the same fluctuations in the strength of the two contending emotions. When the French Revolution began, the desire to be ruled held a general supremacy, and induced a certain carelessness of foreign conquest, which weakened the opposition to French aggression. But in most countries, individualist tendencies were also both powerful and evident, and those tendencies served to convert many from an attitude of negative indifference to one of positive friendliness. Revolutionary ideas spread rapidly. In most of the lands which they invaded, the French were at first regarded rather as deliverers than as enemies; a cordial welcome was extended to the apostles of liberty. In Belgium and in the Rhine provinces, in the districts of northern Italy, the inhabitants offered no voluntary resistance to the invaders.

But the welcome, never universal, was everywhere short-lived. From the very first, the violence of the Revolution produced a revival of internal Universalism beyond the French frontiers. In Russia, Catherine II was able to abandon her tentative reforms. In England, Pitt exchanged a liberal policy for one of severe repression. Generally, those who held and expressed individualist views were regarded as "Jacobins," suspected of a predilection for wholesale murder. And as France gradually abandoned her original cosmopolitanism, the ascendancy of Universalism was further enhanced. The continent appeared to be threatened with subjection, and the very individualists themselves began to fear the consequences and results of their own theory. Whereas the revolutionary armies had been welcomed, they came to be regarded with hatred and aversion. Districts which had applauded now cursed their self-styled liberators, when they learnt that no choice of ruler was to be conceded to those lands which had once accepted French government, or even to those which had once been occupied by French armies. And in those lands which were as yet free from invasion the strengthening of executive power was advocated by all parties. In such a measure seemed to lie the only safeguard against the last calamity of foreign conquest. An immediate development of internal Universalism was a primary result of the aggressive policy of revolutionary France.

At the same time, the critical nature of the situation, especially after the forced dissolution of successive coalitions, tended to produce a certain atmosphere of conciliation. If the individualists were prepared to accept strong government as a necessity, the universalists were in turn prepared to make concessions to their opponents. Both parties recognised the need for union against the external enemy; they were ready to make common cause that they might avoid common destruction. Individualists realised that anarchy would result from too complete gratification of the desire to rule, and that subjection would follow upon anarchy. Universalists realised that too complete gratification of the desire to be ruled would render them less capable of resistance to aggression from without, would fit them for subjection to a foreign power. The very extremes to which French policy tended seemed for a moment to open the eyes of mankind to the evils of extremes.

Accordingly, while the reaction in France produced the consolidation of Napoleonic despotism, a contrary reaction developed, within certain limits, in other European countries. At an earlier date, Leopold II had abandoned his brother's centralising policy, largely owing to his prescience of coming French aggression; the concession of local liberty to the Magyars appeared to him to be a less evil than the complete overthrow of the Austrian Empire. Faced by a crisis hardly less acute than that which had existed at the death of Joseph II, Stadion adopted a similar conciliatory policy. He even dared to preach nationality in the heterogeneous dominions of the Habsburgs. In Prussia, Stein and his collaborators undertook reforms, the underlying principle of which was the extension of liberties to the people. In

Spain, the Constitution of 1812 was a definitely individualist document; the organisers of opposition to the French were champions of limited monarchy, and, indeed, of monarchy so limited that it was almost anarchy. It may be asserted that the very despotism of Napoleon encouraged this tendency to concession in the countries hostile to him; his enemies were no longer the champions of internal Universalism, but rather of internal Universalism blended with Individualism.

All the concessions made, however, were yet made rather in a universalist than in an individualist spirit. There was no clear assertion of the right of self-government; no deliberate enunciation of popular rights, no democratic propaganda. If the individual acquired some increase of liberty, that increase was the result rather of the consideration of the ruler than of any recognition of the right of the ruled to order their own lives. The concessions amounted to little more than an acceptance of the theory of the benevolent despot, of the idea that government should be for the good of the governed. To the ruler still belonged the right or duty to decide in what that good consisted. Internal Universalism was really maintained; if anything, it was stronger at the end than at the beginning of the revolutionary epoch. For, whatever consideration might be given to the welfare and interest of the subjects, it was still realised or supposed that weak government had destroyed the Bourbon dynasty, it was still regarded as axiomatic that at all costs weak government must be avoided. Fear of revolution served to hamper the development of internal Individualism, to maintain in the minds of the majority of mankind the ascendancy of the desire to rule.

The general result of the revolutionary period, therefore, was to strengthen that ascendancy of the desire to be ruled which had existed when the period began. A longing for permanent peace, and the hope that such peace might be attained by the creation of a satisfactory balance of power, inspired the settlement of Vienna and determined the decisions of the Congress. To avoid a renewal of war, every effort was made to satisfy the aspirations of the great powers, every care was taken that each should receive adequate compensation for any gains made by its rivals. Even the ambitions of the lesser states were not wholly disregarded, though, since their dissatisfaction offered a slighter menace to the duration of peace, they naturally did not receive the same consideration as did their more powerful fellows. The balance of power thus established was also to be safeguarded. In place of the loose and occasional leagues of the eighteenth century, the Quadruple Alliance was formed; by the renewed Treaty of Chaumont, England, Austria, Russia and Prussia agreed to unite that they might "watch over the repose and prosperity of nations." An attempt was made to secure a permanent and effective concert, which should give to the existing order the supreme guarantee of invincible military force. And internally, absolutism was in general restored, and restored to a position of increased strength, because fear of revolution dominated the human mind, producing a desire for peace at any price, intensifying the desire to be ruled.

As might have been anticipated, this intensification of the desire to be ruled found expression in a revival of the Catholic Church. During the eighteenth century, the reaction against internal Universalism had originated in an attack upon dogmatic religion. The prestige of the Papacy, shaken by the Reformation and by the Peace of Westphalia, had declined still further, until it reached its nadir when the Pope had been forced to suppress the Society of Jesus. A cynical attitude towards Christianity became a marked characteristic of literature both in Catholic and in Protestant countries. But at the close of the revolutionary epoch, the revival of internal Universalism involved an equivalent revival of Catholicism, that revival finding expression in the Romantic Movement and in the growth of Ultramontanism. The reign of Pius VII gave renewed influence to the Papacy. He had dared to withstand Napoleon; he had suffered for his daring. His sufferings inspired sympathy and respect; he appeared as the true Vicar of Christ, the champion of conscience against the tyranny of the world. His return to Rome was hailed with genuine delight; it secured the approval even of the Protestants. And the coincident re-establishment of the Society of Jesus afforded a measure of the revived power and prestige of the Papacy. At the same time, in place of that cynical deism which Voltaire had popularised and Rousseau vulgarised, the respectful devotion to orthodoxy, inculcated by Chateaubriand, became the fashionable attitude. A general desire for peace, for relief from the wearying exercise of private judgment, became apparent. Dogmatic religion recovered its former strength; Catholicism after the fall of Napoleon was perhaps more powerful in Europe than it had been since the Reformation. Universalism, if regard be paid both to its external and internal aspect, secured an ascendancy more complete than at any other period of History.

Nevertheless, general as was the longing for peace, prevalent as was the desire to be ruled, the ascendancy of Universalism was incomplete. At no period is the eternal nature of the conflict between man's two emotions more vividly illustrated than in the period immediately following the Congress of Vienna. Europe was weary of war, weary of all change. She had experienced to the fullest extent the evils of international anarchy; she had witnessed in France the calamitous results of too ardent gratification of the desire to rule. Yet she would not admit the absolute triumph of the gospel of peace. No misfortune sufficed to effect a modification in human nature, and without such modification the complete victory of the desire to be ruled was impossible. A tendency to reaction persisted; the desire to rule claimed its exponents and adherents.

Externally, that concert for which the universalists strove proved to be unattainable. Even in the first enthusiasm of their joint triumph, the allies disputed as to the division of the spoils. It was perhaps only the return of Napoleon from Elba that prevented a new European war; England, Austria and France had formed a separate alliance to prevent the accomplishment of Russian and Prussian designs in Poland and Saxony. After the episode of the Hundred Days, it was found advisable to abandon all attempts to solve the Eastern Question; the tentative efforts of Metternich to effect a solution had almost destroyed the Quadruple Alliance. The powers, indeed, were mutually distrustful of one another. Each laboured to discover sinister designs of self-aggrandisement, cloaked beneath the others' professions of friendship. When Alexander I suggested that all states should declare their union in the bonds of Christian brotherhood, and that international relations should be ordered according to " the principles of Christ's holy religion," his idealism was greeted with mingled suspicion and contempt. The Holy Alliance, when not considered to be the mere project of a madman, was believed to be intended to conceal some nefarious plan for aggression in the Near East.

But real harmony between the powers could in no

circumstances exist. Every state contained within it an individualist no less than a universalist element, and if, owing to fear of revolution and dread of renewed war, the desire to be ruled had secured a general supremacy, the desire to rule, the resolve to pursue self-interest, was not the less existent. Austria was the most determined champion of international unity, of the concert of Europe. But Austria would not agree to submit the ordering of Italy to the Quadruple Alliance; she demanded that she should be allowed to act as the mandatory of the powers, and that as mandatory she should possess the fullest liberty of action. She was not less distrustful of Russian or French intervention in Spain. Russia wavered between an individualist inclination to favour liberalism and a universalist wish to create a sincere union of hearts among the states of Europe. But whatever else she might desire, she hardly wavered in her resolve that her right to protect her special interests in the Ottoman Empire should not be questioned by her allies. England might be eager to preserve peace, but she was wholly disinclined to accept the theory, put forward by the eastern powers, that peace depended upon the maintenance of absolutism. The aims of the greater states were, in fact, very divergent; the establishment of a perfect concert was impossible. European solidarity was an idle dream, born of the failure of the universalists to recognise the permanence of any theory save their own.

Nor was the ascendancy of internal Universalism really complete. In most countries, indeed, the exponents of the desire to be ruled prevailed, but in some they failed to do so. The internal Individualism of the Revolution was not utterly extinguished. In France, the downfall of Napoleon served to produce a government far less absolute than that of the Empire. The

Royal Charter established a limited monarchy, and during the Hundred Days the Emperor himself expressed in the *Acte Additionel* his recognition of the fact that the French Revolution had in reality overthrown absolutism. In the new kingdom of the United Netherlands, individualist ideas equally prevailed; the rights of the Belgians were at least safeguarded on paper. Certain of the South German states hastened to avail themselves of the ambiguous Article XIII of the Constitution of the Federation, interpreting it as permitting and even as enjoining the establishment of representative government.

But the ascendancy of the desire to be ruled was far more seriously and permanently impaired by the fact that the French Revolution left an aftermath of violence. For a generation, the strife of parties had been vigorous, acute. For a generation, compromise had been consistently rejected, and its acceptance, when the period of external war had ended, was improbable, if not impossible. The universalists, apparent victors, regarded their triumph as incomplete; they desired to crush their opponents more utterly, they dreamed even of an undoing of the past. The individualists, apparently vanquished, refused to despair; they declined to believe their cause to be hopeless. And since the two parties were thus malcontent with the existing situation, their strife was unceasing. Here again the permanence of the conflict appears. Those who believe in the desire to be ruled, and those who believe in the desire to rule, alike strain ever towards the logical conclusion of their theory; they cannot learn moderation, since the very imperfection of human nature makes the retention of the golden mean impossible.

The French Revolution had proved the evil of anarchy; universalists laboured to avoid anarchy by delivering themselves over to despotism. The rule of Napoleon had illustrated the calamities consequent upon the establishment of unfettered despotism; the individualists laboured to avoid despotism by delivering themselves to anarchy. Neither party displayed any readiness to accept a compromise, and the conflict was only less violent than in the most violent days of the revolutionary period. It did not for a moment cease. Peace might be the rule, but it was a disturbed peace.

The period following the Congress of Vienna, indeed, was marked by the constant recurrence of disturbances in different parts of the continent; nowhere was the dominion of Universalism unquestioned. And these disturbances gradually increased in intensity. Of the factors promoting the desire to be ruled, fear of revolution was the most potent. Men could remember, or at least had learned from their fathers, the violence of the Reign of Terror. The extent and duration of that violence was certainly not minimised by memory, and for a while and in the minds of the majority revolution was inseparably connected with spectacles of unreasoning barbarity and senseless atrocity. It was merely necessary for a government to brand its opponents with the epithet "Jacobin"; forthwith, the sentiment of fear rallied the bulk of the community to the side of law and order, to the side of absolutism and even of tyranny. Any movement towards reform, any project for political change, had to contend not only with the natural force of universalist opinion, but also with a special hostility resultant from the character of one period in the French Revolution.

But this fear gradually diminished; it was at no time universal. From the very first, a section in every country was sceptical as to the danger of revolution, or callously indifferent to it. Revolutionary ideas had permeated the armies of many states, partly because a long period of licence had fostered the desire to rule in the minds of the soldiers, partly because more intimate contact with Frenchmen and with French ideas had produced a more favourable opinion of the Revolution than that so zealously propagated by the chancelleries of Europe. And in the ordinary course of nature, a new generation came to birth, without memory of Jacobin proscriptions or even of Napoleonic despotism. More especially, the German university students, sentimental like all their race, enthusiastic with the vague enthusiasm of imagined intellectualism and extreme youth, eagerly embraced individualist opinions. They resented the repressive conduct of the dominant party; they became ardent, if somewhat unwise and ineffective, champions of the desire to rule.

Disturbances, therefore, early occurred, and increased in importance and extent, as ever wider areas came under the influence of the reaction. But the movements were, in the main, at first unsuccessful. The majority of mankind were still wedded to the idea of peace; the revolts of the minority were powerless to effect any permanent change in the existing system. Even when a passing victory was gained, the alliance between external and internal Universalism was in most cases able to secure the restoration of the *status quo*. That alliance, indeed, was an important factor in checking the reaction. The external universalists, aiming at the preservation of peace and of the balance of power, remembered that the revolutionary war had originated in an attempt by the French to remodel their government. Resolved that no such war should occur again, they eagerly assisted the internal universalists to maintain their ascendancy. And in view of the prevalence of the desire to be ruled, in most lands, the efforts of the Quadruple Alliance, or of the three eastern powers, were usually sufficient to prevent any victorious assertion of internal Individualism.

Thus the riots of the German students, such as that which occurred at the Wartburg Festival, only served to perpetuate the existing universalist system in the states of the Confederation. By the Carlsbad Decrees and by the Vienna Final Act, machinery was provided for the repression of all manifestations of liberalism, the further development of constitutional government was checked, the censorship of the press and the supervision of the universities rendered more effective. The military revolts in Naples and Piedmont were equally unsuccessful. Their organisers were handicapped by that difficulty by which individualists are constantly faced; they found it hard to define their creed, to rally together the supporters of the desire to rule and to win over those who were vaguely opposed to the desire to be ruled. A demand for the "Spanish Constitution" was a singularly unconvincing cry with which to appeal to the Italians, a race long used to foreign domination, habituated to internal Universalism since the fall of the mediæval city republics. It is not surprising that the mass of the population regarded the revolutionaries with apathy or aversion, that Austria proved fully equal to the task of restoring the absolute government of Ferdinand and of Charles Felix. Nor was the success of the similar movement in Spain more than transitory. Though for a few years a liberal government was established, it gained no hold on the people, and the eventual French expedition was so little opposed as to be practically a mere parade to Cadiz.

The desire to rule, however, is as permanent and fundamental an emotion as is the desire to be ruled; and that it should displace the opposing theory in its ascendancy over the human mind was inevitable. The history of the thirty years following the Congress of Vienna is the history of the gradual development of the reaction against the prevalent Universalism. Fear of revolution, the longing for peace, grew weaker; a wish to assert private judgment grew stronger. Whereas immediately after the fall of Napoleon only a few students and soldiers were prepared to risk anarchy in their pursuit of liberty, at the end of a generation all classes of the community in every state were more or less infected by the revived Individualism. Whereas the Quadruple Alliance was, at the beginning of this period, apparently a firm and potent league, at its end it had been almost dissolved into its component elements.

Even in the first years after the Congress of Vienna, Individualism, external and internal, achieved a measure of success, made some appreciable progress. Though military revolts in Spain and Italy failed more or less completely, the negotiations to which they gave rise revealed and emphasised the divergence of opinion among the allies. At the conferences of Troppau and Laibach, the reluctance of England to join in any scheme for the repression of liberalism was indicated. The distrust felt by Austria for Russia and the alarm with which she regarded any concessions to France became apparent. At the Congress of Verona, if the solidarity of the eastern powers was confirmed, English isolation was confirmed also. The projected intervention of Europe on behalf of Spain against her revolted colonies was vetoed by England, and it became clear that the concert by which Napoleon had been overthrown was weakening, if indeed it was not already dissolved. That league which French aggression had called into existence, which the lingering fear of revolution had for a while maintained, had now in reality ceased to exist. Nor was the momentary adhesion of France to the cause of external Universalism any adequate compensation for the defection of England and the consequent disruption of the Quadruple Alliance. France was notoriously unstable. Individualism had always tended to be a characteristic of her foreign policy; it had led her to set the example of rejecting the authority of mediæval Emperors, it had led her to limit the power of mediæval Popes. And it was still alive within her in the first half of the nineteenth century.

Europe found the problems presented to her by Italy and Spain difficult of solution. She was entirely unable to cope with that presented to her by the revolt of the Morea. If the battle of Navarino afforded an example of co-operation between the powers, the earlier and later stages of the struggle for Greek independence afforded much more significant examples of divergence. Alexander I, converted to Universalism by accidental circumstances or by the ingenuity of Metternich, had laboured to maintain that concert. The conferences of Czernowitz and Petersburg had proved abortive; the Tsar had been threatened at the close of his reign by rebellion in Russia, where a tendency towards external Individualism was gaining strength and where there was consequently an ever-decreasing inclination to preserve the solidarity of Europe. Nicholas I gave way to the wishes of his people. He followed the example already set by England, when she recognised the Greek flag, and adopted an independent attitude towards the problems of the Near East. The concert, which had failed to solve those problems at the time of the Congress of Vienna, was in no real sense responsible for the establishment of the kingdom of Greece. In place of that permanent alliance desired by the external universalists, a temporary league between England, Russia and France was formed, a league which resembled the occasional confederacies characteristic of the period prior to the

French Revolution. Nor was it merely in the East that the growth of Individualism appears. At the moment when the Greeks were securing their independence, the futility of the recent restoration of absolutism in Spain was proved. Christina promulgated a constitution drawn up by Zea Bermudez; a regent, threatened by revolt, felt that her power could only be secured by concessions to the majority of her subjects, to the growing individualist sentiment of her country.

And in the next revolutionary outbreaks in Europe, the development of Individualism was still more obvious. It is true that, alike in Italy and in Poland, revolution met with no success, but elsewhere a decline of Universalism was evident. In France, the restored Bourbon monarchy was overthrown. Charles X had become the apostle of the desire to be ruled, at home and abroad. He was deposed, and the government of Louis Philippe, whatever may have been its real character, was at least ostensibly individualist. Externally, though the extreme Individualism of Lafitte was rejected, the moderate Individualism of Casimir-Périer was adopted. Austria was checked in her universalist Italian policy; Portuguese Individualism was definitely supported. Internally, the royal title and the professed spirit of the administration were individualist.

Nevertheless, though the desire to rule thus made some progress, the reaction was essentially imperfect. At home, the popular agitation for wider political rights was repressed with vigour; the period culminated in the accession to office of Guizot, almost the embodiment of the desire to be ruled. Abroad, it is true that France showed little inclination to accept the ideas of the Quadruple Alliance. But that alliance had been originally formed against her; even during the most reactionary period of the restored monarchy she had hardly been accepted as one of the great powers. And if her efforts under Louis Philippe were directed to promote individualist movements, the basis of her policy was universalist. It rested upon peace and the Anglo-French *entente;* the extreme views of Lafitte did not prevail; his successor, Casimir-Périer, was a man of moderate opinions. France would give such help to continental liberalism as she might be able to supply without risking isolation; her external Universalism was only coloured by individualist tendencies. She was peaceful, even when she threatened war.

A more interesting example of the degree to which Individualism succeeded and failed at this time is supplied by the case of Belgium. After the Congress of Vienna, those treaties by which the powers had effected a remodelling of Europe had become the gospel of external Universalism, just as the treaties of Westphalia and Utrecht had been at an earlier date; to their maintenance the efforts of the exponents of the desire to be ruled were directed. Among the provisions of those treaties, one of the most important was that the former Austrian Netherlands and the former Dutch Republic should be united into a single kingdom under the House of Orange, in order that France might be the better held in check. From the very first, however, the union was unpopular in Belgium. The news of the fall of Charles X produced a revolution; the kingdom was disrupted into its component parts, and the external universalists failed to prevent the acceptance of the *fait accompli.*

So far, the movement may be regarded as a victory for external Individualism. Both in the case of France and in that of Belgium, the weakness of the European concert was exhibited. The first professed object of the Quadruple Alliance had been the restraint of France and the prevention of disturbance in that country; yet the allies had not dared to move when the elder branch of the Bourbons was driven out. They were equally unable to support the Dutch. England and France refused to coerce the Belgians; the eastern powers could not act alone. Even so, however, the triumph of external Individualism was limited. The government of Louis Philippe found itself obliged to consider the universalist susceptibilities of Europe; its foreign policy found its basis only in a new alliance. And it was the two western powers, not the rebels themselves, that decided the Belgian question. England and France came to an agreement. Adopting the broad principle of the separation of the two states, they settled the details of that separation. Dutch and Belgians alike were compelled to acquiesce in the Anglo-French solution of the problems of Luxemburg and Limburg.

And if external Individualism secured no complete victory, it is also true that internal Individualism did not do so. This fact was largely the result of the circumstance that neither in France nor in Belgium was the revolution entirely individualist. To every episode in the secular conflict there must be an individualist and a universalist side, since neither desire can ever achieve complete victory, and the exponents of each must therefore be in a greater or less degree dissatisfied with any existing system. In the period after the fall of Napoleon, this inevitable dissatisfaction was intensified, partly by the violence of feeling which had marked the revolutionary period, partly owing to the especial incompleteness of the reaction. Both universalists and individualists tended to refuse to accept as final the external and internal settlement of Europe; both believed that a modification in that settlement would benefit the cause which they had at heart. Hence there was an inclination on the part of the extreme exponents of either desire to combine against those who favoured the idea of compromise. Human nature, by reason of its very imperfection, leads men to reject counsels of moderation; no compromise can end the conflict, since no compromise can effect a revolution in the permanent character of the race. The very preachers of compromise have themselves an inevitable bias towards one or other extreme. In no case can any man hold the balance exactly.

And this hatred of moderation, of middle courses, is especially evident in the history of Europe during the generation following the Congress of Vienna. In France, successive ministers, Richelieu, Decazes, Martignac, and to a certain extent even Villèle, laboured to effect a compromise. They were successively defeated by the force of human nature, which expressed itself in an alliance between the ultra-royalists and the ultra-liberals. And to this refusal of either party to pursue a moderate course the overthrow of the restored Bourbons must be attributed. It may, indeed, be admitted that the actual revolution was not supported by the universalists, but it would never have occurred had not the very universalists themselves been dissatisfied with the restoration monarchy. The mere fact of the accession of Louis Philippe indicates the strength of those who were possessed by the desire to be ruled. In place of a republic, the dream of the individualist, kingship was perpetuated. And in the Orléanist government the universalist element really prevailed. Even the "party of action," the more individualist of the two parties under Louis Philippe, did not display any inclination to concede that degree of popular control over the administration which the advocates of the desire to rule supported.

In Belgium, the alliance of the two extreme parties was more evident; there the revolution was clearly both internally universalist and internally individualist. It was brought about by the union of clericals and liberals, of those who desired to be ruled and those who desired to rule. The former had hoped that the overthrow of Napoleon would be followed by their recovery of their former ascendancy; they had been painfully undeceived. A more or less individualist régime was created; toleration was proclaimed, education was to a great extent taken from the control of the Church. Yet, though the universalists were thus angered, their opponents were not contented. Preference was given to the Dutch in the use of their language, in the situation of the capital, in taxation and in representation. The two parties therefore combined, each hoping to find its own triumph in the destruction of the existing system. The kingdom of the United Netherlands was disrupted, not by the isolated action of the individualists, but by a league between them and the universalists.

Nevertheless, when a generation had passed, that ascendancy of external and internal Universalism which had prevailed since the fall of Napoleon was breaking down. Externally, such unity as existed between the great powers was becoming occasional rather than permanent. The Quadruple Alliance, the real European concert, which was the universalist ideal, early failed; even the more restricted league of the three eastern monarchies did not endure. Each successive problem which demanded the attention of Europe produced new and temporary alliances, akin rather to the league of the eighteenth century than to the concert suggested in the Treaty of Chaumont. England, France and Russia combined to deal with the question of Greek independence; England and France joined to defend liberalism in the Iberian peninsula and to solve the Belgian difficulty. Yet there was no definite recasting of alliances. England and Russia intervened in the quarrel between Egypt and the Porte, devising a compromise and enforcing its acceptance, though they were brought thereby into more or less direct conflict with France. Austria had not been generally associated with the western powers, but she joined England that she might save Mehemet Ali from complete destruction. In fact, love of peace, fear of revolution, was potent enough to prevent any open conflict between the powers, to secure a limited degree of external Universalism. It was not potent enough to secure a complete universalist ascendancy, the maintenance of a permanent and effective concert.

Internally, the ascendancy of the desire to be ruled was equally insecure. Even when fear of revolution was at its strongest, some had been eager for change, some had been restless under the absolutist régime. Secret societies were formed, with the object of modifying the existing system. The Carbonari in Italy, the Charbonerie in France, the Freemasons in Spain, laboured to secure an increase of political liberty. Nor were these societies the less revolutionary because their programme was vague, because they tended to dissociate themselves from the principles of the French Revolution. They were always opposed to the existing absolutism, always individualist. And as time went on, their Individualism was emphasised; Mazzini's "League of Young Italy" frankly advocated the destruction of monarchical institutions and the creation of an Italian republic. Though the outbreaks organised by the secret societies failed, the programme for which they stood was yet in a measure adopted. France under Louis Philippe was ostensibly a liberal and popular monarchy; the ruler was "king of the French," not "king of France." In Portugal, political liberty was more or less established. In Spain, insecure as was the position of liberalism, the most obvious champions of absolutism, the Basques, were led to support Don Carlos by their very Individualism; they wished to preserve their local immunities.

The most significant indication of the decline of Universalism, however, is to be found in the growth of the national spirit. Nationality is essentially individualist, and it had been disregarded or crushed by the dominant universalists at the time of the Congress of Vienna. But the disregard was vain, the coercion ineffective. The desire to rule was bound to continue; it was not less bound sooner or later to find expression. In the years after the Congress there was everywhere a gradual revival of nationalism; it became a vital force and supplied the real policy of the internal individualists. The Greeks asserted their independence, the Belgians followed their example. Even the deposition of Charles X may be regarded as an assertion of French nationality; the Bourbons had been restored by foreign arms, and to foreign powers they were supposed to look for support in event of any conflict between them and their subjects.

Still more noticeable was the development of nationality in Germany and Italy. Since the Middle Ages, those two countries had been politically divided; down to the time of the French Revolution, the tendency had been rather to perpetuate than to heal their divisions. But the victories of Napoleon obliterated existing boundaries; his armies formed a school which tended to reconcile the northern with the southern Germans, in which north and south Italians learned to forget their differences and to realise their practical identity of race. At the time of the Congress of Vienna, the realisation of racial identity was still incomplete both in Germany and in Italy. In neither country was resistance offered or much resentment felt at their continued partition into independent states, at the fact that "Germany" and

"Italy" continued to be regarded as mere geographical expressions. National feeling, however, had been aroused; during the next generation it grew in intensity. An agitation for deliverance from foreign rule began, and presently supplied the inspiration of the individualists in each country. Nor was this agitation confined to Germany and Italy. The various races of the Austrian dominions began to claim recognition of their diversity, acknowledgment of their national existence. Magyars and Slavs alike were moved to resent the really foreign domination of the German Habsburgs. But this development of the national movement was merely an indication that the desire to be ruled was losing its ascendancy, that the inevitable reaction was making definite progress.

The culmination of this reaction was reached in the series of revolutions inaugurated by the overthrow of the Orléanist monarchy. More or less serious outbreaks of disorder took place in most European countries; almost everywhere absolute government seemed to be trembling on the verge of dissolution. Both in the fact that a much greater area was affected, and in their essential character, these movements differed from those which had already occurred in the period since the Congress of Vienna. The earlier revolutionary attempts had at first been purely military; they had later assumed a more political character; to leaders such as Morelli or Riego, men like Thiers had succeeded. But in most European countries the mass of the population had still remained subject to the desire to be ruled. At the time of the fall of Louis Philippe, a distinct change may be observed. Discontent with the existing system had become widespread; all classes of the community were infected by it. The desire to rule had secured numerous converts; nationalism, the expression of that desire, in many lands received the support of a majority.

Yet when discontent at last developed into active resistance, only in Sardinia, perhaps, did Individualism secure a real triumph. Victor Emmanuel, despite the menaces and blandishments of Austria, there maintained a liberal system and a limited monarchy. On the other hand, in Prussia, though a constitution was granted and survived, its character was rather universalist than individualist. The franchise was deliberately constituted to prevent any popular control of the administration; the changes made rather afforded an example of the generosity of despotism than asserted the right of the people to govern themselves. In France, though the Orléanist monarchy was destroyed and the Second Republic created, the victory of Individualism was transitory. The movement ended in the establishment of the Second Empire, of a government more autocratic than any which had existed since the fall of Napoleon.

Elsewhere, the failure of the revolution was still more complete. In Italy, Austria recovered her possessions; the Roman and Venetian Republics were destroyed, absolutism was everywhere restored. And after the restoration, rulers, such as Pius IX, who had displayed liberal tendencies, resorted to despotic methods; tyrannies became more tyrannical. The attempt to secure German unity was frustrated. After a brief and ineffective life, the Frankfort Parliament was dispersed, and its dispersal was hardly regretted even by the extreme individualists, so completely had it failed to impair the ascendancy of Universalism. In the Austrian Empire, the revolution at first achieved striking success, but ended in complete disaster. Magyars, Slavs and Roumans were alike brought once more under German control; the rule of Schwarzenberg was more, not less, universalist than had been that of Metternich.

Indeed, the revolutions would be relatively unimportant, were it not that there is a particular significance in the manner of their defeat. Generally speaking, that defeat was the result, not of the unaided efforts of the internal universalists, but of an alliance between the internal and external universalists. Even in France, where there was no trace of foreign intervention, the accession of Napoleon III must be attributed largely to the fact that he gained the support of the external universalists. He declared that "The Empire is peace," and thereby made an effective appeal to those who dreaded international anarchy, who disbelieved in that individualist foreign policy which, rightly or wrongly, they imagined to be inevitably characteristic of republicanism, or at least of French republicanism. To this party of peace, rather than to the individualists, rather even than to the internal universalists, the Second Empire owed its existence, little as it justified the expectations formed of a cessation of war.

This alliance of external and internal Universalism is more obvious in other countries. Absolutism was restored in Italy by the arms of Austria and France. A threat of armed intervention from Schwarzenberg secured the final defeat of the revolutionary movement in Germany; the submission of Manteuffel at Olmütz was not the result of the unaided efforts of internal Universalism, but of fear that the Habsburgs would impose their will by force, if persuasion proved ineffective. Pursuit of Individualism seemed to threaten Prussia with foreign subjection, and therefore Prussia, in a sense, allowed the Confederation to fall for a while under foreign rule, that by so doing she might preserve her own independence. The conquest of the Hungarians was equally made possible by the action of Russia. The weakness of internal Universalism within the Habsburg dominions was illustrated by the failure of the Unitary Edict, a definite attempt to secure that centralisation and consolidation which the universalists desired. Had it not been that Nicholas I, true to the universalist conception that the internal affairs of each state are the concern of all states, lent military aid to Francis Joseph, the cause of Individualism in Hungary at least might have prevailed.

But though the alliance between internal and external Universalism was thus triumphant for a time, the ascendancy of the latter was declining. Of the original members of the Quadruple Alliance, only Austria and Russia remained united. England had long since parted company with her former allies; her sympathy with Individualism was notorious, and formed a factor aiding the internal reaction in every country. Prussia had long been the docile follower of the other eastern powers, but during the revolutions she had displayed a tendency to separate herself from them. Her king had even worn the red cap of liberty; he had become a wandering star in the firmament of sovereigns. Nor was the forced submission at Olmütz calculated to persuade her to join cordially with Austria or Russia in the future; rather, the disgrace was felt and remembered, though the time of vengeance might be postponed. And meanwhile the fear that any war was bound to lead to universal and unending strife was losing strength. Though renewal of conflict was still dreaded, the struggle between Austria and Sardinia in Italy suggested that the flames of conflict need not necessarily spread; the action of Schwarzenberg at Olmütz indicated that war was felt on occasion to be a less evil than the sacrifice of national interest, that the champions of external Universalism were sometimes prepared to adopt an externally individualist attitude. Indeed, the lesson of these revolutions was that the prevalent love of peace among the powers alone maintained the ascendancy of the desire to be ruled, and that this love was growing cold.

War actually followed upon the crushing of the revolutionary movements; that general peace which had prevailed since the fall of the first, was broken soon after the accession of the third, Napoleon. At Olmütz, it had become clear that practical subjection was liable to be the outcome of external Universalism. Prussia, weak and unaided, had given way. She had accepted the humiliating terms dictated to her by Austria. But the submission of Manteuffel was the beginning of the end for the supremacy of the desire to be ruled. It needed only that the external universalists should attempt the coercion of some power capable of resistance, for resistance to be made, for war to begin. Such coercion was attempted in the case of Russia. She was forbidden to regulate her relations with the Porte according to her own will, and when she had displayed at least a limited readiness to concede this point, England and France proceeded further to attempt the regulation of her military and naval position in the Black Sea. The limit of endurance was thus reached; Russia refused to submit and the Crimean War followed. For two reasons, that war was of paramount importance. In the first place, the unreality of the European concert was revealed. The western powers had formed ideas as to the necessities of the Near Eastern situation, which did not commend themselves to Austria and Prussia. Consequently, though the four powers at first acted together, they soon ceased to do so; in the attack on the Crimea, the two absolutist states had no part. In the second place, the war served to dissipate the existing fear of conflict. Though first-class powers were engaged in it, it did not produce any general conflagration, nor was it greatly prolonged. For the future, war was the less dreaded; the ascendancy of the desire to be ruled was proportionately weakened.

The result soon appeared. External Universalism had owed its decided supremacy to the bitter memories of the revolutionary period; it was feared and expected that any disturbance of international peace would result in a prolonged, general war. And since the French Revolution had begun in a movement towards mere internal reform, any such reform movement was dreaded, as being likely to lead to an interruption of European tranquillity. The successive changes in the government of France had proved that this dread was largely illusory; the Crimean War proved that a conflict between some of the great powers need not necessarily extend to the rest of Europe, need not necessarily be prolonged. Thus the ascendancy of external Universalism was impaired, as that of internal Universalism had already been impaired; the way was opened for a more rapid reaction towards Individualism both at home and abroad.

The outcome was a new alliance of forces. As the exponents of the desire to be ruled had united, so now the exponents of the desire to rule united, and from this union resulted those national wars by which the second half of the nineteenth century was marked. In her foreign policy France is always potentially individualist, even in her most universalist moments; the French people are essentially human. And France, naturally less susceptible to fear born of the experience of the French Revolution, set the example of disregarding the supposed danger of individualist foreign policy. At the Congress of Paris, the powers, urged to consider the state of Italy, had replied by the expression of pious hopes of a change for the better. France presently went to the help of the Italian nationalists. A short war with Austria gave victory to the cause of Individualism; once more, no general conflict resulted, despite the murmurings of the universalists, illustrated by Prussian mobilisation.

And the defeat of Austria in Italy encouraged the individualists of Germany. Their agitation against practical foreign control grew in strength, and Prussia put herself definitely at the head of the national movement. Nor was this surprising. The very existence of the Prussian state depended upon her rejection of universalist ideas; she had been early obliged to free herself from Polish suzerainty, and her progress had been rendered possible only by denial of such obligations as might result from the inclusion of Brandenburg in the Holy Roman Empire. She had been individualist during the period of the French Revolution; she had tended to pursue the same policy in more recent disorders, and by her attitude on the Schleswig-Holstein question had indicated her devotion to her own interest. Hence Prussia undertook the championship of German nationality, of Individualism. The Seven Weeks' War accomplished the extrusion of Austria from the Confederation; it secured the defeat of the champion of external Universalism.

The importance of these individualist wars, of this further decline in external Universalism, soon became apparent in the Austrian Empire. The German element had hitherto been enabled to triumph over the Magyar and Slav elements, owing to the universalist spirit in the army and the aid received from the external Universalism of Europe. France had not dared to intervene seriously in Italy, while Radetzky re-established

Austrian control; fear of a general European war had stayed her. The same fear had led Russia to intervene in Hungary. But the Crimean War had greatly weakened the forces of external Universalism; no power was ready to support the Habsburgs when they were brought face to face with the individualist tendencies of the peoples over whom they ruled. The German element, the advocates of the desire to be ruled, were driven to rely only upon the strength of that desire within the Austrian Empire, and that desire, in view of the extreme divergence of race, had to be, as it were, both external and internal, in order to be effective. It was therefore almost necessarily weak. All unitary attempts, indeed, were doomed from the moment of the victory of Napoleon III. The individualists learned the weakness of the forces opposed to them; they realised their own strength, they refused any longer to be coerced. And their numbers were increased by the mere fact that the existing system had failed to hold its own against foreign aggression. Even before the Seven Weeks' War, it was inevitable that some concessions should be made to the local prejudices of the Magyars; as a result of that war, dualism was adopted.

And the establishment of union in Italy and of disunion in the Austrian Empire were alike illustrations of the reaction against the ascendancy of the desire to be ruled. Italian unity implied the destruction of foreign control of the peninsula, and so far was an individualist triumph. Dualism involved the concession of self-government to the Magyars; it meant the cessation of German domination over one of the races included in the Habsburg territories. But in each case the reaction was incomplete. If Italy, by the extinction of Austrian power in Lombardy and Venetia, was finally freed from external control, it was at the cost of the simultaneous extinction of the independence of the smaller Italian states; Naples and Sicily, racially distinct from Piedmont, were compelled to accept the rule of the House of Savoy. And though Hungary secured autonomy, the Slavs were left as much as ever under the control of races alien to them. Dualism, in effect, was a bargain between the Germans and the Magyars for the joint repression of the other peoples of the Austrian Empire.

Nor did the reaction ever attain completion. The culmination of the movement against the ascendancy of Universalism may be found in the Franco-Prussian War and in the events which preceded and followed that war. In it, no other nations took part; the growth of external Individualism is indicated by the fact that the powers of Europe did not intervene either to prevent the conflict or to settle the terms upon which peace should be concluded. In other ways also the struggle illustrated the increased influence of the desire to rule. Napoleon III aimed at the extension of French influence over southern Germany; his attempt, individualist from the point of view of France, from the contrary point of view amounted to an effort to establish universalist control over the states which he wished to dominate, and led them to ally with Prussia in defence of their national existence. Prussia definitely became the accepted champion of the external Individualism of the German race. Her victory secured the deliverance of Germany from the danger of foreign control. Yet this victory of Individualism was bought at a price. The German Empire was established, and in it the ascendancy of Prussia was assured; internal Universalism triumphed hardly less obviously than external Individualism.

And the effect of the war upon France was also dual in character. The autocratic Second Empire was overthrown, and in its fall internal Universalism fell also. But the Communards, the real representatives of Individualism, failed to secure the acceptance of their views; the Third Republic was conservative in its very essence, leavened by a perceptible admixture of Universalism. The champions of the desire to rule had hoped that the fall of Napoleon III would produce a condition of things akin to that which had followed the fall of the *ancien régime*. They were disappointed, and the actual reaction was so imperfect as to leave to the executive almost as much power as it had possessed under the Second Empire. Nevertheless, the history of the period of the national wars is the history of a general reaction against that Universalism which had prevailed since the Congress of Vienna.

And, as always, reaction bred a counter-reaction. No sooner had an apparent ascendancy been secured by external Individualism than external Universalism began to revive. Nor is it surprising that the very state which in its foreign policy had most gratified the desire to rule should be the first to tend towards the contrary extreme. The ideal of the Quadruple Alliance had been the maintenance of the *status quo* by means of a permanent and invincible league between the great powers. The realisation of that ideal had been rendered impossible by Prussia rather than by any other state, and Prussia was the first to dread the consequences of her own action, to attempt the reconstruction of that system which she had assisted to destroy. To her, the revival of external Universalism in the so-called League of Emperors must be attributed, and that league was really no more than a return to that attempted concert of Europe which Metternich had endeavoured to create at the time of the renewal of the Treaty of Chaumont. The new alliance was based upon the identical principle by which the Quadruple Alliance had been inspired. Fear of revolution determined once more the policy of the three eastern powers; love of peace was at the root of this new expression of external Universalism.

The League of Emperors did not become permanent. Like the Quadruple Alliance, it was destroyed by the inevitable tendency towards external Individualism in its constituent states, by the conviction that the interests of different states were themselves different. Nor does the similarity in the history of these two universalist attempts end here. Like the earlier alliance, the League of Emperors was wrecked upon the rock of the Near Eastern Question. Russia adopted an independent attitude towards the Porte, and the degree of independence in that attitude is the measure of the ascendancy of Individualism in her foreign policy. But even in Russia and in reference to the Eastern Question, the ascendancy was incomplete. She permitted the revision of the Treaty of San Stefano by the Congress of Berlin; she subordinated her own will to that of Europe. External Universalism gained a victory. And the circumstances of that victory afford another illustration of the fact that the state which has proceeded furthest towards the gratification of one desire is most prone to turn towards the gratification of the contrary desire. Prussia had defied the concert of Europe in order to gratify her desire to rule Germany. She also formed the League of Emperors that the example of international anarchy which she had set might not be followed. She arranged the Congress of Berlin that the solidarity of Europe might not be wholly destroyed; she gave birth, in fact, to that new concert which, down to recent times, served instead of the Quadruple Alliance.

And the conditions, illustrated by the Congress of Berlin, still exist. Externally, there has been a marked reaction from the Individualism which prevailed in the second half of the nineteenth century. There is a concert of Europe, however weak may be the bonds uniting its members. Since the Franco-Prussian War, it has sufficed to maintain continental peace, so far as conflicts between the great powers are concerned. Yet the concert is no union of hearts. The ascendancy of the desire to be ruled is evidently limited. Each state arms against its neighbours; within the concert itself, mutually hostile alliances exist. An atmosphere of extreme distrust prevails; the action of the concert is slow and hampered at every turn by the suspicious jealousy of its members. Russia once proposed international disarmament, and the Hague Conference was assembled. But the proposal of Nicholas II was regarded with as much scepticism as had been the Holy Alliance, nor is there any real evidence that nations are much nearer sincere agreement with each other than they were in the period immediately following the Congress of Vienna.

From this mutual distrust, manifestations of individualist spirit have followed. Italy, however much she might endeavour to conciliate the opinion of Europe, remained firm in her resolve not to entrust her interests in Tripoli to the care of the concert. At the risk of producing a general war, she attacked the Ottoman Empire. A similar disregard for the peace of the continent was displayed by the Balkan League. Not merely did they dare to raise the Near Eastern Question in its most acute form, but they showed a carelessness, amounting to contempt, for the preservation of the *status quo*, maintenance of which lies at the very root of the new external Universalism. Nor could the concert of Europe in either case do more than regulate somewhat the extent and duration of the conflict. It could induce

Italy not to conduct naval operations in the Adriatic; it did not decide the terms of the Treaty of Lausanne. It could create an Albanian state and secure a voice in the disposition of the Ægean Islands; it could not enforce the observance of the Treaty of London, and the Treaty of Bukarest was due far more to the individualist action of Rumania than to the complaints and protests of the great powers.

Internally, there is an apparent ascendancy of Individualism. Every state in Europe has adopted, at least professedly, representative institutions; there is no state in which the right of the people to a voice in their own government is explicitly denied. Yet the degree to which any actual influence is exercised is doubtful. The close organisation of parties, the rise of a class of professional politicians, almost ensures the practical impotence of the electorate, and the existence of that impotence has been realised in Switzerland, where a special device has been adopted to secure that the people should be able to determine legislation and policy. During the eighteenth century, the benevolent despots claimed to decide wherein lay the true good of their subjects. The benevolent despots have passed into oblivion. But in their place there are party leaders who are equally reluctant to submit their conduct to the judgment of those whose servants they profess to be. Nor have the people at large a much greater share in the determination of their fate than they had in the days of a Frederic the Great; they possess little more than the right to choose between two rival despots.

In short, the present age is externally universalist and only internally individualist to a very limited extent. There is no permanent concert, such as was desired by those who secured the overthrow of Napoleon; there is, however, a partial concert, the members of which regard each other with distrust, though ready to combine to preserve the peace of Europe. The theory that government is for the good of the governed prevails. But the right of the subject to determine what constitutes that good is but partially recognised; the ascendancy of internal Individualism is limited. The reaction from the Universalism of the first quarter of the nineteenth century is incomplete. Individualism has made progress and has suffered reverses. The eternal conflict continues, and to neither side is complete victory vouchsafed.

XI

THE CONFLICT IN ENGLAND

THROUGHOUT the general history of Europe, from the dawn of civilisation to the present day, the eternal conflict between the desire to be ruled and the desire to rule may be traced clearly. But European nations have been subject to violent commotions, have been the scene of obvious revolutions; their normal life has been continually interrupted. England, on the contrary, has not experienced such decided changes; she has never known a French Revolution; for her, even the Reformation was placid and orderly. Her history is far less complex than that of any other land; for some fifteen hundred years its continuity has hardly been interrupted. The origin of many of her existing institutions may be traced back to the period at which the English first appeared in the island to which they gave their name; the origin of some may be found even in the earlier days during which the Anglo-Saxons still inhabited the districts of north-western Germany. It is hardly an exaggeration to say that, with the exception of one brief interlude of experiment, her government has always been a limited monarchy. In the most revolutionary periods of her history, and by the most revolutionary leaders, appeal has always been made to the experience of past ages. The creation of an ideal state by legislative enactment has never appeared practical to her statesmen; the most radical reformers have at least professed devotion to the institutions of their forefathers. And if there were any exception to the universality of the conflict of desire, such an exception would assuredly be presented by England. In her history, if anywhere, the theory of persistent progress finds justification. If England has been the scene of unending strife between two ideals, with the implication of a tendency to return to the original starting-point, then certainly that strife would seem to supply the factor explanatory of History.

And it may be asserted at once that England offers no exception to the general rule. On the contrary, the very simplicity and orderliness of her history makes the conflict appear rather more clearly than it does in the history of most, if not of all, other nations. It may be admitted that the conflict has perhaps been less violent; the greater stolidity of the Anglo-Saxon race has freed them from the experience of those rapid reactions and counter-reactions which have been the lot of the French. Change from approach to one extreme to approach to the other has been more gradual; neither extreme has been so nearly reached. The executive in England has never been as despotic as was the French executive under Napoleon I; it has never been so weak as was that of France after the promulgation of the Constitution of 1791. The English villeins were probably never degraded to a position as low as that occupied by the *miserrimi populi Rutheniorum;* the English nobles certainly never attained to privileges such as were possessed by their peers under the *ancien régime* in France. England never came within the orbit of the Holy Roman Empire; she has never been wholly entangled in continental alliances. The authority of the Papacy was never so extensive as to constitute a serious limitation of the power of the government over its lay subjects; independence of attitude has always been a marked characteristic of the Anglican Church. Universalism and Individualism, external and internal, have never come so near attainment of complete supremacy as they have done in other lands. Yet, for all this, English history is as entirely a record of conflict as is that of every other nation; in England, as in all other countries, the desire to be ruled and the desire to rule have been always battling for supremacy.

At the moment when English history may be said to begin, after the Anglo-Saxon conquest, Individualism was supreme. The island was cut off from the continent and divided against itself. But the marriage of Ethelbert of Kent to Bertha of Paris was followed by the mission of Augustine, and these two events inaugurated the process of breaking down the isolation of the country as a whole and of the units of which it was composed. A closer connection with western Christendom and internal consolidation went hand in hand; each made progress despite strenuous opposition and frequent repulses, until external and internal Universalism secured a decided victory at the Norman Conquest. And the reaction towards gratification of the desire to be ruled culminated in the administrative monarchy of the Angevins, in the submission of Richard I to the Emperor Henry VI and in that of John to Pope Innocent III. At home, a practical despotism was established; abroad, England definitely admitted her inclusion in the Christian commonwealth.

The inevitable reaction followed. England lost her continental dominions, largely because she made no real effort to retain them, and the consequent release from foreign entanglements forced or enabled her to pursue an individualist policy. Even the attempt to conquer France in the Hundred Years' War was rather an assertion of the desire to rule than a reversion to the contrary ideal. At home, that cosmopolitanism which had prevailed since the Norman conquest was destroyed; the power of the monarchy was reduced by successful rebellion and by half-voluntary concessions. So great a hold, indeed, did Individualism secure upon the imagination of the people that impatience of subjection produced anarchy. The Wars of the Roses, a period during which there was no foreign policy worthy of the name, marked the culmination of the revolt against governance, and at the same time expressed the growing conviction that governance was a necessity. If the Lancastrians owed much of their unpopularity to the attempted tyranny of the royal council, that unpopularity was enhanced by the very ineffectiveness of the tyranny; the ministers of Henry VI denied the right of self-government, but produced no satisfactory alternative.

And as the combination of external and internal Individualism was found to produce incalculable evils, the nation gave rein to its desire to be ruled. The Yorkists initiated, the Tudors consolidated, a despotic system. In the progress of the reaction against Angevin Universalism, an interlude occurred, and to the fact that they governed vigorously, that they repressed all disorders, the Tudors owed their undoubted popularity. While in her relations with other states England, on the whole, preserved an individualist attitude, and even emphasised that attitude by the rejection of papal supremacy, at home the contrary ideal was favoured. The authority of the king was vastly increased, and the control of the executive over the people was assured by the creation of special courts, of which the deliberate aim was to hold in check such persons and districts as might tend to assert their independence.

Yet, even under the Tudor "despotism," Individualism survived and found expression. If parliament were controlled, it was also used, nor are there wanting indications of a tendency towards reaction. Each successive ruler encountered more or less opposition; the Commons defended their privileges against royal aggression, and the cessation of payment of members suggests that parliament was felt to be something more than a mere instrument for the registration of the royal will. And no sooner had the Tudor régime freed England from the evils resulting from the extreme of Individualism than she began to fear the evils of the contrary extreme. Resistance to the will of the executive gradually developed. The Tudors had been able to appeal successfully to the national spirit among their subjects; their very Universalism conciliated Individualism. But with the accession of the Stuarts the strength of the crown seemed almost to involve alien rule, and, deprived of any individualist support, the executive was faced by difficulties which it was unable to overcome.

The reaction, which produced successively the Great Rebellion and the Revolution of 1688, culminated in the triumph of doctrines of political, religious and economic liberty. The executive was deprived of its more dangerous powers; the attempt of the legislative to establish a veiled tyranny was thwarted, and the successful agitation for parliamentary reform gave to the people at least a voice in the decision of their own fate. The dominant Church was compelled to admit the right of men to decide upon the way of salvation which they would follow; the dominant mercantile class was driven to resign its right to dictate to the consumer where he should purchase his goods. Externally, the attitude of England was, on the whole, individualist. It was only with extreme reluctance that she consented to play her part as one of the powers of Europe, and though pressing dangers drove her momentarily to accept the idea of the Quadruple Alliance, she seized the earliest possible moment for freeing herself from foreign obligations. Indeed, at the time when internal Individualism reached its high-water mark, England was almost reluctant to bear the burden of her colonial empire.

Since that date, a reaction towards Universalism has occurred. Internally, the province of government has been extended. State interference has become more and more general; the economic life of the country has been more and more carefully regulated. At the same time, the power of the cabinet has grown; the increasingly strict discipline imposed upon the two great political parties has served to give the executive the direction of the details, as well as of the principles, of legislation. Externally, the duties of empire have been recognised; it has been contended that the interests of England must even be subordinated to those of her colonies, and that those colonies possess a specific right to share in the government of the whole empire. Towards foreign powers the attitude of England has become less individualist. The Hague Tribunal has, in a measure, been accepted as a body capable of performing functions similar to those performed by the mediæval Papacy. International arbitration has made progress; there has been an increasing readiness to submit all disputes to the judgment of some external power. England, in short, has shared in that general reaction towards Universalism which has occurred on the continent since the close of the Franco-Prussian War.

XII

TENDENCIES OF THE PRESENT DAY

FROM the dawn of Greek civilisation to the present day, History has been a record of eternal conflict between the desire to be ruled and the desire to rule, a record of constant reactions and counter-reactions. Complete supremacy has never been attained by either desire; the proximate victory of the one has been invariably followed or even anticipated by a reaction in favour of the other. And, if the fundamental characteristics of human nature remain immutable, it may be expected, it is indeed inevitable, that this series of reactions will continue, that History will always be the record of the same conflict. If, therefore, the historian can discover the prevailing tendency of the present, if he can decide whether ascendancy is for the moment enjoyed by Universalism or by Individualism, then it is in his power also to predict the nature of the next reaction. And if he cannot so predict, his work is of relatively less value. He may still both amuse and instruct. By recording the past, he may inspire men to emulate the good and to avoid the evil. He may supply to statesmen and to nations some warnings, vague indeed, yet salutary, suggesting at least the most obvious results likely to follow upon a given course of action. But if he can foresee the ultimate tendency of the age in which he lives, his work will forthwith be raised to a loftier plane. To foresee, to predict, is the highest, most permanently valuable function of the historian. History ceases to be a dead science; it becomes instinct with vitality. It gives to man that for which man has always sought, whether by the path of religion, or by the more devious paths of occult sciences; it gives to him some knowledge of the future destiny of the race.

For the historian to be able so to predict, it is clearly the first necessity that he should be able to determine accurately whether Universalism or Individualism for the moment holds the ascendancy. Nor is such accurate determination difficult, since History is nothing more than the record of the interplay of the two desires, and since nothing is more certain than that the reaction from the one desire to the other proceeds with unfailing regularity. At the present moment, it is clear that externally the desire to be ruled prevails rather than the desire to rule. In the second half of the nineteenth century, and in the national wars of that period, Individualism reached a culminating point. Since that date, there has been a sufficiently effective concert among the powers to prevent any actual conflict in Europe, and the general wish to avoid war has been abundantly illustrated. By the creation of the Hague Tribunal to adjudicate in cases not involving the vital interests of states, an attempt has been made to revive something equivalent to the supreme arbiter of the Middle Ages, and one of the most noteworthy characteristics of the present day has been the growth of the movement in favour of international arbitration and the conclusion of arbitration treaties between different states.

Even in such wars as have occurred, the influence of neutrals has been employed with effect to limit either the duration or the scope of the conflict. Spain, in her struggle with the United States, bowed to public opinion by refraining from the issue of letters of marque, the only method by which she might have injured her enemy, refrained, that is, from exercising a right which she had explicitly reserved to herself. During the war between Turkey and Greece, the Greeks, in deference to the powers, refrained from the use of their fleet. In the war between Russia and Japan, the former gave way to international opinion in the case of the *Malacca,* and submitted the action of the Baltic fleet to the judgment of a neutral court. More recently, Italy abstained from naval operations in the Adriatic or against the Dardanelles. The Balkan states, despite the general Individualism of their attitude and their refusal to accept the decision of the powers in favour of the maintenance of the *status quo,* agreed to the creation of the kingdom of Albania and consented to leave the question of the Ægean Islands in the hands of Europe. Thus, though, as might be expected, individualist tendencies may be discovered, yet the general attitude of the world is universalist.

Nor is this less true internally. Absolutism has indeed disappeared; Russia has now received her duma, Turkey possesses a species of parliament. Nevertheless, there is a decided increase in the area of state control, a decided widening of the province of government. And this has occurred not only in every country, but also in every sphere of political life. Economic conditions have been generally regulated by the state. The direction of policy and of legislation is in most cases more exclusively in the hands of ministers; the representatives of the people seem to tend everywhere to degenerate into mere delegates. And the growth of socialism is an indication of the strength of the desire to be ruled, since that creed, in so far as it proposes to nationalise the means of production, proposes also to make the state supreme over the regulation of that which is perhaps the most vital part of national life in every state.

If, therefore, human nature remains constant in its fundamental characteristics, an individualist reaction, both externally and internally, may be anticipated with confidence. It can only be that when Universalism has attained such a measure of supremacy, the satiation of desire should tend to produce the contrary desire. Nor are signs wanting that this expected reaction is occurring. Externally, the preoccupation of the powers in colonial questions has done much to preserve peace on the continent. States have been absorbed in the opening up of new markets and in the acquisition of over-sea possessions; they have gratified their desire to rule at the expense of the subject races. And it is significant that, as the favoured places in the world have been gradually occupied, the likelihood of European war has definitely increased. The very powers of the concert are mutually distrustful, armed against each other. Those states, which from material weakness have least to hope for from the modern doctrine of compensation, have shown an increasing tendency to act for themselves. It was Italy, the least powerful of the so-called great powers, that was the first important state to dare to enter upon an independent war in Europe after the Congress of Berlin. It was the lesser powers that destroyed the *status quo* in the Balkan Peninsula.

Internally, there have been signs of a growing reluctance to submit to authority. Portugal has experienced a revolution; France, at the time of the separation of Church and State, trembled on the verge of civil war. In Germany, there is an ever-increasing agitation in favour of the establishment of really representative government; the dominance of the military caste has been more and more resented. Russia has been the scene of constant Nihilist plots; in Sweden, the exertion of power or of influence by a limited king produced an anti-monarchical agitation. Throughout Europe, anarchist societies have been formed; men have banded themselves together with the avowed object of destroying all constituted authority.

But the tendencies of the present day may be gauged most accurately from the condition of England. In all the revolutions of the past, in all the changes to which political society has been subjected, England has in general pointed the way, and other states have, though often unconsciously, followed the example which she has set. The Angevins created a strong monarchy, while the continent was still the seat of loosely united feudal states. Despite the early existence of modified representative institutions in Spain, England was the first country to adopt a parliamentary constitution. For such a measure of recognised Individualism as England enjoyed even under the Tudors, the continent in general was forced to wait for some two or three hundred years. The Great Rebellion established the doctrine of limited monarchy while other lands were still labouring to escape from almost mediæval anarchy. The English Revolution confirmed the results of the Great Rebellion a century before France, the most progressive state on the continent, threw off the trammels of despotism. Religious liberty, freedom of the press, the reform of the representative, were all accomplished in England while such changes were as yet hardly foreshadowed in other lands.

It is therefore to be expected that the prevailing conditions in England at the present day will afford probably the clearest indication as to that which the future has in store for the generality of mankind. And both externally and internally, the signs of an approaching and even of an existing individualist reaction are obvious. Externally, despite the increase in the use of arbitration and despite the generally peaceful attitude of the English government, armaments are increasing, expectation of war is growing stronger. Still more significant is the decline of colonial sentiment. English imperialism, in its essence, partakes of the nature of Universalism; it involves not so much the government of subject races as a league of almost independent states, and there is in it a tendency to subordinate the interests of the mother country to those of the colonies. The burden of such empire was borne with reluctance in the early nineteenth century; in recent years the heaviness of the burden has once more been suggested. A growing body of opinion holds that the establishment of complete independence in the self-governing colonies is not only a probable event, but would also be beneficial to England. The agitation in favour of colonial preference has made little or no progress; the majority of Englishmen, or at least of the English electorate, have declined more than once to risk penalising themselves for the real or supposed benefit of the colonial empire. It may be suggested that such success as the tariff reform crusade has secured has been due rather to individualist antipathy towards the foreigner than to universalist imperialism. And an equivalent wish to free England from external obligations is to be seen in the suspicion with which alliances tend to be regarded. Though a universalist attitude may be discovered in the alliance between England and Japan and in the *entente* with France and Russia, yet it is becoming increasingly evident that the former is declining in popularity and that there is little wish that the latter should develop into any closer union. Its continuance may, indeed, be attributed to a certain dread that the individualist reaction will culminate in war.

Internally, there has been nothing more remarkable

in recent years than the rapid increase of a tendency to reject hitherto recognised authority. Politically, the agitation in favour of female suffrage has to a certain extent been organised deliberately on the basis of defiance of all law and order. Militancy owes its origin and its permanence to the growth of individualist sentiment. At an earlier date, the fact of resistance to the constituted government of the state would have been regarded as adequate ground for resort to the severest and most extreme penalties. At the present time, the most violent defiance produces only the most moderate retaliation. Though on a very different plane, the resistance of Ulster to the project of Home Rule can be traced only to the same growth of the individualist opinion of the age. That opinion has led the inhabitants of northern Ireland to decline to submit to the government of a majority of their fellow-countrymen, to announce beforehand and in no uncertain terms their refusal to obey the decisions of the imperial parliament. In this protest they have received the support of a large section of the English population. And it may be suggested that the extent of the agitation in favour of Home Rule itself is the measure of the Individualism of the other provinces of Ireland.

Any consideration of the trend of economic movements affords further proof of the growth of Individualism. During the eighteenth century and until after the Industrial Revolution, the labouring classes were more than ready to submit to the control of their masters. But no sooner had the evils of such subjection become apparent, owing to the prevalence of sweating and the repression of every attempt on the part of the labouring classes to improve their lot, than a strong individualist movement began. Trade unions came into being, and if they have a certain universalist element in their character, they are in essence individualist; though the members of a union are in a measure restrained by their association, yet the union as a whole asserts the unwillingness of the employee to submit to dictation from his employer. And the frequency of strikes in recent years has indicated the existence of an almost cynical disregard for contracts, a pronounced inclination, that is, to refuse to admit any restriction upon freedom of action.

At the same time, the recent increase of state interference with the life of the individual, itself the product of the universalist spirit of the age, has led to a reaction which might have been foretold. Prosecutions under the education acts have been frequent; prosecutions under the Shop Hours Act have been more frequent. In both cases individuals have claimed the right to refuse to receive either education or recreation in the manner provided by the state. And the admitted unpopularity of the Insurance Act has been due less to any real reluctance to affix stamps on cards than to the feeling that government has exceeded its legitimate province in compelling the citizens to take precautions against the accidents and casualties of this life.

But nowhere is the spirit of revolt against authority seen more clearly than in the domain of intellectual activity. Just as the Reformation was in a measure heralded by a general rejection of hitherto accepted standards, so a similar rejection heralds the coming individualist reaction of the present day. In religion, new creeds have arisen and are arising; the human race is becoming more and more malcontent with those beliefs which it once accepted without question. In literature, there is a tendency to rebel against the tacit prohibition of the discussion of certain topics; the same tendency appears in the drama, and the agitation against the dramatic censorship indicates the uneasiness of men under the curb of some moral code. In art, the modernist movement is equally pronounced; the futurists and the cubists deliberately outrage the once accepted canons of artistic construction. And in music, the art most affected by every trend of opinion, modernist tendencies, the revolt against the old, against authority, are still more evident. Wagner held at least to the recognised laws of beauty in the construction of his music; his modern successors tend to reject all laws, to pass from a wide liberty of expression to the most entire anarchy. But all this rejection of authority is nothing more than an expression of the individualist tendency in man, the assertion of the desire to rule against the desire to be ruled. It is nothing more than a phase in that eternal conflict which constitutes and which always has constituted the very life of man.

There is, then, every sign of a proximate individualist reaction; that reaction would indeed seem to have begun already, and to be destined to continue until the desire to rule attains a supremacy at least equal to that which has been recently enjoyed by the desire to be ruled. But to the suggestion that such a reaction must necessarily occur, and still more to any suggestion that for all future time the same series of reactions will continue, one proviso must be added. The idea that because History has always been a record of conflict, therefore this conflict must always endure, depends upon the assumption that in its fundamental characteristics the nature of man is unchangeable, that man is always destined to be the prey of two contrary emotions, the subject of strife between his desire to rule and his desire to be ruled. It is clear that great changes have occurred and are occurring in many spheres of activity. Knowledge in all its branches is to-day more widely diffused than it has been in any other period. Civilisation is spread over a wider area; in all arts and sciences, notable advance has been made. It may well seem unreasonable to suppose that man's nature alone will remain immutable.

At present, men act oftentimes irrationally; they fly from extreme to extreme; they are unstable. Life is a perpetual conflict, in which no victory is ever gained, since, though some may delight in extremes, the majority weary of anything approaching complete gratification. And nations act as do individuals; they are equally unable to pursue a moderate course. But it does not therefore follow that this will always be so, nor are there wanting those who hold implicitly that a change will occur.

For this change, some look to the gradual development of human intellect. A child cannot be expected to act with the considered judgment of a man; the human race has been, as it were, a child, but the race is growing up as a child grows up, so that every century sees an increase and a deepening of the human intellect. Eventually, mankind will be more able to foresee the ultimate consequences of their actions. They will be able to avoid errors and to hold fast to the true path of happiness whether that path is to be found in the fullest possible gratification of one of man's two desires, or whether it is to be found in the blending of the gratification of each desire.

Others hold a less optimistic view of the human intellect. The brevity of life gives to each individual but little time in which to train and to develop his mind. The present lack of all exact knowledge of the future suggests that man will never be able to gauge the ultimate consequences of his conduct. Yet many of those, who are thus pessimistic as to any development of human intellect as a result of normal growth of the human mind or as the result of human effort, none the less anticipate a change. It will come, it may be indeed that it has already come, by the mighty working of the hand of God. Throughout the ages there have been some men who seem to have been beyond and apart from their fellows. Such men have experienced the influence of the divine will upon them; they have been chosen out of the world to exemplify in their lives and even in their deaths the omnipotence of the Deity. As time passes, more and more men will be so influenced; mankind will be brought into closer and closer communion with God, until at last that which is divine in man triumphs over that which is earthly.

And if human nature is so changed, then History will cease to be a record of conflict. Individuals and nations alike will act with reason and with wisdom; attaining happiness, they will have also the power to hold fast to that happiness. But in that case, though the world still endure, though individuals and nations still exist, there will be no History. For History, being a record of conflict, is also a record of mingled joy and sorrow, mingled success and failure, and a world of perfect joy could have no History.

APPENDIX

THE CONFLICT IN THE FUTURE: THE WAR OF THE TRIPLE ENTENTE

HISTORY is the record of an eternal conflict between the desire to rule and the desire to be ruled, and in the existence of this conflict its explanatory factor is found. Herein lies the ultimate cause of all human action, of the conduct of every individual and of every nation. Herein, also, is to be found the true explanation of that real or apparent alternation of progress and retrogression, discoverable in every sphere of man's activity. Between the causes of any two events superficial divergences may be detected, but of all events there is only one ultimate cause. Everything that has occurred, is occurring and will occur, while the nature of mankind preserves unchanged its secular characteristics, is nothing more than an expression of the undying strife between Universalism and Individualism.

And in no period, perhaps, has this truth appeared more clearly than in the century which has elapsed since the fall of Napoleon. The First Empire was the expression of the external Individualism of France; it was made possible by the prior occurrence of an individualist reaction; it was destroyed by an alliance between the exponents of the two contrary desires. But of the two elements in the spirit of the Quadruple Alliance, one, Universalism, attained an ascendancy, with the result that, in the period immediately following upon the Congress of Vienna, the desire to be ruled appeared to have gained a victory more entire than any which it had gained before. That victory, however, was incomplete. The despotism of governments at home, and the despotism of the three eastern powers abroad, alike met with opposition; the inevitable individualist reaction found its expression in a series of national movements. Those movements produced violent external conflict. Europe was once more plunged into war, from which emerged united Italy and united Germany, standing witnesses to the impossibility of maintaining permanently a universalist régime.

But though men tend to hasten from one extreme to the other, they also tend to realise the evils resultant from their own violence. A weariness of self-assertion was produced by the frequency of armed conflict. A reaction towards external Universalism occurred, and became vigorous as soon as smaller nationalities attempted to emulate the achievements of the Italians and the Germans. The so-called " League of the Three Emperors " was formed to check any further development of Individualism. The Congress of Berlin was summoned and, in obedience to the renewed ascendancy of the desire to be ruled, postponed for some forty years the satisfaction of the hopes and aspirations of the Balkan peoples. And in deference to this same spirit, a European concert was gradually evolved. The six great powers tacitly agreed that they would console themselves for the frustration of many of their own designs by coercing the weaker states. From the individualist maelstrom of the period of national wars, Europe passed into the universalist doldrums of the period of the concert.

Yet the eternal conflict knew no real cessation. A reaction against the prevalent Universalism began almost before the concert had come into being. Actual war between the great powers was indeed prevented; little more than this was accomplished. The concert sufficed neither to solve those problems which undermined its own existence nor to maintain uninterrupted peace on the continent. In other words, it effected no revolution in human nature. The spirit of external Individualism endured, and its existence was rendered palpably obvious by the persistent dread of war, by the obviously intense jealousy with which power regarded power, by the elaborate preparations made on all sides for the anticipated struggle. And within the concert itself, more intimate leagues were formed. The Triple Alliance was answered first by the Dual Alliance and then by the Triple Entente. The great powers ranged themselves in different camps; their professed unanimity became ever more unreal, and though external Universalism still preserved its ascendancy, that ascendancy trembled on the brink of overthrow.

A fiction, which has once gained currency, is dispelled only with the greatest difficulty, nor is this less true of international politics than it is of internal politics or of the private life of an individual. In all ages, accepted myths have been exploded again and again; yet they have still won one credence. Even to-day thousands believe that Alfred allowed cakes to burn in the neatherd's cottage, that the guillotine fell upon the neck of Louis XVI to the words, "Son of St. Louis, ascend to Heaven!" The fiction that the Roman Empire was eternal subsisted long after it had been deprived even of the merest simulacrum of truth. The fiction that an English king rules, as well as reigns, survived the Revolution and the Act of Settlement. The legend of Russian cunning has hardly yet died; the legend of the military virtue of the Ottoman Turks was only destroyed at Kirk Kilisse and Lule Burgas. And the pretence that the powers were filled with cordiality towards each other possessed surprising vitality. It was not killed even when the eirenicon of Nicholas II provoked only suspicion and an increase of military precautions. It was not until Italy had adopted an independent attitude towards the one question upon which concerted action was held to be most essential, that men began to appreciate the existence of an individualist reaction. It was not until the Balkan League had defied the powers with impunity that it was realised how impossible was any really united action by the would-be arbiters of the continent. The reaction from external Universalism, however, was not the less existent and vigorous because it was obscured or denied, because there were some who declared that a new and better age had dawned, that war between the great civilised states had become an impossibility. For human nature had not changed, and while it remains constant, reaction must succeed reaction, culminating from time to time in an outbreak of armed hostility, the supreme expression of the eternal struggle. And those who realised that an external individualist movement was in progress, were perforce driven to realise also that a general war was probable, if not inevitable.

For individualist reactions against the ascendancy of external Universalism possess certain normal characteristics. Though the reaction is common to all states, yet it proceeds more rapidly in some than in others, and in any congeries of nations there will almost inevitably be one which is more intensely affected by the prevalent tendency than are others. The external Individualism of such a state will impel it to aggression; asserting its own complete liberty of action, it will deny that liberty to others, for its pursuit of its own interest will cause it to discard all sympathy with or consideration for any other interest. This is, indeed, an almost invariable concomitant of Individualism. During the period of the Reformation, those who most earnestly proclaimed the right of private judgment, tended to deny the exercise of that right to such as were by it led to accept the domination of the Catholic Church. Calvin was every whit as intolerant as any papalist; the narrow dogmatism of Geneva was relentlessly enforced, and the world has perhaps known no more bitter and cramping persecution than that which was conducted by the Protestant exponents of Individualism. The same illogical outcome of a demand for liberty has marked the development of international politics. With the breakdown of mediæval Universalism, England proceeded to attempt the imposition of her will upon France. At a later date, Louis XIV, the most extreme of external individualists, endeavoured to rivet the yoke of French ascendancy upon the states of Europe. His antitype appeared in Napoleon. After having passed through a period of external Universalism, France reverted to the Individualism of the *ancien régime*, and had her designs been accomplished, the continent would have been reduced to political slavery. It may be admitted that the appearance of such an aggressive state has not invariably characterised individualist reactions; it has, however, done so with sufficient frequency to render it not improbable that the revolt against the system of the concert would be marked by an attempt on the part of some one country to secure for itself the domination of Europe.

It is, however, clear that such gratification of the desire to rule partakes of the nature of Universalism. The aggressor denies to others the liberty of action which he assumes for himself, and originally inspired to pursue a particular line of action by the spirit of Individualism, he meets with opposition from that same spirit. The French, who opposed the English invaders during the Hundred Years' War, were not less externally individualist than their enemies. Those states, by which Louis XIV and Napoleon were defeated, were not less individualist than was France. Indeed, in so far as they displayed no desire to dominate the continent, they were more fully actuated by Individualism. It is true that the Grand Alliance, viewed in one aspect, was a preliminary expression of that new theory of external Universalism which ultimately produced the doctrine of compensation and of the balance of power. In another aspect, in its original inception, it was the outcome of the desire to rule among its members; they were resolved not to part with their freedom as independent and sovereign states. The Quadruple Alliance was always marked by a measure of universalist sentiment. When its triumph had been won, it became obviously the exponent of the desire to be ruled, and it is not improbable that it was little more than doubt as to the eventual issue of the struggle which gave the individualist element in it a certain temporary weight. Yet that individualist element was present, nor can it be denied that the original purpose of the league was to prevent the extinction of European liberty. And here appears a second normal characteristic of external reactions in favour of the desire to rule. As one state, inspired by that sentiment, has often endeavoured to impose its will upon others, so whenever such an attempt has been made, it has been resisted by a league of other states. Those whom aggression has threatened have united in self-defence; being no less inspired by the desire to rule, they have refused to forego the gratification of that desire at the bidding of some would-be master.

Any reaction towards external Individualism, then,

will more probably than not find expression in the appearance of an aggressive state, in the consequent formation of an alliance to resist that state, and ultimately in armed conflict. And an illustration of this fact is supplied by the War of the Triple Entente. That struggle is the natural and normal, if not actually the inevitable, outcome of revolt against the external Universalism which prevailed in the period following the cessation of national conflicts. It is, as are all other events, an episode in the eternal strife between the desire to rule and the desire to be ruled, nor is this less true because the protagonists are all inspired by the individualist spirit. For when external Individualism has been exaggerated beyond a certain point, it partakes of the nature of Universalism.

France, under Louis XIV or Napoleon, demanded that she should be allowed to ignore the ambitions and interests, the rights and very liberty of all other states; she was externally individualist. But if her policy be regarded from the standpoint of her opponents, she forthwith appears rather as externally universalist. The triumph of the desire to be ruled would unite all countries into some type of confederation. The triumph of France would have produced the forced union of the continent under her hegemony, and hence, though it is true that French policy in these periods was the outcome of the spirit of Individualism, it could have won acceptance elsewhere only if other countries had been inspired by an extreme external Universalism. Louis XIV and Napoleon, viewed in one aspect, were apostles of the desire to rule; viewed in another aspect, they were apostles of the desire to be ruled, and they failed because mankind was satiated with gratification of the latter desire. In the wars of the later seventeenth and early nineteenth centuries, both parties were in a sense externally individualist; in another sense, one party bordered at least upon external Universalism.

And up to a certain point, the conditions of the periods of Louis XIV and Napoleon are exactly reproduced in the War of the Triple Entente. All the states of Europe, to a greater or lesser degree, are inspired by the desire to rule; they are, however, so inspired in varying measure. Hence, on the one side, there is found a state aspiring to the completest liberty and implicitly denying liberty to others. On the other side, there is found a league of states formed to compel the would-be aggressor so to exercise his rights and to enjoy his liberty that he does not impede the concurrent exercise of like rights and the concurrent enjoyment of like liberty by others.

Germany, in short, occupies to-day a position analogous to that which France occupied in the days of Napoleon. Her external Individualism has led her to enter upon the path of aggression and to embark upon an attempt to subject the world to her will. She has pursued her own interest, or imagined interest, without consideration for the interests of others; she has displayed a cynical indifference towards the most sacred treaties and the most sanctioned conventions. Since international law was devised to impose some curb upon the free gratifications of the desire to rule by any state, Germany has naturally disregarded that law, and as in not dissimilar circumstances Louis XIV seized Strassburg, so William II violated the neutrality of Belgium.

Nor is the Individualism of German policy really impaired by the fact that this policy is being prosecuted in harmony with allied states. It is clear that in any alliance there is normally a certain universalist element. The very existence of an agreement involves some apparent limitation upon complete freedom of action, some limited acceptance, at least, of the corporate conception of human society. But this is only true of alliances between equals, and the states which are allied with Germany are not united with her upon equal terms. Rather the relationship which exists may be more accurately paralleled in that which existed between Louis XIV and Bavaria, or between Napoleon and the Confederation of the Rhine. In her struggle against the Grand Alliance or the Quadruple Alliance, France in reality stood alone; her friends were her dependants, and their support was rather that of subjects than of allies. The Bavarian government exercised but little influence upon the councils of the Bourbons. The princes of Germany were a source of weakness, rather than of strength, to Napoleon, since prestige demanded their protection and the resultant dissipation of energy probably served to hasten the defeat of France.

In the present war, Germany enjoys a like embarrassing predominance. Austria-Hungary has long been the subordinate ally of the court of Berlin. Her policy has been largely dictated to her; her independence of action has become negligible. The command of her armies has been taken out of the hands of her own generals; the plan of campaign has been dictated to her. The Dual Monarchy, indeed, has almost ceased to have a separate existence; it has experienced a foretaste of the meaning of German external Individualism. And this is still more true of the Ottoman Empire. Germany has secured both economic and political predominance at Constantinople; she has assumed control of the Turkish fleet and army, and the Sultan is hardly more independent of William II than is the king of Bavaria or the ruler of Lippe-Detmold. Indeed, the attitude of Austria-Hungary and of Turkey is due to the fact that those two states are not really actuated by the spirit of

Individualism; it really affords an illustration of the truth that the extreme of external Individualism is akin to Universalism. It was the weakness of the desire to rule in the peoples of those two countries which induced their acceptance of German control, as it was the strength of that desire among the Italians which disrupted the Triple Alliance. Germany is not less an exponent of the extreme of external Individualism because she is possessed of subordinate allies, because, in effect, she has already established her hegemony over Austria and Turkey.

Nor are the enemies of Germany universalist in their spirit, despite the fact that they have made a certain concession to the ideal of Universalism. In their original resistance, the powers of the Triple Entente were clearly inspired by the desire to rule. Had they refrained from opposition to Germany, they would have been subjected to the decisive influence of an alien state. They could have refrained from opposition only if their peoples had been filled with the desire to be ruled, and hence for them so to refrain was impossible unless they had been unaffected by the prevalent reaction against Universalism. But between the conception of external Individualism, of which Germany is the exponent, and that of which the allies are the exponents, there is a deep and fundamental difference. Each member of the Triple Entente claims liberty for itself; each recognises the right of its allies to a like liberty. No one of the three powers aspires to curtail the others' ultimate freedom of action, nor can either Great Britain or France or Russia be regarded as the predominant partner in the league. They have not pressed their external Individualism to that extreme at which it partakes of the nature of external Universalism.

Even that element of Universalism, which is discoverable in the conduct of the Triple Entente, is little more than the outcome of necessity, and is possibly inseparable from any true alliance. The French have subordinated their fleets to the English naval command both in the Atlantic and in more distant spheres of operations. The English have placed their expeditionary force under the ultimate command-in-chief of their allies. Such concessions, however, such seeming admissions of a universalist element, are essential to the efficient conduct of any joint operations; they evidence not the subservience of subordinates but the co-operation of equals. Even the common declaration of the three powers that no one of them will conclude a separate peace is nothing more than the announcement of a conviction that the end in view can be attained only by the most complete unanimity of action, and since that end is externally individualist so the alliance is still an expression of the desire to rule. In short, the protagonists in the War of the Triple Entente are all alike exponents of the reaction against external Universalism.

But they have placed very different interpretations upon that reaction. In the past, when a people has destroyed a despotic régime, there has not infrequently been a certain tendency towards anarchy. There have been some who have appeared to confound liberty with licence, to have declined acceptance even of the most moderate restraint, to have become actual or potential criminals. They have been suppressed or held in check by their fellow-citizens. Yet those who have employed coercion have been individualists no less than the coerced; they have only interpreted the reaction to mean that liberty must be accorded to all and held that this is an impossibility without a certain measure of government. And when a reaction towards external Individualism has occurred, there have normally been those who have regarded that reaction as complete only if it produces the most entire international anarchy; there have been others who have held it necessary to preserve some restraining influence. Both parties have been individualist, but their Individualism has not been of an identical type. To the one party, the desire to rule has implied a state of anarchy and hence the ultimate despotism of the stronger; to the other, it has implied a certain limitation of anarchy whereby the ultimate equality of all may be secured.

To this divergence of interpretation the War of the Triple Entente must really be attributed, and it may be paralleled with apparent exactness from the past. The attempt of Germany to establish her hegemony over Europe has, at least to a certain extent, produced exactly the result which was produced by a similar attempt on the part of Louis XIV or of Napoleon. Under those rulers, France was actuated by external Individualism; the policy which she adopted was the illustration of this fact. And she owed her ultimate failure to the additional circumstance that the desire to rule prevailed also in other lands and hence impelled other states to oppose French aggression. Germany has provoked an identical opposition, and by that opposition she will be overcome. For the maintenance of an hegemony over the continent is possible only when mankind is actuated by the desire to be ruled. The Roman Empire, whether in its original form or as revived by Charles the Great, owed its maintenance to the fact that the spirit of external Individualism was weak. When that spirit had attained development, the union of Europe became an impossibility; Charles V, Philip II, Louis XIV, Napoleon and Metternich successively failed to preserve harmony on the continent. And, at the present time, the desire to be ruled clearly possesses no ascendancy; even the mild authority of the concert aroused resistance. That hegemony to which Germany aspires would be far more complete than was the attempted hegemony of the six powers; it is essentially alien in conception from the dominant reaction, and the resistance to its establishment must therefore be crowned with success. If History teaches anything, it teaches that the War of the Triple Entente will end in the victory of the Allies.

That victory will be the victory of states whose policy was originally inspired by external Individualism. But it does not necessarily follow that the victors will remain external individualists. At least at first sight, indeed, History would seem to teach that they will not do so. There have, in the past, been two cases when a state, moved to aggression by its external Individualism, has been met and overcome by an alliance, and in both of these cases the allies were seemingly converted to external Universalism by their very success. When the Grand Alliance had defeated Louis XIV its members endeavoured to prevent the recurrence of those calamities which appeared to have resulted from the breakdown of the mediæval system. They made no attempt, indeed, to return to that system; the conception of Europe as a federation of Christian states under a human vicegerent of the Deity was abandoned. But they did attempt to create a new system, externally universalist in character; they adopted the conception of a balance of power and the doctrine of compensation.

When the Quadruple Alliance had defeated Napoleon, its members in turn attempted to organise Europe upon a basis of external Universalism; the Metternich system in effect proposed that the four great powers should govern the continent. In each case, experience of the possible outcome of gratification of the desire to rule produced a reaction in favour of the contrary desire. In each case, also, the reaction towards external Universalism had hardly culminated when a reaction towards external Individualism began. The period after the Treaty of Utrecht was marked by frequent wars, all of which served to illustrate the permanence of the desire to rule; the period after the Congress of Vienna ended in a renewal of strife, in national uprisings against the attempted domination of the powers. And in each case, the impossibility of organising international society upon a universalist basis was apparently proved the more completely since the very states, which had seemed to advocate such organisation, themselves contributed to its overthrow.

It is, therefore, not unreasonable to anticipate that the War of the Triple Entente, after the defeat of Germany has been accomplished, will result in a reaction towards external Universalism. The victorious allies may be expected to imitate the members of the Grand Alliance or of the Quadruple Alliance, and to attempt the evolution of a system under which they will possess the real control of the continent. In such circumstances, the ultimate result may also be anticipated. Sooner or later, gratification of the desire to be ruled will produce satiation. The inevitable reaction towards external Individualism will occur; the very conditions which have led to the War of the Triple Entente, will be reproduced, and experiencing the evils of the ascendancy of the desire to rule, the weary continent will once more seek refuge in a reversion to Universalism. There will be no cessation of that eternal conflict of which all History is the record.

Such, indeed, is not merely a possible, and even probable, outcome of the conditions of the present time. It is more. It will indubitably be the future of the race, if human nature remains unchanged, if its fundamental characteristics remain unaltered. From earliest childhood to extreme old age, the mind of each one of us is the scene of never-ending strife between the desire to rule and the desire to be ruled. Seeking happiness always, we fail as perpetually to attain the coveted goal. And since our nature is thus imperfect, so is the nature of every nation likewise imperfect. The mind of each state is the scene of an identical struggle, and states tend, as do individuals, to seek deliverance from the evil of one extreme by flying to the contrary extreme. In their relations with one another, they have oscillated since the dawn of History between an excess of Universalism and an excess of Individualism, and to all seeming the powers of Europe to-day are as little able to discover the true path of happiness as were the states of the continent in the ages of the past. It would appear, in very truth, that a consideration of History and of human nature can lead only to the regretful conclusion that the emergence of humanity out of darkness into light will remain for ever the idle dream of those optimists who blind themselves to the clearest truths.

But in all ages there have been those who have held a less pessimistic view of the ultimate destiny of mankind. They have declined to believe that man has been endowed with reason only that he may be unreasoning; they have refused to admit that human nature is not susceptible of betterment; they have denied the assertion that it has not been bettered. On the contrary, they have declared that the race, however slowly, has advanced towards a truer appreciation of the ultimate source of happiness; they have declared that nations have displayed a gradual decrease of unwisdom, and that though the world is still far from perfect, its imperfection has been sensibly lessened. They deny that the work of all the prophets and teachers of the past has been ultimately vain; they credit mankind with the potentiality of appreciating and obeying the dictates of reason. Those who have held such opinions, have in fact believed that the cessation of the secular conflict is a constant possibility. They have looked for that cessation and they have expected a revolution in human nature as a result of every great crisis in the world's history. To-day, such optimists hold that the occasion has at last arrived. They deny that the War of the Triple Entente will produce merely a reaction towards external Universalism to be followed by a further reaction towards external Individualism. They suggest an alternative outcome. They profess to foresee an enlightenment of mankind, which will enable it to avoid those errors by which in the past its pursuit of happiness has been impeded.

Nor is it enough for an historian to dismiss such opinions with the contemptuous remark that similar predictions of vast and salutary changes have hitherto been invariably falsified. It is not enough for him to point out that the end of war, the supreme expression of the secular conflict, has been in the past frequently and vainly anticipated. To deliver such an answer would be to fall into the vulgar error of arguing that whatever has been, will be. And that error is, perhaps, the most serious of which an historian can be guilty. It is necessary, before all things, that an historian, when attempting to fulfil the highest of his functions and to reveal something of that which the future has in store for mankind, should be prepared to consider all possibilities and to approach with an open mind the book of fate. If he permits his judgment to be warped by prejudice or by too easy acceptance of apparent certainties, then he is unfit for the task which he has undertaken to perform and is unworthy of the name of historian.

Hence, though it is abundantly clear that all History has been the record of conflict between Universalism and Individualism, though it may appear to be certain that the present situation will develop as did the situation in the days of Louis XIV and of Napoleon, it is vitally important for the historian to remember that this presupposes the constancy of human nature and for him to consider whether or no the study of the past affords any ground for doubting that premiss. For if reasons can be discovered for suggesting that though the conflict has endured, yet its character has been gradually modified, and if moreover that modification were seemingly in the direction of a diminution of the intensity of strife, then the opinion of those who hold that a revolution in human nature is imminent or is indeed in process of accomplishment would acquire an added weight and an increased plausibility.

And if the history of the past be carefully considered, there may appear to be grounds for the opinion that, even in its most fundamental characteristics, human nature is not entirely constant. It is assuredly true that the conflict of desire has persisted from the very earliest times; it may also be true that this conflict has undergone a certain modification. In the Middle Ages, the ascendancy of external Universalism was marked by a definite attempt to combine the states of the continent into a species of Christian federation under some definite head. The attempt ended in failure and the lesson of that failure was at least partially learned. That new type of external Universalism which appeared after the Reformation contained in it a certain individualist element, and that element has gradually increased in strength. Such success, indeed, as has attended efforts to discover a *modus vivendi* would appear to have been due to a mingling of the two opposing principles. In other words, a certain abandonment of extremes may be noted as a characteristic of the secular conflict. Thus, when after the Treaty of Utrecht the Triple Alliance was formed to prevent a recrudescence of anarchy, the members of that alliance, though externally universalist in their ideals, were ready to make some concessions to external Individualism, and to the making of such concessions they owed the measure of success which attended their efforts. Mankind would appear to have grasped the fact that the organisation of international society upon a basis of extreme gratification of the desire to be ruled was an impossibility. At least, it was upon such assumption that the Triple Alliance acted. The projects of Alberoni and Ripperdà were checked. But that they were checked without any serious outbreak of war was due to the fact that the wishes of Spain were not wholly disregarded. If the two statesmen fell, their designs were not entirely frustrated; concessions in the matter of the Italian duchies formed the price paid to Philip V for his abandonment of his claim to complete liberty of action. And it was the irreconcilable Universalism of the powers of Europe when brought into contact with the French Revolution that caused the final break-up of that system which had been created after the death of Louis XIV. As soon as the moderation of the originators of that system was abandoned, the human race revolted against the too complete ascendancy of the desire to be ruled.

And in that universalist reaction, which followed the fall of Napoleon, the great powers, or rather the three eastern powers, fell into the error of refusing all consideration to the desire to rule. Their violence brought its natural retribution; it served to hasten the reaction towards external Individualism, and the vigour of that reaction was proportionate to the original completeness of the contrary reaction. To a certain extent, this fact would appear to have been understood. Neither the "League of the Three Emperors" nor the later concert of Europe attempted to exercise that degree of control over the continent which the Quadruple Alliance had demanded. Allowance was made for the existence of external Individualism and the success of the concert, like that of the Triple Alliance after Utrecht, was due to this readiness to regard the aspirations of all states. At the Congress of Berlin, though Russia was compelled to forego the realisation of her historical designs, and though the peoples of the Balkan peninsula were prevented from attaining independence, yet no attempt was made to preserve the *status quo*. In the case of Eastern Rumelia and again in the case of the rejection of Ottoman suzerainty by Bulgaria, the concert gracefully accepted the *fait accompli*. When Crete revolted and the Hellenic government intervened on behalf of the rebels, the powers displayed at least a certain willingness to consider the national ambitions of the Greeks. And whenever the concert attempted to pursue a more purely universalist course, its efforts ended in failure. The powers proved to be unable to modify at all seriously either the policy of Great Britain in Egypt or of France in Tunis. Attempts to regulate affairs by means of international commissions have been almost notoriously unsuccessful. Nor has this truth been ignored. The nations of Europe have apparently realised with ever-increasing clarity that a universalist régime can be maintained only by a certain admixture of Individualism.

But not only is it true that the necessity for a certain measure of compromise has thus been appreciated, it is also true that the significance of extremes has tended to be more clearly understood. When France under Louis XIV entered upon a policy of aggressive external Individualism, the other states of the continent were slow to realise the meaning of that policy. Though leagues were formed against her, they were both weak and transitory. The Triple Alliance accomplished little, and its members, if roused for a moment to a sense of their danger, were easily lulled into a renewed feeling of security. The League of Augsburg was dissolved before its work was really accomplished. Even William III, keen as was his appreciation of the European situation, hardly understood at first the true meaning of French policy. If the Partition Treaties indicate his grasp of the fact that the peace of the continent could be preserved only by making some concession to the external Individualism of France, they indicate also that he failed to understand that a state, resolved to gratify its desire to rule, cannot be held in check by any treaty, unless it is clear that to break that treaty is to court certain disaster.

And in their attitude towards the French Revolution, the allies displayed an equal inability to understand the situation with which they had to deal. They showed themselves to be incapable of realising the supreme necessity of sincere co-operation, if they were effectively to resist the aggression of Napoleon, and successive coalitions were wrecked upon the rock of mutual distrust, itself the outcome of a mal-appreciation of the character of the struggle. It needed Jena and Wagram and Moscow to bring Europe to a realisation of the extremity of its danger. Indeed, paradoxical as it may seem, it is almost true to say that of the causes of

Napoleon's failure, his success was not the least potent.

On the other hand, to-day the meaning of German external Individualism has been far more readily grasped. Even before that Individualism had actually developed into positive aggression, the necessity of resistance to it was realised, and appreciation of its inevitable outcome appeared. The *raison d'être* of the Triple Entente is to be found only in an understanding that the prevalence of the desire to rule in Germany constituted a menace to the remainder of the continent. And when war at last began, not only was the Entente speedily converted into an alliance, but its members marked their sense of the realities of the case by announcing their joint determination to prosecute the struggle in common until victory had been secured. It needed long experience of the insatiable ambition of Napoleon to lead the powers to frame a similar declaration at Chaumont; at the present time, it needed no more than the mere revelation of Germany's resolve to wage an aggressive war. Nor has this accurate appreciation of the situation been confined to the Allies. Louis XIV and Napoleon never attained to understanding of the forces against which they had to contend. Germany fully attained such understanding. She realised even before the struggle had begun the certainty of the formation of a coalition to resist her, and all the efforts of her diplomacy and the whole conception of her strategy were directed to counteract this particular danger.

It is, perhaps, possible to account to some extent for this feature of the present situation by the fact that to-day news is far more rapidly disseminated. In the past, communications between state and state were difficult and often defective. The action of a government was often rendered cautious by uncertainty as to the policy of potential friends and enemies. Negotiations proceeded slowly; a war developed gradually as its circumstances and character became gradually defined. At the present day, all this has been changed. News may be received from the most distant lands in the space of a few hours. Views can be rapidly exchanged. Hesitancy in a government is now rarely the result of inadequate information as to the facts of a situation. And there can be no reasonable doubt that improvement in means of communication has greatly expedited the progress of all international negotiations.

Nevertheless it may well be argued that the increased rapidity with which decisions of policy tend to be reached is not the result only of greater facilities for the acquisition of information. The conduct both of individuals and of states is frequently irrational, but there is at least some colour for the suggestion that to-day it is on the whole less irrational than it was in the past. The dominion of unreason over the mind of the individual finds its most obvious expression in violence of all kinds, in the adoption of extreme opinions and in the performance of extreme actions. There is every ground for believing that at the present day there is a diminution of violence. The coarse language and the brutal conduct of an eighteenth-century squire would be almost impossible in the modern country gentleman. Though crimes of violence still occur, they are less common than they were a century ago, and this cannot be attributed solely to the efficiency of the police. It must be due in a measure to a greater exercise of reason, since even if a man refrains from crime merely from fear of punishment, the fact that he considered the probability of retribution argues that he was not the blind victim of his natural passions, that he has displayed some self-restraint. Indeed, every decrease of violence implies a decrease of irrationality; it indicates that the individual man is a more rational being to-day than were his ancestors a century ago.

But nations are aggregations of individuals. If, therefore, there is an increase of rationality in each individual, there will tend to be a similar increase of rationality in the whole nation, and hence there arises a probability that there will be a certain tendency towards the avoidance of extreme courses, both in internal and in external politics. This tendency to moderation seems actually to be present in modern times. Though reactions and counter-reactions still occur, though the race still oscillates between the gratification of Universalism and that of Individualism, yet there does appear to be a diminution of intensity in the conflict. It may be admitted that violence is still a characteristic of internal politics, and that violence of language has indeed increased. But the most violent language is rarely translated into action; revolutions and civil wars have become less frequent; partisans, however embittered, are content with the use of merely verbal weapons.

And if the external aspect of the conflict be considered, a similar tendency towards greater moderation would seem to be discoverable. Extreme Individualism has, perhaps, always been regarded as impracticable; that extreme Universalism which produced the conception of an eternal and all-embracing empire has long been abandoned. Even when the desire to be ruled has achieved a temporary ascendancy, that ascendancy has been constantly more limited. If in the opinion of its most convinced supporters the function of the Quadruple Alliance after the Congress of Vienna was to dominate the continent, in actual fact its authority was from the very first greatly impaired by the "insularity" of England and the crypto-liberalism of Russia.

The aspirations of the recent concert were far more modest; it secured little more than the exercise of a discreet and moderating influence over the lesser states, since with the will to coerce it so clearly lacked the power. And the champions of external Individualism have been at pains to convince mankind of their detestation of international anarchy, the logical outcome of their own creed. They have denied or have excused their disregard for the law of nations; they have felt or pretended a certain willingness to defer to the opinions of others. If the series of reactions has not been interrupted, yet the devotees of the desire to be ruled and the devotees of the desire to rule have alike indicated their readiness to conciliate their opponents.

Nor are there lacking other arguments in favour of the view that the eternal conflict is losing, and has indeed already lost, something of its pristine intensity. Of that conflict, war is the supreme expression. Almost before one desire has attained supremacy, a reaction towards the contrary desire begins. The violence of that reaction is directly proportionate to the completeness of the ascendancy against which it is directed, and when that ascendancy is as nearly as possible entire, there is a probability, if not a certainty, that the attack upon it will be so vigorous as to produce armed conflict. Accordingly, from the frequency or infrequency of war, the strength of the reaction and the degree to which nations have proceeded to logical conclusions, to extremes, may be gauged with comparative accuracy. In the last three centuries wars have become less frequent; the percentage of years of peace has increased. More than half the years of the seventeenth century were years of war; in the eighteenth century more than half the years were years of peace. In the nineteenth century the general peace of the continent was only disturbed for the space of some twenty years. Between the death of Louis XIV and the final overthrow of Napoleon, there were more than thirty years of war; between the final overthrow of Napoleon and the outbreak of the War of the Triple Entente, only some ten. And if the conflicts which have occurred in Europe during the last hundred years be considered, it will be observed that no one of them has assumed the character and dimensions of a general war. It would obviously be unreasonable to insist too much upon these facts. The violence of conflict cannot be estimated solely from the space of time for which it endures. It may very often be that a brief war entails far more destruction and suffering, and is marked by far greater bitterness, than one which drags its weary course over a much longer period. But in the absence of any conclusive evidence to the contrary, the fact that the intervals of peace have increased in duration creates at least a certain presumption in favour of the view that the violence of the eternal conflict has been diminished, that in the nature of mankind a sensible modification has occurred.

And this presumption is perhaps supported by a consideration of the present economic organisation of the world and of the extent and character of modern civilisation. In the Middle Ages, as soon as a reaction against the original cosmopolitanism of that period had begun, the generality of mankind held it to be axiomatic that trade between lands owing a different political allegiance was a practical impossibility. John, after the French conquest of Normandy, permitted the almost unrestrained continuance of commerce between England and the lost province, and a clause in Magna Charta provides for the reasonable treatment of merchants even if subjects of an enemy country. Such conduct, however, was exceptional. The normal spirit of the age is more accurately illustrated by the case of Edward III, whose motive in embarking upon the Hundred Years' War was largely due to his concern for the trade with Aquitaine and Flanders. And at a later date the conviction that all foreign states were economic enemies was crystallised into a theory. It was the assumption that the profit of one state could only be the loss of another that formed the true basis of the mercantile system.

At the present day, though there are some who incline to believe that this assumption possesses at least a substratum of truth, there are also many who hold it to be entirely false. They assert that international division of labour is as beneficial as internal division of labour and condemn as pernicious all barriers against the free exchange of the product of industry. Even those who regard some restraint upon the economic intercourse of nations as necessary, hardly go so far as to declare that identity of political allegiance is a prerequisite for such intercourse. Indeed, though the sentiment of nationality is assuredly no weaker to-day than it was in the past, though states are perhaps even more jealous of their sovereign rights, it has been very generally recognised that intimate economic relations do not necessarily impair political independence, that the prosperity of one country does not necessarily imply the adversity even of its actual or potential enemies. Nor is this increase of economic toleration seriously discounted by the fact that most states have adopted a protective system. The intention of modern tariffs is not to prevent, but merely to regulate, external trade; their very existence may be regarded as indicative of the increased volume of commerce and of clearer recognition of the fact that no country can be wholly independent of the products of other countries.

But inasmuch as the ultimate spring of all human activity, whether mental or physical, is to be found in the conflict between the desire to be ruled and the desire to rule, this modification of economic opinion argues a certain modification in human nature. The extreme of external Universalism would tend to produce complete free trade; the extreme of external Individualism would tend to produce the cessation of all international trade. To-day the world attempts rather to preserve the mean between the two extremes, and thus into the eternal conflict there has entered a measure of moderation. Mankind appears to appreciate more accurately the evil of excessive gratification of either of its two prevailing desires, Universalism tends to be coloured by an admixture of Individualism; Individualism by an admixture of Universalism.

A similar conclusion is suggested by a consideration of the extent and character of modern civilisation. In the last hundred years, in that period which has elapsed since the end of the last general war, the area of the civilised world has been vastly increased. Japan has entered the comity of nations; North America and Australia have been extensively colonised; Africa has been permeated by the influence of the white races. Regions, then unexplored, are now pierced by railways; once trackless oceans are readily traversed; the whole surface of the habitable globe has been mapped with approximate accuracy. In the mid-Victorian era, the journey from London to Cornwall was regarded as something of an adventure; to-day the journey across the Atlantic is a mere incident. San Francisco is now nearer England than was the Riviera in the days of George III. All nations have been brought into closer contact with one another, and with the resultant increase of mutual knowledge, a better mutual understanding has arisen.

The mere fact that civilisation is more widely diffused suggests a probability that the bitterness of the secular conflict will be diminished, since civilisation in its very essence implies some restraint of passion and hence an increased reluctance to proceed to the extreme gratification of desire.

Nor are grounds wanting for the belief that this probable result has actually been produced. Of all the activities of the mind, love and religion are those by which man is most profoundly influenced. If, therefore, he displays moderation in these two regards, it is hardly disputable that he will probably display a similar or even a greater moderation in all other regards. And there are noteworthy indications that in love and in religion mankind is more prone to avoid extremes. The days when marriage was effected by rape or purchase have long since passed away. The days of excessive parental authority have also passed; the control of husband over wife has been limited by sentiment, and that sentiment has secured expression in legislation. The tendency of the age is in the direction of regarding marriage as a contract between equals; it is far less commonly held to constitute any indissoluble bond. The efforts of mankind have been directed to the discovery of a mean between the rigidity of the canon law and that licence which was advocated by the Hébertists or by the earlier Anabaptists.

In the case of religion, the growth of moderation is still more apparent. Men no longer believe that those who differ from them in theological opinion should be persecuted to the death; they hardly condemn them even to social ostracism. It is no longer a recognised maxim of statecraft that identity of allegiance should necessarily involve identity of religious belief, or even of publicly professed belief. There is a certain inclination to recognise the possible existence of a mean between the absolute negation of God and the unquestioning acceptance of dogmatic religion. Even the Roman Church, the most conservative and unchanging of all human institutions, has modified in practice, if not by explicit admissions, her attitude towards various questions. If the Pseudo-Isidorian Decretals have not been actually repudiated, they are no longer paraded. The Papacy has silently allowed to fall into desuetude its mediæval claim to the lordship of the western world. The famous Bull of Alexander VI would be impossible of issue at the present day; not merely is it certain that no sovereign state would recognise the validity of such an edict, but it is equally certain that no modern pope would advance claims so extensive. Formerly, a rigid insistence upon orthodoxy compelled the excommunication of all heretic princes and the issue of commands for their immediate deposition. To-day the Papacy pursues a policy more akin to that of Innocent XI who assisted to finance the expedition of William III. Benedict XVI is in nowise reluctant to enter upon friendly diplomatic intercourse with the Defender of the Faith, though that ruler owes his position to the Act of Settlement and to the explicit repudiation of the legitimate and Catholic heir.

It is a curious and not entirely unimportant fact that in the present crisis the Bavarian claim to the English crown has not been raised. Germany has used every effort to enlist the sympathy of any disaffected or potentially disaffected elements in the British Empire. Her agents have been active in Egypt and in India; they have appealed to the extremists in Ireland and in South Africa. They have not attempted to win over the Catholics by urging them to support their co-religionist, the legitimist claimant. In the past such an appeal would in all probability have been an effective weapon; it would at least have caused some heartburning among the loyal children of the Roman Church. That the appeal was not made therefore suggests an increase of moderation in Catholicism, and it suggests this the more strongly since the failure to advance it cannot be reasonably attributed to any peculiar insight into the minds of English Catholics. German statesmen and diplomatists have displayed an extraordinary incapacity for appreciating even the broadest characteristics of national temperament in other lands; they confidently anticipated an Indian mutiny, an Irish civil war and a Russian revolution. The futility of urging the Bavarian claim must have been indeed obvious for it to have been realised at Berlin, and hence the increased political moderation of the Roman Church must also be considerable.

And it is impossible to account for this indubitable growth of moderation in the attitude of mankind towards religion on the ground that the race has become coldly indifferent. Nothing could be more untrue than the assertion that the present age is more irreligious than the last. It has been marked by exceptional ecclesiastical activity. Renewed vigour has been shown by the older Churches. Missionary enterprise is general. The Anglicans assert that the number of their communicants has increased; the nonconformist bodies do not deplore any decline in their strength. It is the opinion of the most unprejudiced observers that in France the anti-clerical movement which produced the Separation Law has spent its force and that the Catholic Church to-day is there more popular and more powerful than it has been for many years. The frequent appearance of new sects indicates the continued interest of mankind in the problems and perplexities of theology.

If the number of professed agnostics has increased, this is no proof of indifference. A man inclines naturally to adhere to that creed in which he has been born and bred; if he is indifferent, he is unlikely to discard explicitly the faith of his childhood. Deliberate profession of agnosticism argues at least some thought upon the principles and implications of revealed religion; in a large number of cases, it is not improbably the result of prolonged and even of painful debate.

There would, then, appear to be little ground for the suggestion that the existent increase of religious moderation is the mere expression of religious indifference. It is far more probably resultant from a growing distrust of extremes. But it cannot be denied that in the past men tended to gratify immoderately one or other of their two dominant desires; it is really indisputable that such tendency to excess has been most apparent in the attitude of mankind towards religion. Of all types of controversy, theological controversy has been the most embittered and the most violent. Of all forms of toleration, religious toleration has been most hardly attained. Persecution for conscience' sake was almost introduced into the world by the Christian hierarchy; it has never assumed a more thorough and vindictive character than when devised and carried out by saintly ecclesiastics. If the race displays greater moderation in its attitude towards religion, if in this particular aspect the conflict has become less intense, then there is at least considerable justification for the belief that human nature has experienced a sensible and an important modification.

It is, in short, permissible to suggest that in those mental activities by which he is most profoundly moved, man is displaying a greater conviction of the merit of some intermingling of Universalism and Individualism.

There is a tendency to seek for some mean between that view of marriage which was held by the mediæval canonists and that which was preached by the Anabaptists of Münster. There is a tendency to seek for some mean between Catholicism and atheism. The generality of mankind believes more implicitly that in the middle path true happiness must be sought; it displays less incapacity for seizing and holding fast to the golden mean. But if in its fundamental characteristics human nature is not wholly immutable, if it is susceptible even of the slightest modification, there is at once a presumption in favour of the opinion that to such modification there is no assignable limit. A possibility arises that in the life of each individual the conflict may become less intense; there is even a possibility that the conflict may entirely cease. Nations, however, are aggregations of individuals; their conduct ultimately corresponds to the conduct of every individual. It therefore follows that there is also a possibility that the conflict in the life of nations will cease; it is by no means certain that the world will for all time continue to experience that series of reactions and counter-reactions which have filled the record of the past.

At first sight, indeed, the study of History clearly suggests that the eternal conflict will continue in all its intensity. It would appear to be certain that in the future, as in the past, mankind will tend to hasten from one extreme to another, that the world will ever waver between the exaggeration of Universalism and the exaggeration of Individualism. The unwisdom of humanity has hitherto been far more patent than its wisdom; man's capacity for error is far more clearly proven than is his capacity for right judgment. There are innumerable instances of folly both in nations and in individuals. The most earnest strivings of the race have been constantly misdirected; they have been productive of no apparent results commensurate with the energy expended, and the results produced have been as often evil as good. A philosopher, contemplating the long vista of past centuries, may well be impressed rather by the essential littleness, than by the achievements, of his fellow men. He may well permit himself to smile at the futility of human endeavour or to mourn over the calamitous results of human unreason. Since the dawn of History, ability has been constantly misused. Elaborate schemes have been formed and carried out, only to reach the fruition of a foredoomed failure. Those very institutions, upon the perfection of which most effort has been exerted and in which men have taken most pride, have not infrequently proved to be pernicious, detrimental to the ultimate well-being of the race. The wisdom of one age has only too often proved to be the folly of the next.

It is little wonder that some are tempted to cry with the prophet of old that they are no better than their fathers. It is little wonder that some theologians have pointed an apparently obvious moral, declaring that the whole past history of the world conspires to justify those who have asserted that the betterment of mankind can occur only through the personal intervention of an almighty God. It is still less surprising that many should declare that out of the present evil times no permanent good can come. Even those who admit that the War of the Triple Entente must affect profoundly the future of the world can see little hope of any substantial advance towards better things. They may anticipate some transitory respite from armed conflict, some local advantages for themselves or for others. They anticipate far more confidently a repetition of the errors of the past. They are assured that a brief inter lude of comparative happiness and calm will culminate only in a renewal of turmoil and misery. For whether the teaching of History as to the character of nations, or its teaching as to the character of individuals, be regarded, there seems to be abundant reason for the belief that it is probable, that it is indeed certain, that the eternal conflict will endure, its intensity undiminished. And in this event men and nations alike will continue to prosecute vainly the search for happiness, will continue to gratify unwisely their desire to rule and their desire to be ruled.

But it would be a fatal error for an historian to accept without the closest investigation an apparent truth. It is his primary duty to test all things, to bow to no authority save that of his own intimate conviction. And the record of the past affords abundant proof that the superficially probable has constantly not occurred. Nothing appeared to be more unlikely than that the Swiss could resist successfully the power of the Habsburgs, or that the Dutch could carry their cause to victory despite the strength of Spain. While the world yet accepted the dogmatism of the Middle Ages, it seemed improbable that the human intellect could be delivered from thraldom, that there could ever be such intellectual activity as characterised the epoch of the Renaissance and the Reformation. It was improbable that the preaching of an obscure Augustinian could avail to shake the mighty fabric of the Papacy and to imperil the very existence of an ecclesiastical system, sanctioned by centuries of acceptance, supported by the most powerful interests, and but recently triumphant over a movement which had commanded the assent of many of the princes of the Church. It was improbable that the rancour and bitterness of the so-called Wars of Religion could culminate in the dawn of an era of even comparative toleration. While France was yet ruled by Louis XV, while her very sages and prophets were tainted by the corrupting influence of the court and were ready to prostitute their talents to the adulation of a worthless king and of his effete associates, it might well have seemed to be impossible that her sons should presently arise and preach to the world a new gospel of political liberty. In the face of these and of many other examples of the frequency with which the improbable has occurred, it would be unwise for an historian to assert that an event will not have a particular outcome because that outcome appears to be unlikely. For him to make any such assertion would, indeed, be for him to display the most crass ignorance of the very elements of his subject. And thus an historian cannot with justice declare it to be certain that the War of the Triple Entente will be followed by results identical with, or even by results similar to, those which have followed the general wars of the past.

And if the history of mankind be more closely considered, reason appears for the belief that any such declaration would be indicative of ignorance of human nature. Man is to-day, as man has always been, the plaything of two dominant passions; he submits alternately to the dominion of one or of the other. Seeking for happiness and content, he tends to gratify to excess either his desire to rule or his desire to be ruled. His mind is the scene of a perpetual conflict, not the less real because often unconscious. But while it is true that this conflict has endured through all the ages, since man first became man, there are not wanting indications that its character has not remained as constant as might be supposed. There are grounds for the belief that human nature has been modified, and hence is susceptible of further modification. If a greater appreciation of the evil of extremes, and a consequent increased readiness to consider different points of view, be a good, then there is ground for believing that the modification has been for the better. History has always been a record of ceaseless oscillation, but it would seem that this oscillation has grown less violent. There has been an increasing tendency for the pendulum of human thought to come to rest at some point midway between the extremes of Universalism and Individualism.

In the past the appearance of such a tendency has proved to be merely the prelude to more violent oscillation. It may be that herein lies the true explanation of this apparent tendency to-day. But it may be that the pendulum is indeed coming at last to rest. It may be that the long conflict is at last drawing to its close. It may be that we who now live are destined to witness the final cessation of that weary quest which has occupied the race since the dawn of History, a cessation due, not to the abandonment of hope, but to the glad attainment of the long-sought goal.

The value of History lies most truly in the fact that through its medium alone can man lift even the veriest corner of that dark veil which hides the future from our eyes. Theologians, astrologers, all who in sincerity or fraud profess to be able to reveal the destiny of mankind, are but idle speculators. Men may prophesy, but their words are vain and idle, unless they are inspired by the light which comes from true understanding of the past. All men may guess; the historian alone can know. His mission, therefore, is lofty; it is sacred, not lightly to be undertaken. For its due fulfilment, care and patience, sincerity and zeal, are needed, freedom from prejudice and from the tyranny of preconceptions. And at no time were these qualities more needed than they are to-day. The world is in travail; the pangs of birth afflict humanity, and the desire of nations is to know what shall be brought forth. The historian alone can approach to an answer of this question; to answer it is his highest privilege, his noblest function. If he answers carelessly, if he permits his judgment to be clouded by his private longings, by pessimism or by optimism, he commits a crime against his kind, he sins against the light of reason. He must beware of dogmatism; he must hesitate lest by haste he plunges some into despair or buoys up any with vain hopes. And hence, if he deals faithfully and truthfully with his present task, he must declare this message to the world; that though History seems to teach that the War of the Triple Entente will end in the mere repetition of those errors by which man has been distressed and perplexed in the past, yet it does not teach this so clearly as to preclude the possibility that the War will end in the dawn of a new era, in which the race will be delivered from the dominion of unreason and, triumphing at last in its search for happiness, enter upon a bright age of peace and goodwill.

INDEX

Published by

Facsimile Publisher
Ashok Vihar, Delhi-110052 (India)
Website: www.facsimilepublisher.com

Distributed by

Gyan Books Pvt. Ltd.
5, Ansari Road, Daryaganj, New Delhi-110002 (India)
E-mail: books@gyanbooks.com, Website: www.gyanbooks.com